NARRATING THE NEWS

NARRATING THE NEWS

New Journalism and Literary Genre
in Late Nineteenth-Century
American Newspapers and Fiction

KAREN ROGGENKAMP

THE KENT STATE UNIVERSITY PRESS
Kent and London

Library of Congress Catalog Card Number 2004028468
ISBN-10: 0-87338-826-7
ISBN-13: 978-0-87338-826-9
Manufactured in the United States of America

09 08 07 06 05   5 4 3 2 1

A version of chapter 2, "'To Turn a Fiction to a Fact,'" originally appeared in the *Journal of the American Studies Association of Texas* 31 (2000): 19–46. Reprinted with permission.

A version of chapter 3, "A Front Seat to Lizzie Borden," originally appeared in *American Periodicals* 8 (1998): 45–62. Reprinted with permission of the Ohio State Univ. Press.

A version of chapter 4, "The Evangelina Cisneros Romance, Medievalist Fiction, and Journalism That Acts," originally appeared in the *Journal of American and Comparative Cultures* 23, no. 2 (2000): 25–37. Reprinted with permission of Blackwell.

LIBRARY OF CONGRESS CATALOGING-IN-PUBLICATION DATA
Roggenkamp, Karen, 1969–
    Narrating the news : new journalism and literary genre in late nineteenth-century American newspapers and fiction / Karen Roggenkamp.
        p.   cm.
    Based on the author's doctoral dissertation—Univ. of Minnesota.
    Includes bibliographical references and index.
    ISBN 0-87338-826-7 (hardcover : alk. paper) ∞
    1. Press—United States—History—19th century. 2. Sensationalism in journalism—United States—History—19th century. 3. Reportage literature, American—History and criticism.   I. Title.
    PN4864.R64 2005
    071'.3'09034—dc22   2004028468

British Library Cataloging-in-Publication data are available

For Jay, Simon, and Piper.

CONTENTS

ACKNOWLEDGMENTS

Perhaps it was inevitable, given that several of my close relatives are journalists and that my family shares a general love of literature and history, that I should somehow try to fuse several disciplinary perspectives into one study. This book, at any rate, would not have come about without the support both of those family members and of my professional colleagues.

My deepest gratitude is directed toward my two closest advisors, Edward Griffin and Donald Ross, at the University of Minnesota. Their guidance as members of my doctoral dissertation committee, where they saw the first versions of this book, was surpassed only by their support as colleagues and mentors within the context of the Early American Literature Research Group at Minnesota. They exuded confidence in my project long before I could recognize its value myself, and they continued to offer frank advice and solid insights through final revisions of the manuscript. I cherish the good fortune I have had in knowing them. I also extend sincere gratitude to the other members of the Early American Literature Research Group, particularly Danielle Tissinger, Sarah Wadsworth, and Karen Woods Weierman; their good-humored suggestions and unflagging support enriched my project at each stage of its development.

I am greatly thankful for three other members of the University of Minnesota faculty who nurtured me as doctoral advisors: Toni McNaron, Nancy Roberts, and Hazel Dicken-Garcia. Their superb instruction continually challenged me to construct new paradigms for my own thinking. Collectively, they awakened my interest in journalism history, nineteenth-century gender politics, and interdisciplinary studies.

I owe hearty thanks to my editors at the Kent State University Press. Joanna Hildebrand Craig has demonstrated incredible humor and good faith from our first meeting. She has expressed her positive spirit through situations as mundane as my endless editorial questions and as unusual as her being driven from her office building after a botched animal dissection; she has kept me smiling all the while. Likewise, Kathy Method provided incredible flexibility, not to mention commiseration, during fall 2004. I would also like to thank Michael Robertson, whose cogent remarks on an early edition of the manuscript have proved invaluable.

This manuscript profited from the institutional support I received while I studied at the University of Minnesota. The Graduate School offered significant financial support, which allowed me to complete an earlier version of this book. And Wilson Library at the University of Minnesota continually impressed me with the depth of its collection and its level of courteous and prompt service. Both the College of Arts and Sciences and the Department of Literature and Languages at Texas A&M University-Commerce provided additional support in the final stages of editing.

Finally, I owe a special debt to Simon and Piper, who remind me every day that the best stories are the ones a mother shares with her children, and to Jay, whose unswerving faith in my ability to get things done carried this project to its completion. The three of you are light in the darkness.

INTRODUCTION

Literary Rooms in the House of News

Throughout most of the nineteenth century, New York City's newspapers were housed along a pulsating street named Park Row—unofficially dubbed "Newspaper Row"—which stretched from the corner of Broadway and Ann Street, past Printing House Square at Nassau Street, and on to Chatham Square on the lower end of Manhattan. Adjacent to City Hall, criminal courts, and the Bowery, Newspaper Row electrified the city and molded the narration of news throughout the nation. Large and small papers alike found a home here, including three that changed the course of both American journalism and literature at the end of the century: the *World,* the *Sun,* and the *Journal.*[1]

By the 1890s the very buildings of Newspaper Row had entered into cultural imagination, symbolizing within their walls the swiftly changing print culture they helped produce. The *Sun* building had been a fixture on Newspaper Row since editor Charles Dana had installed his paper there in 1868.[2] Out of its solid, unflappable depths, the daily story of New York had risen for decades. But in 1890 editor Joseph Pulitzer amazed New Yorkers by constructing headquarters that surpassed in scope and brilliance all other structures in the city and that quite literally cast his competition—specifically Dana of the *Sun*—into the shadows. Sixteen stories high and domed in gleaming gold plate, Pulitzer's *World* building captured a new pulse pounding along Newspaper Row. Americans had never seen a structure of this size; many visitors were afraid to ride the elevator to the *World's* top floors. Clearly, this was not a common office building. The *World's* home spoke instead of importance, illustriousness, and *new*ness—it spoke of surpassing all competition and of sheer business enterprise. Pulitzer's building stood as the tallest in New York for a short time, and the *World* was the city's most spectacular newspaper as well until another enterprising "builder"—William Randolph Hearst—blazed into town and introduced an even newer and more spectacular daily: the *New York Journal*. Hearst did not bother to build literally a larger and more impressive structure to tower over his competition. Rather, in a telling move that brought new meaning to the phrase "undermining the competition," Hearst took office space within the buildings of his rivals, including Pulitzer's own *World* tower.[3]

The papers that the *Sun, World,* and *Journal* offices produced were more important, of course, than the buildings that held them. For in the nineteenth century these newspapers developed a novel way of narrating the news that came to be known as "new journalism"—an innovative, commercialized, sensationalistic, and above all dramatic style of reportage. The phrase "new journalism" was coined by Matthew Arnold in 1887 in connection with the energetic editorial style Pulitzer had been championing for over four years, first in St. Louis, then in New York. New journalism "has much to recommend it," Arnold admitted; "it is full of ability, novelty, variety, sensation, sympathy, generous instincts."[4] However, he added, new journalism's "one great fault is that it is *feather-brained*. It throws out assertions at a venture because it wishes them true; does not correct either them or itself, if they are false; and to get at the state of things as they truly are seems to feel no concern whatever."[5]

Arnold recognized the roots of a mass communication phenomenon that was to increase in force as the nineteenth century closed. Facing growing rivalries with one another and within a burgeoning print marketplace more generally, urban newspapers felt pressure to create prose that entertained, and the urge to spin attractive and popular tales sometimes came at the expense of factual information. Indeed, most editors and reporters believed, as they still do today, that one could be both entertaining and factual. But for new journalism the ideal of entertainment was primary, creating within its pages an ongoing dance between the literary (dramatic, sometimes fictionalized, stories) and the journalistic (factual reportage). In essence, as historian Michael Schudson explains, two journalistic systems operated in the 1890s—a "story" model and an "information" model.[6] The latter supposedly conveyed something close to "pure information," or a collection of unframed and unadulterated facts. This ideal is the journalistic standard we are most familiar with today in our own view of American newspapers as agents, theoretically, of "fairness, objectivity, [and] scrupulous dispassion."[7] New journalism, on the other hand, championed the story through an underlying assumption that newspapers should principally provide entertainment. In pieces notably similar to those rolling off the presses of such literary publishers as Harper & Row and Lippincott's, the *Sun,* the *World,* and the *Journal,* among other papers, narrated the news with an eye toward character, plot, setting, dialogue, dramatic pacing, and other literary elements.

Approaching the news with significantly different expectations and standards from those of newspaper consumers today, most nineteenth-century readers embraced this "story" aesthetic wholeheartedly, even if news stories sometimes appeared overtly fictionalized. Journalist Edwin Shuman, writing in an advice manual for aspiring reporters, asserted correctly in 1894 that "if you have a simple, sensible, breezy style with a sparkle in it, the newspaper reader will forgive a great deal of inaccuracy in your matter."[8] Storytelling and fictionalizing within the news staved off the "unpardonable sin" of "dullness," and inaccuracy itself was "excusable as long as the imaginative writing is confined to nonessentials and is done by one who has in him at least the desire to represent the truth."[9] Indeed, Shuman advised his protégés,

> This trick of drawing upon the imagination for the nonessential parts of an article is certainly one of the most valuable secrets of the profession. . . . Truth in essentials, imagination in non-essentials, is considered a legitimate rule of action in every office. The paramount object is to make an interesting story. If the number of copies sold is any criterion, the people prefer this sort of journalism to one that is rigidly accurate.[10]

As Shuman's remarks suggest, new journalism was characterized not by dry or even inherently newsworthy content and presentation, at least in our modern conception of the word, but by an amalgamation of "event, idea, and 'story' or drama."[11] Journalism historian Hazel Dicken-Garcia has demonstrated how journalistic practices correspond to particular social structures and contexts. Our understanding of proper standards for the delivery of the news is constantly evolving as cultural circumstances and market pressures themselves change. As a result, some of the hallmarks of new journalism scarcely resemble those of later American newspapers, particularly once the field was professionalized and standardized under the banner of "objectivity" in the early twentieth century.

In fact, new journalism was much more closely tied to American fiction than scholars have traditionally recognized or than most readers would assume today. The dramatic presentation of news defined the industry, and "the story" in late nineteenth-century journalism was "a product that was marketed and sold," with a central plot "around which drama was woven to create the thrill that would make people want to read and therefore to buy the newspaper."[12] The big business of urban newspapers, in other words, depended for its success on the reporters' narrative skills and their ability to mold information—sometimes factual and sometimes not—into dramatic and skillfully told tales. Furthermore, newspaper reporting became an attractive profession into which aspiring novelists entered in hopes of achieving fame in the literary world. A natural and fluid connection existed between literature and journalism in terms of style and profession, and editors and reporters alike self-consciously reinforced the ideas that one textual venue bled into the other and that the pages of the newspaper contained within them a particular literary aesthetic.

The aesthetic of new journalism found fertile ground for reproduction in 1890s New York. In 1830, only sixty-five daily newspapers existed in America, with a total daily circulation of about 78,000. Just ten years later, 138 dailies reached a total circulation of about 300,000. That number had exploded to 574 dailies by 1870 and 2,600 by 1900, with circulation rising to an astounding 22 million by the end of the century.[13] If printed in book form, one critic noted in 1903, just a single year of American newspapers "would make a library" of close to four billion volumes.[14] Newspapers were "crowding out the books" in the late nineteenth-century literary marketplace, and "many wealthy men with great libraries in their houses . . . read scarcely anything but the daily journals from one year's end to another."[15]

Literary critics recognized the power behind these numbers, and many celebrated the newspaper's possibilities. Walt Whitman, for instance, asserted that newspapers were "the mirror of the world," the "reality of life."[16] Nathaniel Hawthorne, an avid penny-press reader and self-proclaimed consumer of "all sorts of good and good-for-nothing" writing, proclaimed, "It is the Age itself that writes newspapers and almanacs, which therefore have a distinct purpose and meaning."[17] William Dean Howells, who called city journalism "the school of reality," noted that in Boston "journalism desired to be literary" while in New York "literature has to try hard not to be journalistic."[18] Literary critic and novelist John W. De Forest asked whether "a society which is changing so rapidly" could "be painted except in the daily newspaper."[19] Columbia University professor and novelist H. H. Boyesen observed that "the average American has no time to read anything but newspapers."[20] The newspaper had "become the king of the realm of letters" in late nineteenth-century America.[21]

Yet despite the newspaper's extensive audience and its recognition by critical voices, the study of this print form, the "school of reality" that so vividly narrated American progress and shaped national reading experience, has suffered within modern academia because of the strictness of disciplinary boundaries. Literary scholars have ignored newspapers almost entirely, seeing them as little more than the repository of an ephemeral record of daily life in the city and across the nation. Newspapers, literary history has told us, hold inferior, unimportant writings, a view that overlooks the fact that new journalism, for instance, operated explicitly within models of dramatic storytelling. A few literary historians have studied newspapers, but they largely focused on a handful of canonical figures who enjoyed careers in journalism, notably William Dean Howells, Stephen Crane, Mark Twain, Theodore Dreiser, and Ernest Hemingway.[22] Historians of journalism, conversely, have regarded the more sensationalistic and dramatic aspects of new journalism with something close to chagrin, marking the period as a time of extravagant experimentation that ultimately gave birth to the staid, inverted pyramid style of modern newspapers. They have likewise ignored the "other" discipline, failing to recognize and theorize the intentional use of "literary" technique by nineteenth-century journalists: the strong characterization, the plot motifs, the symbols, the language, the description, and the appropriation of genre conventions.

What both journalism and literary scholars have missed in these predominant, discipline-bound assessments is the dynamic interplay among journalism, fiction, and a mass communications marketplace in which both participated during the late nineteenth century. New journalism, invested as it was in dramatizing stories, appropriated popular literary genres to frame the news for readers. Reporters and editors rewrote current events into stories laced with the familiar motifs of hoaxes, scientific and travel adventures, mystery and detective tales, and historical romances, to name just a few genres, in effect revising and resurrecting these popular fictional forms as news items. Using current events as their source documents, reporters fashioned their own dramas based on those that readers recognized from a broadly drawn literary culture, and they populated these dramas with such rich character types as the female adventurer, the accused murderer, the dashing hero, and the damsel in distress. As newspaper workers felt out an aesthetic of composition—one based on "the real thing"—they posed their works of "art" in explicit competition with fictional prototypes. What reporters manufactured was something that looked a lot like fiction, read like fiction, and entertained like fiction but that was ultimately, they argued, better than fiction, because it was, after all, "real."

This newspaper realism begs for attention, particularly in light of the growing interest in the history of publishing and readership. More than a history of literature or of journalism strictly defined, this study looks more generally at part of the history of mass print communications, which was itself the central phenomenon—and problem—of late nineteenth-century print culture. Thousands upon thousands of people read newspaper narratives every day; comparatively few read imaginative works with similar regularity. For large numbers of Americans, in other words, the imaginative works most frequently encountered were the stories produced in newspapers. The face of literary history was inevitably influenced by what this mass audience read. The literary marketplace was in fact shaped by a constant, dynamic conversation between imaginative writing and periodical culture in the late nineteenth century, a periodical culture that included magazines and newspapers alike. But this conversation within literary history has been largely ignored, often because of where news stories appear and the ostensible circumstances under which they were written. Literary scholars have assumed, incorrectly, that newspaper stories—by nature composed under deadlines—are inherently transient and ephemeral. Readers in the 1890s, by contrast, recognized that reporters were witnesses to the richest vein of story material: "the tragedy and comedy of human life, its cynicism and toadyism, its passionate struggling and feverish ambition, its sham and subterfuge, its lavish wealth and gasping poverty, its joy and sorrow, its good deeds and its most hideous crimes."[23] Readers also recognized that they would find these epic human issues translated into pathetic, tragic, comedic, thrilling stories in the daily newspaper. For the way in which reporters saw and described events was affected by the fiction that they in turn read. Popular literary genres of the late nineteenth century offered the familiar plot situations, character types, and settings upon which reporters and editors drew to frame their own news stories. These were the stories millions of people encountered daily, and these were the stories that impacted the imaginations, attitudes, and actions of readers across America.

Although new journalism eventually became a nationwide phenomenon spanning several decades of the late nineteenth and early twentieth centuries, this study concentrates on three major New York newspapers of the 1890s. My choice of New York as a center of focus is rather obvious—the city's papers boasted the largest circulation, and much of what was produced in New York disseminated through the syndication networks and news agencies that emerged in the nineteenth and early twentieth centuries. Furthermore, while such editors as Joseph Pulitzer and William Randolph Hearst initiated their journalistic innovations in western cities (St. Louis and San Francisco, respectively), they recognized that their efforts were incomplete unless they moved those innovations onto the scale that New York offered. Neither of these editors was content to be "the chief" in a smaller, less influential city. New York represented to editors and readers alike the ultimate narrative stage. I chose three specific New York newspapers—the *World,* the *Sun,* and the *Journal*—not merely because of the style of reportage and the operational missions each espoused but also because of the competition among the editors of these papers. In the later decades of the nineteenth century, Charles Dana held the city captive with his precursory form of new journalism until Joseph Pulitzer brought even fresher innovations to eastern readers—and stole much of Dana's staff in the process. Later, upstart William Hearst undermined Pulitzer's efforts with his rendition of the news, once again stealing other newspapers' staffs (including Pulitzer's) in the process. Simply put, no love was lost among these three editors, but their lives and their newspapers were linked elementally. Finally, I focus on the 1890s because this was the single most significant decade in terms of the development and practice of new journalism. Joseph Pulitzer "invented" new journalism in the early 1880s, but in the 1890s storytelling in newspapers grew richer, circulation figures rose dramatically, and "fictionalizing" became so extreme that it ultimately brought a critical backlash that changed, once again, the face of the profession and its narration of the news.

The bulk of this book is devoted to case histories and specific media events that expose the competitive and reinforcing interplay between specific literary genres and their journalistic revisions. Here I examine the narrative behind and within some of the most infamous moments in newspaper history. Chapter 1 turns to earlier history and sets the scene with one of the best-known cases of journalistic storytelling in America, "The Moon Hoax," concocted in 1835 by the *New York Sun.* This journalistic fabrication, which presages the appearance of new journalism several decades later, also introduces the complex figure of Edgar Allan Poe, who, in his multiple roles of editor, imaginative writer, newspaper columnist, scientist, and hoaxer—and in his grappling with more basic questions of "the real" versus "the artificial"—introduces key issues about narrative genre, mass readership, and periodical culture. Chapter 2 brings attention back to the 1890s with the tale of Nellie Bly, sent by Joseph Pulitzer's *World* to beat the travel record set by Jules Verne's imagination in *Around the World in Eighty Days.* In her journey, Bly challenged not just Verne's record but the very status of fictionality in an age of news. Chapter 3 turns to the case of Lizzie Borden and explores how reporter Julian Ralph's writing in the *New York Sun* adapted conventions of the newly popular detective story by offering readers a critical view into a sensational trial. Ralph transformed the figure of Lizzie Borden into a complex persona, fleshing out her character in an act of resistance against other news portrayals of the young woman.

Chapter 4 visits the saga of Evangelina Cisneros, a young Cuban ingénue who was rescued from her Spanish captors by reporters for William Randolph Hearst's *Journal,* in a fabulous reworking of medievalist romance. Placing their own adventure story beside the literary offerings of both past and contemporary authors, *Journal* writers proclaimed their romance "real" and ultimately more captivating than fiction. Chapter 5 pushes history forward nearly a century, closing this study by returning to the issues of hoax, truth, and invention. This chapter explores Janet Cooke's 1981 Pulitzer Prize–winning newspaper "hoax" and traces how the relationship between fact and fiction in the paper changed over time as professional standards developed and as new models of reportage, based on information rather than entertainment, emerged. These case histories are complemented by broader cultural analyses that touch on vital topics by introducing some of the central issues surrounding both the literature and the journalism—realism, professionalization, gender, and expansionism.

Ultimately, new journalism's significance reaches far beyond what it tells us about the reading culture and materials of late nineteenth-century

America. For the impulse to turn the news into a story continues to this day. A study of the standards and practices of 1890s news writing inevitably leads to questions about how our own standards and practices have—and have not—evolved since the past century. In what way is journalism of today a reaction against what came before? In what way does journalism continue its intricate dance with literary forms? In what way does the blending of fact and fiction in contemporary newsmaking entertain and manipulate readers on a mass scale? As we embark on a new century, one that has seen the manufacturing of news and the dramatic presentation of current events grow increasingly important, a study of new journalism and its own grappling with these issues serves as a relevant guidepost to understanding the phenomena of contemporary media. This study, then, offers neither a history of literature nor a history of journalism exclusively but an enriched chapter in the history of mass communications itself, one that stretches well into our own century.

CHAPTER ONE

———————

The *Sun,* the Moon, and Two Balloons

Edgar Allan Poe, Literary Hoaxes, and Penny Press Journalism

Shams and delusions are esteemed for soundest myths, while reality
is fabulous.
                    —Henry David Thoreau, *Walden*

Introduction

This study of 1890s new journalism does not open by examining the
1890s or new journalism. Rather, it begins with a much earlier development in the nineteenth-century press—1830s penny papers—and one
author's relationship to that form of periodical literature, for here were
laid the foundations that made new journalism possible. The questions
raised in this chapter about truth, invention, fact, and fiction cast a shadow
over subsequent chapters, as these questions became central for new journalists and their critics at the end of the century.

Penny papers of the 1830s and 1840s introduced a new fluidity between literary and journalistic forms in the daily newspaper, a fluidity
that functioned even more dramatically two generations later. Fueled by
new printing technologies and increasing literacy rates, the number of
newspapers published in the middle decades of the nineteenth century
skyrocketed. Shrewd newspaper editors recognized the untapped market
of an urban mass readership and catered to the needs of this audience by
selling exciting newspapers for one penny, thereby undercutting the efforts

of older, more conservative, six-cent newspapers. Egalitarian in nature where the six-penny papers were elitist and specializing in sensationalistic and violent human interest stories where six-penny papers focused on politics and economics, such periodicals as Benjamin Day's *New York Sun,* established in 1833, quickly earned large audiences and tidy profits as well as the ire of the more established New York papers. Unlike earlier newspapers, penny papers specialized in news that could easily be confused with fiction. Through a readjustment in the public's standard for judging newspapers, the penny press smeared preconceived borders between fact and fiction in the antebellum literary marketplace. Indeed, the very roots of 1890s new journalism lie in the penny press, and examination of these early newspapers offers a glimpse into the inception of later dramatic news styles and practices.

Penny paper stories frequently appeared to be lifted straight from popular fiction. One detailed article, to provide a random example, described how "a young gentleman, the oldest son of a distinguished baronet in England," returned home from school, fell in love with an orphan, ran off with his beloved, suffered disinheritance, regained his rightful title following his father's death, and finally faced a charge of incest brought by his younger brother. Perceptive readers might notice the smallest of verbal clues—the word "recent," for instance—and infer that the story was a news item rather than wholesale fiction.[1] Otherwise, the story's plot, characterizations, and descriptions might well have appeared within the pages of an early nineteenth-century novel. Adding to the confusion between fact and fiction, penny papers frequently published—without commentary—fictional works adjacent to factual ones.[2] Stylistically speaking, only essentially nominal differences existed between these pieces; the reader herself would need to determine which was factually verifiable and which was not. However, for the most part, readers did not seem to desire any clear indication in the papers of what actually happened and what was imaginary.

For their part, aspiring fiction writers were forced to recognize the appeal of the newspaper as a dramatic medium and to court the enormous audiences that purchased penny papers. Most American writers after the 1830s depended on the periodical press as a venue in which to publish at least a portion of their work. From the early decades of the century onward, "daily and weekly newspapers were the first medium in which aspiring writers were able to break into print and begin to forge a name for themselves" before a wider reading public.[3] Without the attention afforded by the newspaper, writers risked utter anonymity. For authors who desired something more than anonymity, the newspaper became "both symbol and product of the new publishing industry," combining "different forms of meaning into a single package that could be disseminated to a great mass of readers."[4]

But movement into that new publishing industry disrupted some of the oldest ideals about fiction writing. Many authors expressed intensely ambivalent feelings about the demands placed on artistry within the increasingly consumer-oriented culture. Perhaps most vividly, Edgar Allan Poe, with his own confused attitude about the literary marketplace, provides a rich opportunity to highlight the industry of popular publishing and reading. Poe and other writers were attuned to the beat of the newspaper, and they studied how to tap its sources. But many writers—and perhaps especially Poe—never made that study without both envy and bitterness. For Poe, conceding to the mass media "transformed" him "into a strange synthesis of art and commerce," someone at once eager for the popularity the newspaper world could bring yet contemptuous of it.[5] At once hoaxer and rationalist, imaginative writer and journalist, Poe serves as a touchstone for central questions about composition and aesthetics that new journalists themselves later addressed. His multifaceted identity as a writer in a changing popular marketplace presaged the fundamental issues that emerged forcefully some forty to fifty years later.

Spotlighting Edgar Allan Poe and his relationship with America's first penny paper, Benjamin Day's *New York Sun,* this chapter locates a precedent for the 1890s blurring of fact and fiction in New York newspapers. Poe and the *Sun* are linked by two famous instances of that intermingling—the "Moon Hoax" (1835) and the "Balloon Hoax" (1844), cases that chart how penny-paper journalism operated and what the journalistic standards it shared with its readership signified. The chapter also considers how Poe, as an important literary figure, negotiated an increasingly commercial literary marketplace. Ultimately, Poe's uneasy negotiation of that marketplace points to questions underlying both penny press journalism and 1890s new journalism: What is the role of factuality in the newspaper, do imaginative writings and news writings derive from different inspirations, and to what degree does news narrative offer a distinct aesthetic?

Day and the Sun

Benjamin Day stood first in a line of revolutionary newspaper editors of the 1830s and 1840s. Originally the owner of a New York printing shop, Day decided to experiment with a novel kind of newspaper after his regular business began to fail. The first edition of his *New York Sun* came off the press on September 3, 1833, offering to "lay before the public, at a price within the means of everyone, all the news of the day, and at the same time afford an advantageous medium for advertising." The paper would present news not for the privileged classes alone; rather, it would print items that went beyond business and politics. The newspaper would adopt a lively style and offer stories of interest to all classes of readers— especially those whom the competing New York papers had marginalized. Day's experiment paid off quickly. Within just a few months, the *Sun* boasted the largest circulation in the city at five thousand copies a day. By 1835 its daily circulation had risen to fifteen thousand copies.[6]

Day's penny paper provided a space for literary experimentation and entertainment but not necessarily for the dissemination of truth in any "objective" form ("objective" not being a word used to describe the media in 1833). News items slid naturally and without warning into items of pure invention. Furthermore, as the example of the English nobleman's tale cited above illustrates, countless news items looked as though they had been ripped from the pages of popular novels. Indeed, the very practice of publishing news of human interest was the invention of Day and his competitors. The exclusive, six-penny mercantile and political papers printed shipping accounts and reports from political parties, but penny papers exposed what happened within police stations and before judges, as well as behind the doors of private residences. Such tantalizing fare was shared in a colorful and captivating style utterly unlike that of the more expensive newspapers. One brief article, for instance, "A Case of Conscience," told the moralistic tale of a man who had vowed to end his addiction to drink, writing in his Bible, "I promise from this day never to drink grog or blaspheme in the name of the Almighty." But, alas, when "his passion for liquor overcame his resolution," the man was haunted by his broken vow, and with "circumstances preying on his mind . . . he cut his throat."[7] Another article joked about a neighboring town's new "Anti-Cow-breaking-into-gardens-Society," which had "hired a man to take up every cow that shall be found at large after nine o'clock in the evening,

and pound them according to law," in order to prevent the further de-
struction of local vegetable gardens. New York City, the *Sun* writer observed, had a greater problem with broken "heads, houses, stores, and
windows," leading him to recommend an "Anti-head-house-store-and-
window-breaking-Society . . . with the privilege annexed of *pounding* all
offenders, law or no law, until they beat their head, house and window
breaking propensities out of them, by breaking every bone in their bodies."[8] As if illustrating the need for such a society just one week later, the
paper rather humorously recounted the misfortune of a peddler who
"was attacked by two women . . . who forced him into a small grog shop,"
knocked him down, and robbed him.[9] Although the phrase was not yet
used, "human interest stories" would describe newspaper items of this
type, and editors often stressed "interest" at the expense of reality.

Readers recognized—and delighted in—the interplay in penny papers
between fact and fiction, storytelling and news briefing. In this sense, penny
papers corresponded to an antebellum American society that was "a jam-
boree of ballyhoo, exaggeration, chicanery, sham, and flim-flam," a society
invested in "humbug" and hoaxes.[10] Did the failed temperance man really
cut his own throat? Did the peddler actually suffer assault and robbery at
the hands of women? To penny paper readers, it hardly mattered if such
stories were real or imaginary, for the very question of actuality was part
of the appeal. Readers expected that this journalism would present "true
things" alongside fabrications; the point of the paper, at some level, was
not to provide only fact but to pose a sort of challenge to the reader.
Fabrication, in other words, turned into something of a game, in which
the newspaper story might attempt to trick readers into thinking a fictionalized story was true. Indeed, penny papers specialized in outright humbugs and hoaxes, for editors understood that readers would literally and
figuratively buy "a spectacular story, preferably one slow to unfold, in which
a mere germ of plausibility and a great deal of excitement stood substitute
for any amount of fact."[11] Perpetuating a literary hoax was but one way to
create a spectacular story—and guarantee spectacular circulation figures.
In this way, the newspaper hoax created a community of readers joining in
good-spirited competition against editors and "reveling in the heady thrill
of choosing for themselves whether or not to believe."[12]

Poe, like the hoaxing penny paper editors, enjoyed creating works built
on "a pattern of delusion, a seemingly solid system that offers its victims
tenets of belief" that appeared to include a believable and "comprehensible

structure."[13] On at least two significant occasions, Poe's interest in literary hoaxing coincided with and even collided against hoaxes perpetuated by the *New York Sun,* collisions that echo a much more basic pattern of interaction between antebellum literature and penny-press journalism. Poe's relationship with these new urban periodicals, however, was complicated. He publicly rejected the literary value of newspapers, yet he craved the mass audience and financial potential represented by success in the press. Poe, in this sense, was "at the center of the expanding publishing industry and more attuned than many of his fellow writers to the vagaries of the marketplace and its effect on the entire panorama of literary production."[14] Though he railed against the pervasive influence of the periodical press and particularly against cheap newspapers like Day's *Sun,* he nevertheless recognized their cultural capital.

Like other serious authors of his time, Poe still believed in an ideal of artistry. He conceived of literary invention as a phenomenon outside the influence of commercial interests, a craft perfected in privacy for the benefit of genius itself, and perhaps for a small circle of appreciative and cultured admirers as well. The growth of the literary marketplace—and specifically of the periodical press—upset that ideal spectacularly. The terms of creation were ripped out of the idealized realm of the coterie into the very public and impolite world of transaction, mass readership, and market demands. The question of how to reconcile the artistic ideal with the market reality posed no small problem to a writer of Poe's ilk. At once contemptuous and envious of the enormous audience penny papers commanded in urban areas, Poe sought the benefits of marketing within this new medium. He yearned "for the ideal poetic life" yet was "profoundly influenced by the forces of commercialization he tried to resist."[15] This dual consciousness is strikingly evident in Poe's involvement with the *New York Sun*—first in his protest against the *Sun's* 1835 Moon Hoax and then in the publication of his own 1844 Balloon Hoax in the same newspaper.

The Moon Hoax

The so-called Moon Hoax, written by journalist Richard Adams Locke and published in the *New York Sun* August 25–31, 1835, reigns as one of journalism history's definitive moments. Locke had been on the *Sun* staff only a few months when he authored a story about life on the moon, and Day recognized in the tale a priceless opportunity to hoodwink his readers and competitors alike.[16] Having casually announced an upcoming special report from the *Edinburgh Courant* four days earlier, the *Sun* on 25 August began reprinting on its front pages the latest scientific "news" from world-famous astronomer John Herschel. The *Sun* article announced that the *Edinburgh Courant* had recently located these "scientific reports" in the *Edinburgh Journal of Science* (an actual journal that had, unbeknownst to *Sun* readers, suspended publication several years earlier). The reports were strikingly technical and official in tone—they were, in other words, utterly believable.

The Moon Hoax described a powerful telescope Herschel had erected at the Cape of Good Hope, with which the astronomer had zoomed in on lunar mountains and forests, replete with the vivid vegetation of a "mountainous district of highly diversified and romantic character."[17] The telescope had picked up "a beach of brilliant white sand," green marble, and "grotesque blocks of chalk or gypsum" before revealing "mounstrous [*sic*] amethysts . . . glowing in the intensest light of the sun."[18] Even more amazing, Herschel's report noted, were the "herds of brown quadrupeds," which looked like "diminutive bison," sporting "a remarkably fleshly appendage over the eyes" to protect from the "extremes of light and darkness."[19] More geographical and animal wonders (including a unicorn-like beast) appeared within the lens of the telescope, all sprinkled among a lush lunar landscape uncovered bit by bit over several consecutive issues of the *Sun*.

No discovery, however, was as wondrous as the one revealed in the August 28 edition of the *Sun*. Readers that day were astonished when the paper divulged Herschel's greatest discovery yet—his observation of "beings in human shape" walking "both erect and dignified" across the moon's surface.[20] These creatures, which looked rather like "large orang outang[s]," "averaged four feet in height, were covered, except on the face, with short and glossy copper-colored hair, and had wings composed of a thin membrane."[21] Fantastically, they "were evidently engaged in conversation" and "appeared impassioned and emphatic," leading Herschel to call them "*Vespertilio-homo*," or "man-bats."[22] The *Sun* even obliquely suggested that Herschel had observed lascivious conduct among the man-bats, the most sexualized and scandalous of which the paper supposedly deleted from the original source, ever mindful of protecting readers' morality.

Readers were left gasping for more information about these incredible lunar discoveries, and in the few days the moon story ran, the *Sun* became a chief topic of conversation on New York streets and beyond. Contemporary accounts assert that the *Sun* office was "positively besieged with crowds of people of the very first class, vehemently applying for copies of the issue containing the wonderful details."[23] Presses ran ten hours a day to meet the demands of an ecstatic reading public, titillated by the thrilling discoveries. The *Sun* rushed to print pamphlet versions of "Herschel's" text, with the more technical sections conveniently edited out for the lay reader, along with a series of lithographs also supposedly copied from the "original" *Edinburgh Journal of Science* article. Benjamin Day proclaimed that circulation had topped out at 19,360, a record for newspapers and some four times higher than that of the nearest six-penny competitor. An admiring P. T. Barnum later calculated the *Sun* also made at least $25,000 from Moon Hoax paraphernalia.

A surprising variety of readers were fooled by the hoax, not just the (supposedly) lower- and middle-class regular readership of the penny papers. Caving in to public interest in "Herschel's discovery," six-penny papers were forced to make note of the "reprints" from the *Journal of Science,* and they did so with varying degrees of credulity. Additionally, an array of notable figures enthusiastically admitted their belief in the story. Edward Everett proclaimed that the discovery of humanoid life on the moon was going to change the world; Harriet Martineau remarked on the special story in her diary; and a group of Massachusetts ladies reputedly opened a fund "to send missionaries to the benighted luminary."[24] Even members of highly educated scientific communities found themselves wondering if Herschel had not in fact made such discoveries. When Yale University dispatched a delegation of scientists to view the "original" edition of the *Journal of Science* from which the *Sun* claimed to have copied its articles, Day and Locke had to send the visitors on an ingenious wild-goose chase across the city to prevent them from discovering that the *Journal of Science* no longer existed. After spending an exhausting day running from printing office to printing office in search of the nonexistent original article, the scientists finally returned to New Haven empty-handed but no less assured of the absolute truth of the story.

Though it may seem remarkable to readers in the early twenty-first century that so many people believed the Moon Hoax, the status of scientific and technological knowledge in the 1830s went far in supporting the basis of Locke's work. By the 1830s, the "language of technical explanation and scientific description" was "a form of recreational literature" within newspapers, magazines, stories, and short stories, a trend that grew through the century.[25] Scientific and pseudo-scientific description became popular discourse, and a number of the important astronomical works that had been published in the years preceding the Moon Hoax (some of which supplied verbatim copy for both Locke and Poe) fed the conversation. The American edition of John Herschel's *Treatise on Astronomy*, for example, appeared in 1834. Similarly, such fictional works as "Leaves from an Aeronaut" in the January 1835 *Knickerbocker Magazine* and George Tucker's novel *A Voyage to the Moon* (1827) supplied an imaginative environment conducive to astronomical hoaxes.[26] The scientific discourses used in nonfictional works were the same as those used in fictional works, and it was this general delight in technical description and language that made American readers susceptible to hoaxes. To some extent, intentional literary trickery was prevalent in the early nineteenth century because readers were "easy targets for pseudoscientific explanations, for detailed descriptions of fictional machinery, for any fantasy that was couched in the bland neutrality of a technological vocabulary."[27] Readers wanted to believe in scientific and technological advances, and if the language and description of a narrative rang with the expected tones of authority and assurance—as they did in the Moon Hoax—readers were willing to label the work "true."

Even after suspicions about the veracity of the moon stories spread in September 1835, the *Sun* refused to admit publicly that it had pulled off an elaborate hoax at huge profit. Locke reputedly confessed his authorship of the hoax to a fellow journalist after that reporter applied to him for a full copy of the "original" text for his own paper. Locke, wanting to save his friend later embarrassment, warned that the moon stories were a hoax, and the next day the competing newspaper unmasked Locke as author of the "great astronomical discoveries."[28] After additional competitors accused the *Sun* of inventing the story, Day wryly asserted that, accusations aside, almost all American newspapers "congratulate us on having afforded the world much intellectual amusement, if not, indeed, much theoretical instruction."[29] In fact, Day added, even newspapers that now considered the moon story untrue nevertheless praised it for "its ingenuity and talent."[30]

Day's claim that his readers actually appreciated being hoodwinked seems oddly accurate. One factor in P. T. Barnum's success in the early nineteenth century, after all, involved his own recognition that "a complicated hoax" established a pleasurable "competition between victim and hoaxer, each seeking to outmaneuver the other, to catch him off-balance and detect the critical weakness," and finally "to discover how deception had been practiced."[31] Even the person whose name stood at the center of the hoax—John Herschel himself—enjoyed the story. He told a fellow scientist: "Since there are some people silly enough to believe any wild story anyone sells them, we must wish that the stories should always be as harmless as this; in any case, I am not disposed to complain seriously."[32] Likewise, Lady Herschel called the Moon Hoax "a very clever piece of imagination" that "is so well *clenched* with minute details and names . . . that the New Yorkists were not to be blamed for actually believing it as they did. . . . It is only a great pity that it *is not true.*"[33]

It was precisely this public admiration for Locke's ingenuity and skillful prose that Poe envied deeply, and his involvement in the Moon Hoax of 1835 offers an entry point into examining how this case travels beyond the bounds of antebellum journalism history and prefigures an exchange between literature and journalism that would become even more influential by century's end. The *Southern Literary Messenger* had published Poe's story, "Hans Phaall—A Tale,"[34] in June 1835, calling the work an imaginative parody fit for "these ballooning days . . . when we hear so much of the benefits which science is to derive from the art of aerostation" and a propos of a near future when "a journey to the moon may not be considered a matter of mere moonshine."[35]

The text of "Hans Pfaall" involves a Dutch bellows maker who, seeking to flee an unhappy marriage and the harassment of creditors, secretly constructs a balloon to carry him to the moon. On April 1 (of course), Pfaall loads up his invention, along with "a telescope; a barometer: . . . a thermometer; an electrometer; a compass; a magnetic needle; a seconds watch; a bell; a speaking-trumpet; etc. etc. etc.," cuts the "single cord which held [him] to the earth," and shoots "upward with inconceivable rapidity."[36] After several mishaps with his breathing apparatus and close calls with meteors (all described with numbing technical detail and explained in the most scientific of tones), Pfaall's balloon approaches the moon, affording a look at not only volcanic mountains and strange vegetation but a fantastic city filled with "a vast crowd of ugly little people," with noses "prodigiously long, crooked, and inflammatory," eyes "full, brilliant, and acute," chin and cheeks "broad, puffy, and double," and bodies of "a routundity [*sic*] highly absurd."[37] The tale is framed by the arrival and departure of a messenger—one of the "ugly little people"—who has been sent back to Rotterdam (via a newspaper-covered balloon) to negotiate Pfaall's return to earth. "By late accounts from Rotterdam, that city seems to be in a high state of philosophical excitement," the opening of the story declares, in the tone of a breaking news dispatch.[38] Indeed, the narrator confides, "phenomena have there occurred of a nature so completely unexpected—so entirely novel—so utterly at variance with preconceived opinions—as to leave no doubt in my mind that long ere this all Europe is in an uproar, all physics in a ferment, all reason and astronomy together by the ears."[39]

Poe's fictional Europe may have been in an uproar, but despite the inclusion of page after page of factual, technical detail—and regardless of Poe's claims to the contrary in subsequent years—"Hans Pfaall" was not originally intended to stand alone as a widespread hoax, as the Moon Hoax was.[40] Rather, Poe's hoax as constructed for the pages of the *Southern Literary Messenger* operated on more subtle levels. Modern critics contend that the story functions not as a trick transparently intended to fool readers but as a philosophical statement on the ultimately intangible nature of reality, the "inevitable state of deception" in which humankind is trapped.[41] Whatever level of hoaxing Poe originally intended, only a few southern periodicals took notice of "Hans Pfaall" in July 1835, those few calling it "a capital burlesque upon ballooning" and moon speculation, and "one of the most exquisite specimens of blended humor and science that we have ever perused."[42]

Poe should have felt gratified by such praise. Instead, his satisfaction with his own moon story was short-lived once the *Sun*'s hoax captured the attention of the reading public by the end of August and—potentially, at least—diverted attention away from Poe's own lunar work. If Poe had created a story of life on the moon, the *Sun* seemed to be uncovering the reality of that life, and an invented world simply could not compete with the (apparently) real thing. Poe reacted to the *Sun* story immediately with outrage and distrust. He seemed less concerned about the satiric or artful effect of his tale than about Locke's having written a story that was gathering an enormous readership and notable financial success. Poe had planned to write a second part to the Hans Pfaall story for the *Southern Literary Messenger* the following month, and he felt the nagging urge to justify his own position vis-à-vis the mass market moon story. "Have you seen [Locke's]

'Discoveries in the Moon'?" he asked one companion. "Do you not think it altogether suggested by *Hans Phall?* It is very singular,—but when I first purposed writing a Tale concerning the Moon, the idea of *Telescopic* discoveries suggested itself to me—but I afterwards abandoned it. I had however spoken of it freely, & from many little incidents & apparently trivial remarks in those *Discoveries* I am convinced that the idea was stolen from myself."[43] Poe, who had essentially cribbed notes from Herschel and other authorities on lunar travel in constructing his own tale, quickly turned to one of his favorite accusations—that someone, in this case Richard Adams Locke and the *New York Sun,* had plagiarized his work.[44]

Poe's sense of persecution grew when northern papers provided only oblique mention of his story, and then always in comparison to Locke's. The *New York Transcript,* for instance, apparently attempted either to launch its own lunar hoax or to parody the *Sun* by reprinting "Hans Pfaall"— having first deleted Poe's name as author—under the title "Lunar Discoveries; Extraordinary Aerial Voyage by Baron Hans Phall, the Celebrated Dutch Astronomer and Aeronaut."[45] If, in the increasingly commercialized marketplace of antebellum letters, writers like Poe understood that "the reputation of the author rather than his literary merit sells the work," the *anonymous* publication of his work on a major urban stage must have been especially galling.[46] Despite his repeated posturing of himself as an artist—a man above the tumult of journalistic writing and the mass market—Poe thirsted for a name, which, increasingly, was most easily captured through the penny papers. The moon episode frustrated Poe because he had been usurped at his own lunar games. Where he had attempted to craft a story burlesquing hoaxes, the *Sun,* which already enjoyed more readers and financial stability than Poe could ever hope to achieve, had enraptured readers with an entirely different kind of hoax, one that had fooled the public beyond Poe's wildest dreams.

Poe licked his wounds by scoffing at the *Sun's* success and reasserting the artistic and scientific merit of his own tale. Though he later retracted his statement that Locke had pirated his work, Poe nevertheless insisted rather defensively that his creation was superior to anything found in the newspaper and that it deserved at least as much attention as did the Moon Hoax. He positioned himself as the "correct" reader of the hoax, the one who finally could not be deceived, unlike the public rabble that had purchased the *Sun* rather than the *Southern Literary Messenger.*[47] In the 1839 edition of "Hans Pfaall," Poe added an appendix that placed his story head to head with Locke's creation: "The author of 'Hans Pfaall' thinks it necessary to say, in *self-defense,* that his own *jeu d'esprit* was published . . . about three weeks before the commencement of Mr. L.'s."[48] Having established the precedence of his own "hoax," Poe educated his readers about "why no one should have been deceived" by the inferior nature of Locke's scientific prose.[49] Poe continued to defend the superior quality of his hoax and denigrate the Moon Hoax in his article on Locke for *The Literati.* Once again he maintained that his ideas for a lunar hoax had been brewing long before 1835 and that he had in fact wisely rejected the telescope idea that forms the centerpiece of the *Sun* articles before falling "back upon a style half plausible, half bantering . . . to give interest . . . to an actual passage from the earth to the moon."[50] The two works, he conceded, were together an amazing public achievement, given that "nothing of a similar nature had ever been attempted before these two hoaxes, the one of which followed immediately upon the heels of the other."[51] But, overall, his story was still vastly superior in terms of both science and artistry. After establishing his own precedence and importance, Poe complained that though he had written "an examination of [Locke's and the *Sun*'s] claims to credit, showing distinctly its fictitious character," he "could obtain few listeners, so really eager were all to be deceived."[52] The Moon Hoax was finally only the "greatest *hit* . . . of merely popular sensation—ever made by any similar fiction either in America or in Europe."[53] But if the *Sun*'s work was a popular hit—the ephemeral product of tasteless and thoughtless throngs of readers—Poe's own work offered both better science and better art. Only a person who genuinely understood the fundamentals both of art and of science, only a person of true and diverse literary abilities—a person like Poe himself— could finally separate fact from fiction in American writing.

The Balloon Hoax

Poe's response to the penny-paper world in 1835 was characterized first by jealous defensiveness, then by aloof attack. Despite this posturing, nine years later Poe attempted to mimic and manipulate the very popular success he had criticized in 1835, by writing another hoax and publishing it in, of all places, the *New York Sun.* Early in 1844, Poe, finding himself in dire financial straits, had moved from Philadelphia to New York to seek new fortunes. Hoping to spark a public sensation and earn the wide audience and public reputation that he simultaneously disparaged and craved, Poe attempted a large-scale hoax modeled on Locke's earlier work. For fifty dollars he sold to the *Sun* a factual-sounding story about an unexpected and unprecedented crossing of the Atlantic Ocean by balloon. In keeping with Locke's inclusion of Sir John Herschel in the Moon Hoax, Poe chose "real life" characters for his story, including Monck Mason, a well-known experimental balloonist, and Harrison Ainsworth, a contemporary British novelist.

Ballooning and moon exploration continued to prove extremely popular reading subjects in 1844, as they had in 1835. Mason, for example, published a popular account of a balloon voyage he had completed in 1836, and he also brought out a pamphlet describing the potential of his new dirigible balloon in 1843.[54] Even more directly, Charles Green had published the results of his balloon experiments in the April 1840 *Burton's Gentleman's Magazine,* which Poe was coediting at the time.[55]

Hoping to capitalize on this widespread interest in aeronautics, Poe launched his hoax by printing an announcement in the April 13, 1844, *Sun* advertising an "extra" edition to run later that day. This broadside would detail the "astounding intelligence" of how "the Atlantic Ocean [was] crossed in three days!!" That afternoon the *Sun's* extra appeared, as promised, complete with an engraving of the balloon that had supposedly completed the fantastic voyage across the ocean. Claiming to be an "authentic and accurate" verbatim copy of the "joint diaries" of Mason and Ainsworth, the story describes the balloon in intricate detail, combining the breathy tone of an exciting news scoop with the kind of technical description a reader might find in a regular news feature about aeronautics. Even a short quotation gives a sense of the whole story:

> The balloon is composed of silk, varnished with the liquid gum caoutchouc. It is of vast dimensions, containing more than 40,000 cubic feet of gas; but as coal-gas was employed in place of the more expensive and inconvenient hydrogen, the supporting power of the machine, when fully inflated, and immediately after inflation, is not more than about 2500 pounds. The coal-gas is not only much less costly, but is easily procured and managed.[56]

Poe uses technical jargon to establish the accuracy and believability of the report, then incorporates a vaguely epistolary style to introduce the most dramatic portion of the hoax—hour-by-hour journal accounts. An example of the "journal entries" reveals how he weaves excitement into his tale: "The last nine hours have been unquestionably the most exciting of my life. I can conceive nothing more sublimating than the strange peril and novelty of an adventure such as this. . . . One single gale such as now befriends us . . . and the voyager will be easily borne . . . from coast to coast."[57]

Poe may have crafted his "Balloon Hoax" with the utmost tone of accuracy and just the right amount of drama, and he may have modeled it consciously on the *Sun's* earlier hoax, but by most accounts the story was a resounding failure as a hoax. An excited crowd did gather to purchase the *Sun's* extra on the afternoon of April 13, but apparently other New York newspapers were not fooled by the *Sun's* latest hoax. Few papers even bothered to mention the hoax, "except in derision."[58] Backtracking as they never had with Locke's work, *Sun* editors admitted the very next day that the story was imaginary—though, they insisted, its technical information did give "great pleasure and satisfaction" to readers.[59]

Intriguingly, Poe himself may have escorted his hoax to its early grave. One contemporary account suggests that Poe,

> crazed by a glass of wine, stood on the walk before the publisher's door, and told the assembled crowd that the extra was a hoax, as he personally knew, for he had written it himself. The crowd scattered, the sales fell off, and the publisher, on going to the door, to ascertain the cause of failure, saw his author making what he conceived to be the necessary explanations.[60]

This account, if true, nicely illustrates Poe's ambivalent attitude toward the penny press. Poe felt a need both to be a part of and to stand apart from the commodifying and fictionalizing process of commercial journalism. He apparently wanted to observe the sensational effect of his balloon hoax, to bask in the popular success unfolding before his eyes. Simultaneously, he distanced himself from mass-produced texts by taking the role of the "superior creator," the hoaxer made uncommon "because of his mind, his ingenious intellect, . . . keen perception and creativity."[61] Here we see Poe within a literary marketplace commercialized by the penny press, acting out a compulsion to present himself as a "specially endowed" person, a creative genius who created art and not a "tradesman" creating mere news stories.[62]

Once again, and more significant than Poe's immediate reaction to the literary hoax within a newspaper, was his later, revised story of the hoax's reception and his insistence that the work was just as remarkable—and marketable—as the Moon Hoax had been a decade earlier. In the summer of 1844, when Poe was employed as the New York correspondent for the *Columbia Spy,* a small Pennsylvania newspaper, he tried to renew interest in what had in fact been the flat failure of the Balloon Hoax. He boldly (not to mention inaccurately) proclaimed in one of his letters to the *Spy* that the Balloon Hoax had "made a far more intense sensation than anything of that character since the 'Moon Story' of Locke," and that when the *Sun* announced its extra, the "whole square" surrounding the building "was literally besieged, blocked up, ingress and egress being alike impassable."[63] For this *Spy* article—itself a kind of hoax—Poe invented a duped crowd frenzied with excitement, ready to pay any price to read the hottest news straight off the press. "I saw a half-dollar given, in one instance, for a single paper," the correspondent confided to his readership, and "I tried, in vain, during the whole day, to get possession of a copy."[64]

Poe gushed with praise for the "brilliant" hoax and for writing that could enrapture readers so markedly. But he also characterized himself once again as the rare and careful critic, seizing the opportunity to compare this hoax to Locke's decade-old achievement. Once more criticizing the earlier work's technical flaws, Poe proclaimed that the Balloon Hoax contained "positively" no "internal evidence of falsehood" unlike the "more generally accredited fable of Locke," which "would not bear even momentary examination by the scientific. There is nothing put forth in the Balloon Story which is not in full keeping with the known facts of aeronautic experience—which might not really have occurred."[65]

Poe added to his own mythology in a note he appended to the Balloon Hoax for the Griswold edition of his works, published shortly after his death. He insisted in his note that the story sold out in extra editions, concluding that the Balloon Hoax "fully subserved the purpose of creating indigestible aliment for the *quidnuncs* during the few hours intervening between a couple of the Charleston mails. The rush for the 'sole paper which had the news,' was something beyond even the prodigious."[66] Here perhaps Poe struck what he might have considered the final blow against what was actually the more successful hoax. When put to scrutiny and the test of time, he suggests, only the more artfully done work sur-

vives—and it survives, ironically, because it is finally "truer," both aesthetically and technically.

Poe's editorial remarks about the Balloon Hoax and the Moon Hoax
correspond nicely to the theories he developed in such works as "The
Poetic Principle" and the "Philosophy of Composition." If we read these
essays as serious attempts to animate an aesthetic for reading and writing,[67]
we can likewise read Poe's defense of his hoaxes as an attempt to define a
rather similar aesthetic. Dennis Pahl suggests that Poe's "Philosophy of
Composition" is comparable to such tales of ratiocination as "Hans Pfaall,"
"The Mystery of Marie Rogêt," "The Purloined Letter," and others in
which "the art of analysis is put prominently on display."[68] Thus, the "Philosophy of Composition" attempts simultaneously "to idealize the poetic
process" and "to demystify the romantic view of the poet as one who is
utterly divorced from the world of work."[69] The superior literary work
must be artistically flawless and capable of captivating, or fooling, the reader
with the creation of another world, another setting, and unfamiliar characters. But the ultimate literary work must also, sometimes paradoxically,
be "true," quite literally. The ultimate artist creates in print an artificial
object that is somehow more real than reality itself. Of course, even this
simultaneous idealization and demystification could also be another of
Poe's postures. Given his always precarious financial state, Poe's theoretical
works, like his hoaxes, most probably arose out of "both self-promotion
and needed funds," not merely out of "critical-aesthetic considerations."[70]
The enigmatic positioning that critics sense in the "Philosophy of Composition" and "The Poetic Principle" is at play in Poe's defense of his
hoaxes as well. He wished to present his writing as something aesthetically
pure and beyond the reach of the marketplace, yet his very crafting of his
own humbugs indicated his obvious dependence on mass appeal.

To what degree can Poe, seemingly that most puzzling, contradictory
of antebellum individuals, point us in the direction of the news culture
that prospered several decades after his death? Most basically, the very
paradox Poe encapsulated in his own attitudes tantalizingly foreshadows
some of the predominant issues animated by the 1890s new journalism.
Where Poe scrambled to define himself against and above the "fictionalizing" of news, new journalists embraced that process fully. Where Poe
struggled to mask his thirst for popular success, new journalists celebrated
theirs. And where Poe both worried about and manipulated the crossover

between imagination and factuality within newspapers, new journalists manipulated that crossover wholeheartedly.

The appropriation of literary conventions became one way editors could market new journalism, but marketing is only part of the story. While new journalists of the late nineteenth century were convinced that writing was a commodity craft within an efficient literary market-place, they also attempted—consciously or not—to reserve a space for artistic creativity in that increasingly regimented marketplace. In their attempt to manufacture news stories that would produce mass appeal and phenomenal monetary success, journalists of the 1890s, like Poe, were feeling out an aesthetic of their own, one based on the ideas that news writing was the purest form of literary realism possible and that truth could be sometimes stranger—and frequently better—than fiction.

Conclusion

Poe stressed early in his career that "magazines and journals overall out-classed newspapers and that literary men who became newspapermen pandered to the masses."[71] Nevertheless, Poe's involvement in two of the many literary hoaxes that appeared in penny papers suggests his attraction to this forum that welcomed a blending of fact and fabrication, realism and romance. His uneasy posturing unmasks the difficulties he faced in negotiating his authorial identity in a changing antebellum marketplace, where newspapers were fast becoming a literary force of their own. At once craving and despising the mass readership afforded by a New York newspaper audience, he both catered to that audience and placed himself well above it.[72] Moreover, his work with hoaxes suggests that the literary hoax as produced by an "artist" could be the twin of the literary hoax as produced by a journalist, and that readers of penny papers did not draw fundamental distinctions between the "journalistic" and the "literary."

If penny papers were an experiment to decipher which journalistic standards and practices an urban public would embrace, and if they inte-grated the purely factual with the purely imaginative, then perhaps Poe discovered the papers were not, after all, such a far cry from his own compositional ideals. In an 1849 letter to Evert Duyckinck, Poe described his interest in a "plausible or verisimilar style" of writing, which would "attempt a kind of realism in which the events are supposed to be true."[73]

Here he defined the very ideal at the center of the literary hoax and penny paper journalism generally—the ideal that formed the nucleus of 1890s new journalism as well. As the nineteenth century ended, editors and journalists adopted Poe's commitment to the manufactured story and applied it to "real news" or to events that really had happened (or at least to events that *appeared* to have happened). Outright hoaxes still existed in 1890s journalism, but, unlike Poe and to some degree Richard Adams Locke and the *Sun,* new journalists labored to present their stories— regardless of how much had been invented—as writing that was unquestionably superior to the idealized art Poe finally celebrated. Moreover, new journalists wholeheartedly rejected the ideal of the privately laboring artist in favor of the writer as an agent to the masses. They took up the same mantle of "the real" that Poe toyed with and that fiction writers developed themselves in the late nineteenth century, altered it to suit the stories of the city, and created their own aesthetic of composition for narrating the news.

American Literary Realism and
the Cult of the Real Thing

But to get at the real thing! It seems impossible! . . . We can never
tell life, one to another, although sometimes we think we can.
——Stephen Crane, "War Memories"

If Americans in Poe's time were attracted to scientific and technical discourses, Americans of the late nineteenth century were all the more committed to the ideal of "the real thing," a phrase that echoed powerfully
through the parlance of the era. It seemed evident to readers and writers
that reality could be replicated and enclosed "in manageable forms,"
whether those forms were the leaves of a novel, the pages of a newspaper,
or the borders of a photograph.[1] Indeed, the very words "fact" and "real"
took on "mystical" qualities as they "became the point of fusion between
social and literary motivations."[2] "The real thing"—which included the
most sensational elements of human life—was manifest in nearly every
mode of expression: journalism, architecture, interior design, photography, social work, visual art, imaginative writing, and so on. Advertisements assured buyers that a product was the "real thing," just as imaginative writers "trumpeted the 'truth' or 'reality' of their fictional works."[3]
Likewise, photographers referred to their craft as "the real thing itself."[4]
The "real thing" became, in the words of one 1887 commentator, "the
state of mind of the nineteenth century," affecting "the poet, fictionist,
humorist, journalist, essayist, historian; the religionist; the philosopher;

the natural scientist; the social scientist; the musician; the dramatist, the actor, the painter, the sculptor."[5]

In the context of new journalism, however, the influence of "the real thing" on fiction proved most influential. A common appreciation of "the real" over "the imaginary" nourished both new journalism and American literary realism, the late nineteenth-century fictional method that appeared to provide a factually verifiable record of "real life." Realism sought to create stories that were mirrors of everyday life. Likewise, new journalism sought to present stories that recreated reality. Both forms of writing grew out of a common cultural milieu, and the imaginative and the journalistic drew upon each other in forming their respective stories. Chapters 2, 3, and 4 examine specific instances in which new journalists appropriated fictional conventions in writing their forms of realism, even as they argued that purely imaginative realism was insufficient in comparison to journalism. But here I provide a brief survey of the more generalized literary mode and public attitude against which new journalism situated itself. By surveying the conflict-laden quest for facts in American literary realism of the 1880s and 1890s, this section paves the way for my subsequent explorations of how newspapers played upon the conventions of fictional genres.[6]

The realists took as their mantra not "beauty is truth" but "truth is beauty." Though a commitment to authenticity and actuality had been manifest in American literature for decades (indeed, we see this commitment in Poe himself), the claims of mimetic writing resonated more loudly within a culture fully devoted to scientific facticity. Realists believed that if only they looked carefully enough—if only they studied society scientifically—they could identify "the real thing" and recreate it in fictionalized print. Ideally, their efforts would even provoke desirable social, political, and economic reforms. The novelist thus became, within the realist aesthetic, an "unattached observer" who "convert[ed] the stuff of life to fiction" and studied "the world dispassionately, as if it were under a microscope."[7] The fiction writer's notepad became something of a laboratory, and fiction writers were themselves the "scientists uncovering the economic and political facts of industrial life more boldly, more clearly, and more 'realistically' than anyone had done before."[8] Once uncovered and rendered fictionally, these facts would, in Henry James's words, "catch the colour, the relief, the expression, the surface, the substance of the human spectable."[9]

America's late nineteenth-century realism accompanied intense social and economic upheaval, culminating in an unprecedented explosion in America's urban population. In 1860 only sixteen American cities had a population of more than eighty thousand; by 1910 that number had jumped to eighty. Between 1870 and 1920 eleven million Americans left farms and rural villages for cities, and eleven million immigrants made their homes in American cities during the same period.[10] As these native and immigrant Americans gathered in overcrowded, diseased cities, they discovered they had traded the ideal of a life's work based on craft and skill for the new ideals of the factory: mechanistic efficiency, productivity, and dehumanization. The changes attending industrial urbanization in the United States destabilized many of its citizens, and literary realism became a way for intellectuals to process this unease. Novelists "felt the impulse to explain, or at least to record, the ongoing changes" as accurately as possible, and fiction based on recognizable daily life became a popular way to detail "life as it is."[11] Influenced by William Dean Howells's 1886 call for "an objective, accurate picture of who and what [is] out there," realists crafted literature designed to "make us known to each other in our own common political and social progress," a goal that seemed to make realistic portrayals particularly suitable for addressing some of the most challenging problems facing Americans as the century ended.[12]

Realists viewed their writing as a solidly democratic practice and suggested "that through such activit[y] they could transcend the divisions and fragmentations that had accompanied capitalist development."[13] From his seat in *Harper's* "Editor's Study," Howells, for instance, advocated stories that celebrated the lives of "real" people and literature that spoke "the language of unaffected people everywhere" without resorting to obvious artfulness.[14] Hamlin Garland enthusiastically followed Howells's call, celebrating in 1894 the "drama of life" that "stings, arouses, fires with exultant and awakened humanitarian religion."[15] For these writers, the "urban world of social thriving and social acting" in which real native and immigrant Americans lived "provided the theater of cultural realism," presenting "poetry, romance, tragedy, and a palpitating force" in a "flood of the real."[16] Novels and short stories translated that reality into fiction through the use of entertaining plots, provocative language, and strong characterization.

It was this "flood of the real," however, that lent an air of controversy to realism. Outspoken critics of the genre believed literature should deal only in ideal, "eternal," and uplifting subjects. Realism, quite in contrast, "crowd[ed] the world of fiction with commonplace people; people whom one would positively avoid coming into contact with in real life," as one critic sniffed in 1885.[17] Howells outraged many intellectuals when he used his influential position at *Harper's Monthly* to editorialize for writing that seemed to undermine "fundamental and eternal beliefs about God, man, and society" in favor of radical treatments of morality, social class, and sexuality.[18] Perhaps ultimately unwilling to address the crucial reform issues that so many realistic novels raised, critics of realism focused on virtue, advocating literature that promoted lofty social tone and moral uplift among the great mass of immigrants and working-class Americans—if they addressed those people at all. For these critics, literature was *literary* only if it remained artful and avoided identification with the increasingly fractured society in which authors and readers lived. Realism, quite in contrast, was merely an unimaginative imitation of a disturbing world—not "the real thing" at all.

By the 1890s realists and their more risqué offspring—such naturalists as Stephen Crane and Frank Norris—engaged in open revolt against idealistic and romantic literary traditions, which they considered insufficient to meet the demands of a rapidly and radically changing nation. The post-Howellsian realists placed even more emphasis on the "tangible realities" of life instead of the "spiritual and poetical ideals" embodied by sentimental and genteel fiction.[19] "The world has grown tired of preachers and sermons," asserted Clarence Darrow in 1893. "To-day it asks for facts. It has grown tired of fairies and angels, and asks for flesh and blood."[20] Novelist Joseph Kirkland noted, "The romantic and the realistic are engaged in a life-and-death struggle."[21] The trade publication *Journalist* boldly suggested that "the idealist pure and simple hardly exists at all," for "the taste for the fantastic and impossible is plainly dying out."[22]

Many realists also took issue with the idea that literature should remain safely ensconced within the realm of fine art, which they associated with weak, feminine tastes. William Dean Howells, Stephen Crane, Jack London, and others strove to reclaim a masculine edge to fiction writing, fearing that such terms as "literature" and "artistry" had been tainted by the effeminate sentimentalism of previous decades and by some current popular literature. They privileged literary realism—and newspaper reportage, as well—as a masculine endeavor, ensuring that the realist was "anything but an 'artist'" and "neutralizing" their own status within a culture "intensely suspicious or contemptuous of 'art' and the 'artistic.'"[23]

It was this move to reclaim fiction as an "unartful" artifice that led some realists into conflict with the newspaper world. The emphasis placed on documenting life and producing works that could almost stand alone as fact meant that the fictions that realists produced could be virtually indistinguishable from the stories newspaper reporters created. As magazine and newspaper editors and fiction syndicates came to view fiction writers as workers who produced a marketable commodity, boundaries between people who, in theory, wrote for profit alone (i.e., journalists) and people who, at least in the lingering romantic imagination, did not (i.e., novelists) wavered.[24] These blurred boundaries stirred significant unease among such literary critics as Howells and James, and, as my concluding chapter will explain, the overwhelming urge toward newspaper stories that looked like fiction and fiction that looked like newspaper stories finally destabilized the mainstream acceptance of new journalism in the early twentieth century.

Until that breakdown occurred, however, realists, like so many other Americans, embraced a scientific ethos in pursuit of "the real thing." When journalism adopted "science" and modernity in a contest against literature itself, as chapter 2 demonstrates, the results were phenomenal.

CHAPTER TWO

"To Turn a Fiction to a Fact"

Nellie Bly, Jules Verne, and Trips Around the World

"Oh Fogg, good-by," said Nellie Bly,
"It takes a maiden to be spry,
To span the space twixt thought and act
And turn a fiction to a fact."
          —1890 advertisement for Schenk's Mandrake Pills

Introduction

In June 1887 Joseph Pulitzer, editor of the *New York World,* tried to capture the nation's attention by staging an elaborate transportation-based stunt. He proposed sending a hot-air balloon westward from St. Louis; reporters at the newspapers he owned in both these cities would then keep readers captivated with mile-by-mile accounts of the journey. A cub reporter from Pittsburgh named Nellie Bly applied to Pulitzer to travel on the balloon, only to be rejected promptly. Reading audiences, to Pulitzer's surprise, in turn rejected the *World*'s stunt. The balloon was sent off "to much fanfare," but both the planned journey and the story "sputtered out long before [their] expected completion date[s]."[1]

Although Pulitzer's first attempt at a travel stunt failed, the publisher and practitioner of late nineteenth-century new journalism learned from his mistakes. On November 14, 1889, the *World* brought to center stage another travel stunt, which became one of the most widely discussed expressions of new journalism and set the stage to dramatize an explicit competition between literature and journalism. Reporters announced that the newspaper was sending its pluckiest "girl" reporter, Nellie Bly (Elizabeth Cochrane Seaman), the very woman rejected for the earlier balloon journey, on a trip around the world to see if an actual voyager could beat the fictional record of circumnavigation imagined by novelist Jules Verne in his novel *Around the World in Eighty Days.* Published thirteen years earlier,[2] Verne's lighthearted adventure had described the exciting journey of the intrepid Londoner Phileas Fogg, who circumnavigated the globe within eighty days. Transcending a series of unforeseen challenges and dangers, Fogg manipulated various forms of transportation to triumph in a celebration of modern technology over imposing geography. Verne's novel had proved a spectacular success in Europe and America, but until the *World* announced its stunt, no one had attempted to make Fogg's fictional travel "real" in such public fashion.[3]

The *World* was poised to change that. Pulitzer, who had introduced the concept of new journalism to New York six years earlier after purchasing the struggling *World,* was prepared to challenge Verne's art and not only imitate it but improve upon it. Where Verne had sent a man, assisted by a faithful servant, on an imaginary trip, Pulitzer would send a young woman, unescorted, and in actuality. Where Fogg had required eighty days to complete the voyage, Bly's itinerary predicted only seventy-five were necessary. Pulitzer anticipated that the race around the world and against time would become a race against the very idea of fictionality as well; the newspaper, if successful, would emerge as the superior medium for a revision of Verne's romance. Nellie Bly's tale would be as electric as Phileas Fogg's, with an equal number of hair-raising adventures and mad dashes, but in the end its thrill would in fact surpass the thrill of the novel, because it would be real.

Bly herself acted as protagonist in this new(s) story, for Pulitzer cast her as both author of and protagonist in the journalistic tale. Bly posed as heir apparent to Verne, who, in the newspaper's framing, represented an aged literary tradition outmoded by that journalism. In his turn, Verne attempted to use the paper's travel writing and his perceptions of modern journalism to link his imaginative writing with journalistic practice and to position himself not as a stodgy artist but as a vitally modern contemporary storyteller. This chapter surveys Pulitzer's conception of new journalism and describes the mission of the *New York World* before examining the paper's positioning of Bly against Verne's fictional backdrop. Most of the narratives discussed in this chapter were written by anonymous reporters for the *World*. Because of the limitations of communication networks in 1889, Bly's own full account of the trip was not published in the *World* until after she returned; this account ran in Sunday issues of the *World* between January 27 and February 23, 1890, before it was published under separate cover as *Nellie Bly's Book*.

Bly's own framing of her travels, written after the fact, is less informative than the *World*'s presentation of its heroine during her actual trip. For while Bly traveled, the *World* became the "corporate author" of a new kind of adventure story in which the conventions of scientific fiction were combined with those of travel narratives and given new life under the banner of actuality. In his turn, Verne, an author incalculably indebted to Poe, would seek a reversal of the newspaper's message that fiction paled in comparison to the stories of the news. Assured of the authority and relevancy of fiction, Verne labored to demonstrate that his own mode of writing—itself a perpetual crossover between various generic boundaries—was significant and relevant, especially in light of this extraordinary competition between literature and journalism. Taken together, the "two sides" of the story of Nellie Bly and Jules Verne accentuate the ligature between fictionality and factuality as they appropriated discourses from each other and sought to claim a space in the late nineteenth-century literary marketplace.[4]

Joseph Pulitzer's New Journalism

Any discussion of new journalism in the 1890s rightfully begins a decade earlier with Joseph Pulitzer, owner and editor of the *St. Louis Post-Dispatch* and the *New York World*. Although other newspaper editors around the nation were moving in the same direction as Pulitzer as they turned increasingly to sensationalism, human-interest stories, punchy writing, and engrossing illustrations, Pulitzer must be credited with almost single-handedly normalizing those techniques, primarily because his methods were widely copied by other editors nationwide. Thus, while Pulitzer did not "invent" new journalism per se, he was its first practitioner par excellence, the standard against whom others—most notably William Randolph Hearst and in an inverse fashion Charles Dana—measured themselves.

Pulitzer, born to a genteel Hungarian family in 1847, immigrated to the United States in 1864 and enlisted in the Union army. After serving in the Civil War, he settled in St. Louis as a reporter for a German-language newspaper and soon purchased a joint interest in the periodical with money he had saved from successful investments. Pulitzer brought financial stability to the German paper and bought the *St. Louis Dispatch* (which merged shortly with the *Evening Post*) in 1878.

Under Pulitzer's influence the newly combined *Post-Dispatch* produced a fresh kind of journalism. It was "bright, sharp, irreverent, surprising" and a "trifle shocking"; it "breathed a quality" of sensationalism.[5] Pulitzer—who in the characterization of one biographer was "innately excitable and dramatic"—built the St. Louis paper into both a source of sheer entertainment and moral crusading, a paper enjoyed by businessmen, workmen, and housewives alike.[6] The newspaper became a place to dramatize both events and people whom other newspapers had ignored—the immigrants, the working classes, the "common man." Pulitzer turned ordinary characters and situations into extraordinary stories. Reviving the strong characterizations, colorful writing, and intense plotting that distinguished Benjamin Day's *New York Sun* in the 1830s, Pulitzer altered the very nature of Midwestern journalism and saw his fortunes rise exponentially. He revitalized the entertainment value of the newspaper, spotlighting such innovations as sports and women's pages, large headlines, illustrations, and crusading investigative reports.

These innovations worked well in St. Louis. Pulitzer, however, trained his ambitious eye on larger markets and sought to acquire a New York stage on which he could display his new journalistic techniques to wider audiences.[7] When Jay Gould's faltering *World* came onto the market in 1883, Pulitzer recognized his opening and willingly paid substantially more for the paper than its apparent value. With the purchase of the *World,* Pulitzer could finally expand his news-making practices on a much grander scale. His venture most certainly succeeded. The paper had a daily circulation of only fifteen thousand in 1883; by 1898 it boasted a stunning circulation of 1,500,000.[8]

In his New York newspaper Pulitzer spotlighted sensation to an unprecedented degree, feeding his readers a steady fare of "sex, crime, and tragedy," all displayed within revolutionary layouts, generous illustrations, specialty pages, and in enormous Sunday editions.[9] As with his St. Louis publication, however, Pulitzer did not desire merely to titillate readers and earn a fortune for himself. Rather, like his predecessor Day of the *Sun,* Pulitzer held complex and sometimes contradictory ideas about the role of sensation in newspapers and, more basically, about newspapers in American society. Writing in his first editorial column, he asserted:

> There is room in this great and growing city for a journal that is not only cheap but bright, not only bright but large, not only large but truly democratic—dedicated to the cause of the people rather than that of purse-potentates—devoted more to the news of the New than the Old World—that will expose all fraud and sham, fight all public evils and abuses—that will serve and battle for the people with earnest sincerity.[10]

Pulitzer's goal, as an immigrant himself, was to "speak for as well as to the masses of people who patronized the *World,*" specifically underprivileged populations, which needed more accessible and affordable reading material than the other papers offered.[11] More generally, Pulitzer prided himself on taking the political and social side of all working-class Americans. Social change would arise out of the audience of immigrant and native working-class readers that the *World* courted. The way to attract those readers, Pulitzer argued, was not through explicitly political news, rendered in a dry, intellectualized manner but through sensation and articles of human interest. Theoretically, page one would grab the attention of readers and encourage them to keep reading so that the editorial section on page four could educate them. What resulted in the *World* was "a unique blend of colorful reporting and crusading zeal."[12] What also emerged was writing of incredible vigor and even artistry, as Pulitzer's authors sought (in the memory of former *World* reporter Theodore Dreiser) "The Facts—The Color—The Facts!"[13]

The paper teemed with stories that read nearly like fiction, with vivid characters, evocative settings, narrative presence, and descriptive language.[14] The facts of any given news event certainly were present in most stories, but color—or the way a story was told—was critical, especially in the human-interest pieces in which the *World* specialized. Reversing the familiar terms somewhat, anything considered "literary," in Pulitzer's words, should "be judged by standards not too different from those applied to newspaper feature articles. It should tell a story, and in doing so use all the tricks of plot development and lively prose to hold the reader's attention."[15] One *World* reporter added:

> It is possible . . . to select certain particularly picturesque or romantic incidents and treat them symbolically, for their human interest rather than their individual and personal significance. In this way news ceases to be wholly personal and assumes the form of art. It ceases to be the record of the doings of individual men and women and becomes an impersonal account of manners and life.[16]

When actual happenings failed to provide material that could be transformed into artistic narratives, Pulitzer, like Day in 1835, provided the material himself by manufacturing the news or by staging stunts on which the paper could then report. The trick was to select subjects that would seem representative and animated, just as a novelist's key to success lay in creating representative and animated plots. Nellie Bly's trip around the world became a premier example of such manufactured animation. It was the prototypical newspaper stunt, a hallmark of new journalism in its creation of a plot into which a dramatic and even symbolic character could fit. The trip, that is, was not an abstract report on the worldwide transportation industry in 1889. Manipulating manufactured news, Pulitzer's writers told their revised tale of world travel artfully, incorporating plenty of adventure, exotic locales, and indefatigable characters, all the while asserting that the modern newspaper story was superior to the *wholly* manufactured, or imaginary, story.

Around the World with the World: *Linking Fact to Fiction*

Both the motivation and timetable for Nellie Bly's race around the world arose from the unbroken record of circumnavigation that Verne had imagined in *Around the World in Eighty Days*. The *World* boldly proposed to "undertake the task of turning" Verne's "dream into a reality" and to travel, both literally and figuratively, where no newspaper story had ventured before.[17] Despite the novel's sizable readership—it had been extremely popular in America, eventually selling nearly a half million copies in Verne's lifetime—"thousands upon thousands" of readers had "been content to stop with the reading and curiously enough," a *World* reporter wrote, "not one seems to have carried out the idea" of racing around the world. The paper recognized an opportunity to animate the trip—and to manufacture some highly profitable news—with a cheeky proclamation that "it remains for THE WORLD to lead the way in this as in so many other paths."

To make the race against Verne's fictional record particularly magnificent, managing editor John Cockerill[18] chose as the circumnavigator (or, as one reporter put it, the recipient of the "romantic assignment") Bly, who was by now busily crafting a name for herself as one of a new "breed of American writer" and who served as "a symbol and repository of new national values," particularly "strenuosity" and "the outdoor life."[19] Employed by the *World* only two years, Bly had already gathered appreciable fame with her seemingly fearless investigative reporting and candid interviewing. Presenting herself as "young, charming, outspoken; modern and adorably bold," Bly thrilled readers with insider exposés of life in an insane asylum and the hardships faced by young women looking for work in the city, to name just two stories.[20] Hers was precisely the sort of persona the newspaper could manipulate to turn a stunt into a story.

Women were just appearing as professional journalists with some regularity in the late nineteenth century, though most were still employed as society reporters or fashion editors.[21] Bly envisioned a different newspaper career for herself. Born Elizabeth Cochran in Cochran's Mills, Pennsylvania, in 1864, she had entered journalism in 1885 when she responded with displeasure to a disparaging *Pittsburg Dispatch* article entitled "What Girls Are Good For." The paper's editor, impressed with Bly's verve, offered her a job as a reporter. Bly enthusiastically accepted, adopted a pen name from the popular Stephen Foster song "Nelly Bly," and entertained Pittsburgh readers for two years with her sharp humor and startling exposés. Still, Bly's unabashed yearning for fame led far beyond the relatively small market of Pittsburgh—by 1887 she "felt ready to crash the gates of New York City."[22] Dismissing the difficulty faced by men, let alone women, in breaking into the New York newspaper business, she demanded interviews with editors across the city, finally setting her sights on the *World*. One Bly legend recounts that after front office staff at the *World* ignored her, she simply let herself into Pulitzer's *sanctum sanctorum,* where he was meeting with John Cockerill. Impressed by her brass and daring, the two men bent their usual policies and hired a woman reporter.

Bly was a perfect fit for Pulitzer's new journalism. Seeking ever-more sensational angles on the news, editors at the *World* and other papers gradually realized the advantage of keeping women on staff. To Brooke Kroeger, Bly's biographer, "it was the advent of both the stunt girl" like Bly and "the large separate women's sections" in newspapers "that created the first real place for women as regular members of the newspaper staff," bringing "women, as a class, out of the journalistic sideshow and into the main arena."[23] Bly became one of the earliest performers in this arena and proved one of the best. In most of her New York newspaper projects, her thirst for sensation stretched the boundaries of social acceptability for women in late nineteenth-century America. The proposed trip around the world was no exception. In that era, white, middle-class women neither worked as reporters nor traveled alone with any regularity, and those who did were magnets "for diverse and complicated reactions."[24] Predictably, then, when Bly proposed an idea for her most sensational exploit yet—an unescorted trip around the world—her daring seemed to reach almost mythic proportions. Bly later took great pleasure recounting how she introduced the idea of world travel to Cockerill:

> "I want to go around in eighty days or less. I think I can beat Phileas Fogg's record. May I try it?"
>
> To my dismay he told me that in the office they had thought of this same idea before, and the intention was to send a man. . . .
>
> "It is impossible for you to do it," was the terrible verdict. "In the first place you are a woman and would need a protector, and even if it were possible for you to travel alone you would need to carry so much baggage that it would detain you in making rapid changes. . . ."
>
> "Very well," I said angrily, "Start the man and I'll start the same day for some other newspaper and beat him."
>
> "I believe you would," he said slowly.[25]

Here was the stuff of legend; here appeared a heroine too intrepid to be real, a young woman as compelling as any fictional heroine in her apparent ability to defeat whatever obstacles stood in her way. Yet she *was* real, and public reaction to the race was immediate and palpable.

That Bly would not only travel alone but would engage in a physically and mentally draining race—and as a professional woman, no less—was itself enough to ensure that spectacle would surround the reporter and her sponsoring paper. But Bly would also strive against a daunting fictional goal in the process. Though she would not necessarily keep Verne's "record" as "the uppermost thought in her . . . endeavor," she would nevertheless "make the trip in the shortest possible time and tell all she can interesting about it," the *World*'s editors assured their readers.[26] Placed beside the entertaining character of Phileas Fogg, she, a mere "modest little woman travelling all alone," would be equally entertaining and meanwhile "demonstrate that the trip can be made in five or six days' less time" than Verne had imagined possible.[27] The gender transformation was key, not only because women simply did not travel alone (and in such adventurous ways) but also because Bly's journey radically rewrote Verne's plot, in which the only female character, Aouda, appears as the helpless victim of an Indian suttee, rescued in the nick of time by male travelers.[28] Verne and Bly even joked together about such "plot revisions" when they met en route. When the author asked Bly why she did not plan to visit Bombay, as Fogg had, Bly laughed that she was "more anxious to save time than a young widow." Verne replied that Bly "may save a young widower before you return," to which Bly merely smiled with, as she put it, "a superior knowledge, as women, fancy free, always will at such insinuations."[29] Almost inevitably, then, Bly became the symbolic centerpiece of young American vigor, feminine ingenuity, and most importantly, journalistic derring-do as the newspaper recast the plot and characters of Verne's novel, manufacturing a new story and the news simultaneously.

This overt challenge to test fiction and revise it into an entertaining and true story became the focus of writing in the *World* from November 1889 through January 1890. Repeatedly, *World* writers used the benchmark motif of "imagination versus reality" as rhetorical justification for the trip, and the subtext girding these references reveals a steady privileging of "the real thing" in modern reading practice. Bly's character entered the class of what Wilson calls America's "high priest of 'experience,' the expert on 'real life.'"[30] By the late 1880s, reporters in general were considered people who could travel to all branches of society and to all corners of the world and see "real life" as it was "really" lived. Thus, one article gloated that while the "romantic Frenchman" Verne "will stay at home and dream," this "nervy, plucky, go-head little girl will push on to add" a new "episode" to the story of new journalism.[31] Verne's novel might well have served an earlier generation of readers who had not required firsthand knowledge. But within an increasingly fact-based society, the accuracy of

Phileas Fogg's journey demanded empirical testing. Fancy alone would no longer suffice. One article in the *Pittsburg Press* posed a modern scenario to support the need for Bly's trip—what would happen, the writer mused, if Andrew Carnegie needed to return to the United States from Hong Kong to attend to pressing business matters? Not to worry. With "Bly's model of rapid transit to guide him," he need not rely upon "the untried fictional notions advanced by Jules Verne."[32]

The juxtaposition of the newspaper's fact and Verne's fiction suggests that editors conceived of the race around the world as a way to appeal to public faith in the "scientifically provable" idea. One article boasted that the "boys and girls in the schools pore over their atlases with much deeper attention and interest than they did" before Bly's trip. Indeed, "the entire population has been greatly benefited by the project," and "everybody will be to some extent improved by the Nellie Bly tour."[33] Other articles emphasized how the trip would advantageously test new transportation technologies and networks—students at Johns Hopkins had even begun studying the trip for this purpose, the *World* proudly mentioned.[34] While in reality the scientific value of the trip was negligible, these references were hardly accidental. Rather, reporters used them in conjunction with the figure of the aging Verne to transform what could be dismissed as a mere journalistic stunt into something of purported real-world value. Placing a scientific and realist spin on the narrative was a strategy, we shall see later, to which Verne himself turned in order to lend credibility and timeliness to his own fiction.

Editors rightly assumed that tying the journalistic story to technological progress would refresh the worn path of travel writing that Bly inevitably traversed. Indeed, the article announcing the trip conceded, "Since Cook's day the number of globe trotters would make a good-sized army. Every now and again somebody becomes imbued with the idea that the surest road to fame is to run around the globe and then write books to crowd upon the shelves of libraries. Few of them are ever read."[35]

Bly's trip, in other words, was to some degree indebted to a much older and decidedly less glamorous tradition of travel writing. *World* articles exuded confidence that this journey would yield a more significant story because of the nature of the travel and the character of the traveler. It would be timely, sped-up, and as sensational as the newspaper in which it was recorded. Under the banner of new journalism, which cast itself as the most timely print medium available in 1889, a different kind of travel adventure could be initiated—one in which the speed of the trip, the celebrity of the traveler, and the triumph of actuality over mere imagination, rather than the sights seen or the escapades experienced en route, became the story. This narrative would be delivered not to already overburdened and dusty bookshelves but daily to the parlors and breakfast tables of thousands of American readers, who were almost guaranteed to read it.

Since Bly was unable to publish her own story in the *World* as she traveled, other reporters told her story during the seventy-two days of the trip, tracing her route and speculating on the adventures she might experience at various ports of call. The race against Verne's fiction remained the central motif in these articles. One report, for instance, crowed that Bly's pace was bound to "throw Jules Verne and his London hero entirely into the background of both fact and fiction," while another saw Bly making Verne's fiction into "a stern reality."[36] The *World* quoted the remark of one U.S. senator: "Jules Verne did not have the New York WORLD in contemplation when he made the schedule for circumnavigating the planet world, otherwise he would have cut down the time to about sixty days. The WORLD's pace is becoming too fast for even the imagination of a Verne."[37] Other coverage asserted that "when Jules Verne's imaginary character made the tour in eighty days it was looked upon as a feat in keeping with the vivid imagination of that wonderfully imaginative author, but nothing more."[38] Headlines—including one reminding readers that "M. Jules Verne" was bound to be "outdone" and one pitting "Bly Versus Verne"—continued to position "the real" and "the imaginary" in a pivotal contest.[39]

Pitting the journalistic voyage against the imaginary one even more dramatically, *World* editors arranged a meeting between Bly and Verne once she arrived in Europe.[40] The meeting appeared upon the pages of the *World* as an explicit juxtaposition of the fictional figure of old and the factual heroine of modernity. This relationship represented for its reporters a passing of the narrative torch from earlier imaginary constructions to new journalistic realities, and in it they read something of a patrilineal blessing bestowed by "fiction" upon "fact." The *World*'s London and Paris correspondents, and later Bly in her own narrative, detailed her pilgrimage to Verne's home at Amiens, France. In their framing, Verne was cast as a kindly and somewhat frail grandfather, humble enough to share a toast with Bly, open his writerly inner sanctum, and wish her a hearty *bon voyage* as she rushed to meet her next train. Verne, the story revealed, approved of the modern tastes that privileged realism over fantasy; he specifically praised American newspapers, proclaiming the *World* "to be the most American of them all."[41] The novelist's admiration for Pulitzer's new journalism and for the reporter representing it was seemingly endless. He gushed that in "no other country in the world" could one "find a young lady who would venture to do what you are doing and certainly none where a newspaper would go to the cost of backing her in such an experiment for its scientific value."[42]

But the visit to Verne's home became more than a single, charming stop on Bly's blitzkrieg itinerary, for the *World* continued to deploy Verne's name—and the fictionality he represented—long after Bly's journey had led her away from France. This manipulation of Verne's character suggests that news makers recognized the importance of adjoining Bly's name to Verne's during the actual travel so as to highlight what the story indicated about new journalism's status in relation to fiction. Sizable follow-up articles in the *World* reintroduced Verne as a character in the drama, reminding readers of his literary projects and gauging his reaction to Bly's real-world progress. One article, for instance, originally published in the *London Pall Mall* and reprinted by the *World,* quoted Verne lauding Bly as the "prettiest young girl imaginable. . . . Nobody, to look at the quiet, ladylike little thing, would have thought for a moment that she was what she is and that she was going to do what she is doing. Yet I must say she looks built for hard work."[43]

Further, on January 26, 1890, the day after Bly completed her record-setting journey, a long story about Verne's reaction to the accomplishment stretched over three of eight front-page columns, and an additional front-page column was composed of telegraph cables between the *World* and Verne. As Verne's prominence on the front page attests, *World* editors read his congratulation as an implicit concession on his part. His name reminded readers about the momentous question behind the more superficial adventure plot: which narrative form is "the real thing," fiction or journalism? Verne's "hurrahs," the *World*'s front-page layout suggested, acknowledged the victory of fact over fiction. The articles themselves asserted this victory as well. One gushed that Bly "has turned the dream of a French fiction-maker into sober truth" and that the "fact of today has made the fancy of a quarter of a century ago seem like a twice-told tale."[44] Now, the article continued, "the ghost of Phileas Fogg" had only to "sit and skip ghostly hopscotches somewhere in the realm of fancy."

Nellie Bly greets a line of defeated globe-trotters, including Jules Verne's fictional character Phileas Fogg. Vivid, exciting prose detailing the victory of fact over fiction surrounds the symbolic illustration. *New York World,* January 26, 1890.

Editors even added a front-page illustration of the triumphant Bly greeting a rank of former male world travelers, among them a rather resigned-looking Phileas Fogg. The implication was clear. Bly and the *World* had appropriated Verne's materials, and where the romancer had faced only the boundaries of imagination, new journalism had turned art into life and made it, paradoxically, even more ideal than it had been in its original, artful form.

As further proof that real life could be better than even the most realistic fiction, *World* writers lifted a breathtaking scene almost directly from *Around the World in Eighty Days.* In chapter 28 of the novel, as Fogg races across America on the transcontinental railroad, the train reaches a precarious suspension bridge at Medicine Bow. Rail watchmen forbid the train to proceed, warning that the bridge's cables are broken and that its collapse is imminent. "With the devil-may-care attitude of the Americans," Verne slyly observes, "one can say that when they play safe, one would be crazy not to play safe as well."[45] The race against time seems hopelessly lost until one "true Yankee" has the idea of "sending the train hurtling along at full speed" in order to place minimum weight on the bridge, cross the chasm, and resume the journey. This novel proposal instantly sways the trainload of hearty Americans, though to Fogg's uneasy companion Passepartout, "the idea still seemed . . . a little too 'American.'" Unwilling to heed Passepartout's logic, the engineer races the train down the track and sends it leaping over the gulf "just like greased lightning." Ignoring no opportunity for thrills, Verne reveals that "hardly had the train crossed the river than the bridge, now completely demolished, crashed noisily down into Medicine Bow Rapids."

Surely the scene proved exciting for novel readers. How much more harrowing it was, then, when Nellie Bly herself faced a similar situation. The January 23, 1890, *World* recounted how Bly narrowly escaped "a terrible death" when a train "running at the rate of over fifty miles an hour" across New Mexico dashed toward a section of track under repair on a bridge spanning a deep canyon. A special dispatch to the *World* breathlessly related that the rails, "only held up by jackscrews," remained miraculously intact as "the engine and car went thundering over the ravine." Though the "rails bent under," the "structure did not give way" to the train and its precious cargo.[46] Clearly, the railroad workers "who witnessed the train flash past on its straw-like structure" agreed, this was an "interesting bit of realism."[47]

Verne's subtle mocking of brash Americans is turned on its head so that the trainload of earnest but incautious "true Yankees" become heroic, objects of celebration, able to leap deep chasms in a single bound. Furthermore, by the time Bly got around to providing her version of the story in her own book, the incident's facts had been improved upon, so that the bridge reportedly falls immediately after the train zips across the chasm. In Bly's rendition, a lucky rabbit's foot given to her by an admirer seems to keep the travelers safe at this critical juncture. "Well, I don't know anything about the left hind foot of a rabbit," Bly remarks, "but when I knew that my train had run safely across a bridge which was held in place only by jackscrews, and which fell the moment we were across, . . . then I thought of the left hind foot of a rabbit, and wondered if there was anything in it."[48] Once more life could both imitate and improve upon art, transforming it into a dramatic and "real"—if somewhat embroidered—tale.

The *World*'s use of Verne as an icon—and even the use of a scene that directly revised Verne's novel—showed how expertly its editors marketed

Bly, her character, and her occupation. In essence, they manufactured a story about how news stories themselves were fitting for a modern narrative age that already privileged factual discourses, generally speaking. The framing of the sensational circumnavigation as a race between literature and journalism became a "point of fusion between social and literary motivations" for a "growing middle-class culture that valued objectivity increasingly."[49] By usurping the imaginary with the provable, the *World* generated reader interest in Bly as representative of writing that took its start from artifice and then improved upon it and made it "the real thing."

In Verne's World: Imagining the Facts

If the *World* manipulated Verne's role to establish journalism as the new and improved story, Verne and his agents in turn used Bly's persona to rejuvenate the novelist's waning career and emphasize the real-life relevance of his fiction.[50] Verne recognized the extensive publicity potential of Bly's journey; he readily understood the mass attraction of new journalism. He also realized that his own fiction, despite the *World's* implicit devaluing of it, was nourished by a common vein of facticity. Early in his career, Verne had composed articles on scientific topics for a Paris magazine. The process of "poring over various reference books, scientific magazines, and newspapers" had led him "to envision the possibility of incorporating all this documentation into a new and innovative type of novel whose narrative format would simultaneously blend fiction with fact, adventure with didacticism, and literary motifs with scientific data."[51] Verne considered his fiction "geographical" and "scientific" in nature and claimed that he merely clothed that "science in the charming robes of romance."[52] Throughout his career he merged imagination with science, always blurring lines between fact and fiction. Now recognized as a father of scientific fiction, or the *roman scientifique* (as opposed to the more fantastically based science fiction), Verne endeavored, in his words, "to make even the wildest of my romances as realistic and true to life as possible," utilizing "with advantage my scientific education to blend together science and romance into a work of an advantageous description that might appeal to the public taste."[53] While some of his works delighted in wildly imaginative and purely fantastic scenes, others, including *Around the World in Eighty Days,* were romances "not so very far in advance of sober, solid fact after all."[54]

Verne's work, then, consistently negotiated and problematized the boundaries between "the real" and "the literary." If both American and European literary realisms thrived in the nineteenth century "as a means for neutralizing anxieties about the writer's status" within cultures that were "intensely suspicious or contemptuous of 'art' and the 'artistic,'" Verne's creations rested firmly within the realm of "the real."[55] Realism, after all, was a "claim" for "the real," or a "socially normal . . . activity" that lessened public "suspicion" about art.[56] Verne's imaginative claims drew strength from scientific and journalistic discourses, which could render even his wildest adventures relevant, not suspiciously artistic. Furthermore, through this discourse he differentiated himself from writers like H. G. Wells—who, Verne said, constructed his ideas "entirely from the realm of imagination" rather than science—and positioned himself and his literary production closer to apparent actuality.[57]

It was in this commitment to actuality that Verne lay close to his literary progenitor, Edgar Allan Poe. Verne read Poe in translation by 1856 and under this influence began his *Voyages Extraordinaires,* the eventual collection of fifty-four novels constituting the core of his *oeuvre.* Fond of sprinkling references to other writers into his own stories, Verne used Poe's name more than that of any other author and frequently borrowed scenarios, characters, and ideas from his American alter ego. Notably, Verne picked up Poe's cue about travel to the moon and balloon transportation in numerous stories and in the novels *Five Weeks in a Balloon* (1863), *From the Earth to the Moon* (1865), and *Round the Moon* (1870). In the second of these novels, a group of Baltimore gun club members and Civil War veterans, depressed over the end of the war, apply their munitions expertise to space travel. The president of the gun club recounts the history of moon narratives and includes in his chronicles the "discoveries" of Hans Pfaall, à la Poe. "Cheers for Edgar Poe!" the club members roar.[58] In addition, in 1864, as he wrote his lunar travel novels, Verne also completed a serious critical study of Poe entitled "Edgar Poe et ses oeuvres."

Most directly, one of the sources for *Around the World in Eighty Days* was Poe's "Three Sundays in a Week," a riddle tale that provided the climactic idea of gaining a day of travel time by journeying in an easterly direction.[59] Poe's story includes a character who feels "repugnance to 'the humanities'" in comparison to "what he supposed to be natural science," and while Verne obviously did not share this revulsion, he revealed his own biases by infusing natural science into his stories and novels.[60] As

Poe built such fictions as "Hans Pfaall" and "The Balloon Hoax" around contemporary scientific discourses, granting them plausibility and forcing his readers to question the essential nature of fact and fiction, Verne blended generic lines so that even the most futuristic and fantastic of his works maintained a foothold in possibility.

From the beginning of Verne's career, readers and book reviewers acknowledged this realistic appeal.[61] His first novel, *Five Weeks in a Balloon*, took its lead in part from Poe's "Balloon Hoax." The story about a London penny paper backing a balloon expedition led some Parisian newspaper readers to believe "that the book described a real journey," because "it was as up to date as the next day's paper."[62] A review for *Five Weeks in a Balloon*, perhaps written by Verne himself, stated that the author, like Poe, "knows how to link fiction to reality in proportions so exact that one does not know where one begins and the other leaves off."[63] Another reviewer for the 1864 novel *A Journey to the Centre of the Earth* remarked:

> In reading we at times forget the utter impossibility of the adventure for the travellers, and fancy ourselves reading merely the account of ordinary travellers. Indeed, highly sensational as some of the hairbreadth escapes of the different explorers appear to be, they might be paralleled by some of the miraculous escapes of our modern Alpine climbers.[64]

Similarly, some original readers of *Around the World in Eighty Days* forgot that Verne's writing was a fiction. British and American newspapers ran translated excerpts of the novel as it was serialized in France, leading certain subscribers to believe Fogg's journey was actually occurring. As a result, "bets were placed, and international liner and railway companies competed" for participation in the "journey."[65] Adding to the delightful confusion, during the time *Around the World in Eighty Days* was being serialized in *Le Temps* of Paris, Thomas Cook was publishing in the *Times* of London factual accounts of his own much-publicized tourist trip around the world (which was to have taken only 102 days but ended up lasting seven months).[66] An older Verne likely enjoyed recalling these testaments to his own veracity. Having once traveled himself to gather scientific and geographic data for his novels, by 1889 the now elderly man traveled "only in imagination" and through the maps and almanacs that littered his library table.[67]

If Verne's age persuaded him to leave actual travel to plucky young reporters while he remained in the library, his mind still concocted unusual narrative journeys, toward which he needed to draw readers' attention. The meshing of his work with Bly's—juxtaposing imagination with actuality—brought such attention in a remarkably public fashion. Most obviously, Bly's trip renewed interest in Verne's novel, which, as he often asserted, had itself been inspired in part by "a tourist advertisement seen by chance in the columns of a newspaper."[68] One January 1890 *World* article recorded that ten new editions of the novel had been issued since the start of Bly's trip; at least thirty-eight American and British editions were to appear between 1890 and 1899, about twenty more than during the previous decade.[69] A story that had found international popularity when first serialized some fifteen years earlier in *Le Temps* was newsworthy once again, piggybacking on the interest generated by its even more fabulously serialized journalistic offspring.

Verne and others who profited from his work seized this novel amalgamation of fact and fiction as an opportunity for additional marketing, arguing that fiction's utility had not truly been defeated, given that Verne's art was already so faithful to the facts. The manager of Paris's Chatelet Theatre reopened the company's *'Round the World in Eighty Days,* despite his admission that the production had previously been "quite played out" and that "the last time it didn't pay expenses."[70] But with Bly's trip, the old became new(s) once again; the manager discovered "a great actuality now" that compelled him to restage the play "in compliance with a very general demand." Demand was in fact so great that already in early January, as the *World* proudly related, all seats for the opening performance— which was to "coincide with the reception in Paris of the news of Miss Bly's arrival on time in New York"—had sold out. The theater manager even hinted that he might add lines alluding to Bly to the script: "We certainly owe her some recognition."[71]

Verne lent his hand more directly to similar rejuvenation efforts. As Bly dashed around the world, he repeatedly granted newspaper interviews in which he bubbled with enthusiasm about Bly and the *World.* "Ah, yes, Miss Bly of the New York WORLD, the brave young lady who is going to show the world that my novel of a journey round the world in eighty days is by no means an impossibility"—attempts to reinforce the pertinence of his fiction (and plug his own book by title) for a reality-hungry reading public.[72] Similarly, when Bly completed her journey successfully, Verne cabled immediately to the *World* office in New York, "Hurrah for her and for the Director of the *World!* Hurrah! Hurrah!" This telegram had the effect of placing Verne within the circle of triumph and reminding readers about the *World*'s source of inspiration—as well as diminishing the idea of a race or contest between his writing and the *World*'s.[73]

Verne had good reason to compliment the American newspaper and its star reporter. As an avid consumer of periodicals himself—he took subscriptions "to over twenty newspapers," and his library table groaned under "a mass of newspapers, reviews, and scientific reports"—he recognized the attraction of the medium, especially in its modern incarnation.[74] Verne had saved articles "for future reference," believing this laborious effort kept him "thoroughly abreast of the times with regard to matters of scientific interest."[75] Keeping abreast of the news was, he argued, "the only satisfactory means of fitting an author to deal with the kaleidoscope progress of modern events," a modernity necessary for crafting relevant fiction.[76] Clearly, Verne understood the importance of newspapers and their implied facticity, in terms not only of gathering ideas for himself but of gathering an audience. In 1890, when his publisher, Jules Hetzel, reported some discouraging sales figures, Verne asserted that a reading public *did* exist, but primarily for newspapers rather than novels.[77] Verne's self-identification with the news, then, should be read as multilayered, at once embracing his own scientific approach to fiction (which was itself informed by external social and marketplace forces) and anticipating and expanding "the boundaries of the consumer's reading experience."[78]

Surely Verne's involvement with the *World* was not entirely self-interested or motivated by his designs for increasing readership. Verne's compliments to the *New York World* certainly seem sincere, and he sharply protested any suggestion that he wrote merely for profit. Still, his enthusiastic praise for Bly echoed positively in the halls of the *World* building and may have ensured additional interviews, articles, and publicity about Verne. Such articles, published first in the *World* and then reprinted widely in other American papers, reminded the public about Verne himself, whose career by 1889 had seen much better days. The elderly author was still producing the two volumes per year his publishing contract demanded, but the new books were not nearly as popular as previous ones had been, and he felt, according to his grandson, "that he was becoming a has-been."[79] Sales for Verne's new novels were soft during the 1880s, and he faced an increasing pool of imitative competitors in the scientific romance genre.[80]

An attempt to recapture audience interest during Bly's travels might be seen in one *World* article in which Verne plugged his latest romance, *The Journey Backward,* as "a trip through the north of America, Alaska, and the Bering Strait."[81] Additionally, Verne's "Topsy Turvey," which appeared in the Sunday *World* of January 19, 1890, was a story that, as the paper's masthead had declared two days earlier, Verne himself "told Nellie Bly to read." Rumors even circulated that Verne planned to write Bly as "a very sprightly character" into his next novel, which would, if his writing pattern held true, once again stretch the boundaries of fiction.[82]

While Bly never did appear as one of his central characters, Verne began work on *Claudius Bombarnac, or the Special Correspondent* following his meeting with her in November 1889.[83] In this slight novel a newspaper correspondent for the evocatively named *Twentieth Century* is sent upon a rapid-fire journey across Asia on the Trans-Asiatic Railroad (a fictional line modeled on the trans-Siberian route). Verne seems to have fixed upon the idea of another travel novel soon after meeting Bly, and he structured this one to include, once more, the theme of record breaking and modern journalism. The author told one London reporter in 1889 that Bly's record would probably fall once a railroad across Siberia was built, and his remarks, filled with details about where the line would run and how many days of travel it would trim off a circumnavigation, suggest he was already plotting *Claudius Bombarnac.*

Verne's novel teems with gentle parodies of sensationalized journalism (Bombarnac cries that "a minute lost is ten lines of correspondence" and thus loss of profit) and of travel-writing conventions, especially when those conventions are employed for stuntish news races ("I have no time to deliver myself in a remunerative torrent of descriptive phrases," Bombarnac once remarks breathlessly, almost mocking Nellie Bly's own narrative style. "Let us hurry off to the railway station"). Always on the lookout for the interesting travel tidbit—and seeking "Novelty! Novelty! The unforeseen! The appalling!" for his correspondence—Bombarnac eyes an American traveler suspiciously, fearing that he too is "a special [correspondent], perhaps for the *World* or the *New York Herald,*" someone who "has also been ordered off to do this Grand Asiatic [tour]. . . . He would be a rival!"[84] Provocatively, the novel also offers its own record-paced globe-trotter, the Baron Weisschnitzerdorfer, who is out "to rival Miss Nelly [*sic*] Bly" in a thirty-nine-day circumnavigation. "I shall be much surprised," Bombarnac sniffs, "if this German beats an American at globe-trotting."[85]

If Verne had hoped references to Bly, journalistic sponsorship, and American globe-trotting would bring widespread attention and financial payoffs to his novel, he was mistaken. *Claudius Bombarnac* is hardly one of Verne's better works, although its choice of characters and subject matter is provocative in terms of the Bly story. By keeping his own name attached to Bly's and to newspaper stunts both during and after her circumnavigation, Verne manipulated what Christopher Wilson has called "the modern cult of celebrity."[86] Articles reinforcing Verne's connection to the eminently popular and famous Bly—along with reminders of his fictional travel adventures and their meshing with Bly's nonfictional voyage—presented an opportunity to convince readers that his fiction could still compete with the newspaper's manufactured stories. If the *World* used the literary celebrity of Verne's name, in other words, to position new journalism as superior to fiction, Verne used the celebrity of Bly's name, all that she represented about new journalistic practice, and the intertwined discourses of literary and newspaper enterprise as "'property' to keep steadily in the public eye."[87]

At Journey's End with Bly and Verne

Despite the celebrity Verne drew upon to publicize his own writing, interviews with the writer revealed that he felt mistreated by the *World* once the frenzy over Bly died down. According to Robert Sherard, the *World*'s Paris correspondent, who claimed to have arranged the meeting between Bly and Verne, the old man believed "it was very strange that after he had served the purpose of the paper not a word of acknowledgment had been made to him."[88] Sherard repeatedly sought a "letter of thanks" for Verne from the New York office but was "told that the 'old man had got good advertising out of it and had no reason to complain.'"[89] Verne's sensitivity was shared by Bly herself. She left the *World* abruptly at the end of 1890, because she too felt the paper's managers had mistreated her. She complained she had not been given a bonus or raise, or even a token gift from Pulitzer, all of which she had enjoyed after producing her earlier sensational exposé *Ten Days in a Mad-House*.[90]

Bly did, however, reap financial rewards Verne could only dream of. In addition to various gifts from admirers, one of which was real estate valued at $1,500, she embarked on a national speaking tour that netted some

$9,500, a sizable sum by 1890 standards.[91] Meanwhile, the book version of her narrative, which she had first published in the *New York World* after her return, sold out its first edition by August 1890.[92] Further, Bly drew upon her journalistic celebrity and the interweaving of fact and fiction that had fueled her journey to earn a lucrative contract to write novels. She had already published in 1889—first in the *World* and then under separate cover—*The Mystery of Central Park,* based on a real murder she had covered as a reporter, and intended to launch a "Nellie Bly Series."[93] After her circumnavigation and lecture tour, she signed with the *New York Family Story Paper* to write serial novels for ten to fifteen thousand dollars a year, a contract Bly never fulfilled.[94]

That Bly's novel-writing career quickly stalled and then died altogether is a point for consideration. Bly's biographer attributes the almost immediate failure to Bly's basic ineptitude in such skills as plotting and characterization. More than that, I would point to the lack of a newspaper's "corporate authorship," which had once served to edit and structure Bly's efforts. With the help of Pulitzer and his new journalism, she had participated in taking a point of imagination, acting upon it, and surpassing it on a very public stage. Without this new breed of "author"—the newspaper itself—Bly became little more than one of many reporters trying to use their journalistic experiences as launching pads for wholly imaginative work. Part of what made Bly so remarkable, in other words, was the new aesthetic and the cultural authority she represented through the medium of the newspaper itself. Poe had invented his moon and balloon stories in an era of independent writers and editors, but by the end of the century journalism had become the province of corporate authorship. Stories were still invented and news was still manufactured, but as the result of the efforts of teams of usually anonymous workers, not necessarily of identifiable individuals. In other words, the woman who could so readily serve as a character type for other reporters and editors as they wrote the *World*'s new journalistic story could not ultimately infuse enough imagination into her own writing to make it more imaginative than factual—or rather, to make the facts more artistic than "art" itself.[95] If Bly took as a fictional starting point real stories she had encountered as a reporter, she finally could not make the fictional aesthetic more compelling than the real thing. Truth proved, once again and quite literally, better than fiction.

Bly's own forays into the fiction marketplace aside, what lingers from her 1889–90 adventures and, more specifically, from the *World*'s framing of this media event is a forceful message about textual values and the standards American readers were beginning to hold for mass-market newspapers. Despite his efforts to defend a space for fiction in the context of this race, Jules Verne finally served as little more than a point of juxtaposition for the newspaper's own fabricated story. Verne was an individual who imagined; the newspaper was an agent that acted and that proved "scientifically"—and it did so with the strongest elements of characters, plots, settings, suspense, and so on. Bly and Verne, without question, both won worldwide renown. Yet, in this particular context and pitted against the presence of the corporate author, they both signaled failure on the part of the individual author of fiction within this changing literary marketplace. Only the newspaper—which could write the "fiction," make it real, and add all the weight of its own actuality and authority—met with the most significant kind of success. For above all else, and despite Verne's claims, Pulitzer's stunt challenged the very idea that works of imagination held sway over reading audiences, at least when compared to the equally imaginative yet "true" offerings of the daily paper. In framing Bly's journey as a race against an imaginary or fictional record, the *World* also framed a contest against imagination or fiction writing itself. The triumph of Bly signaled a triumph not only of the daring young female spirit and modern transportation networks but of the emerging aesthetic that new journalism encapsulated.

Where Bly failed in her efforts to expand that aesthetic into fiction by herself, however, another journalist—Richard Harding Davis—would win accolades with his own version of new journalism, and he would do so with a most curiously intertwined style that forged his identities as fiction writer, journalist, author, and character into one.

Journalist as Hero

Richard Harding Davis and the Cult of
the Reporter in 1890s America

How vast and alluring is the work that stretches before the enthusiastic writer!
—Edwin L. Shuman, *Steps into Journalism*

Nellie Bly's meteoric rise to celebrity status emblematizes the position of
new journalists as public heroes in late nineteenth-century America. Along
with other reporters, such as James Creelman, Annie Laurie, and Stephen
Crane, Bly achieved national cult status through the profession. Though
journalists as we think of the term had been around since the penny-
press era, the profession grew and changed dramatically in the 1880s and
1890s. The new journalists in particular rose in prominence as their reporting style thrived, forming the catalyst for a professional authorship
through which stories became real and newsprint became a serious rival
to the bookmaker's stock. It was through journalists themselves that new
journalism became a social phenomenon, and we can best comprehend
the cultural impact of new journalism by studying its most notorious
practitioners. This section introduces one such figure—Richard Harding
Davis, whose career neatly epitomizes the way that new journalism at its
best blended life and art and cast the late nineteenth-century professional
reporter into a dramatic role.

Before the 1880s and 1890s, reporters for mass-market dailies had generally been considered by most Americans "as bohemian at best, and other-

wise as ne'er-do-wells, fly-by-nights, and, especially, drunkards."[1] The stereotype pictured the "old" reporter as "uneducated and proud of his ignorance; . . . regularly drunk and proud of his alcoholism."[2] Though not
necessarily drunk and uneducated, editors James Gordon Bennett and
William Cullen Bryant had helped to reinforce this negative characterization by a series of very public, physical, and verbal brawls with other editors and community leaders in the 1830s and 1840s. Journalists achieved
more respectability during the Civil War era, when they became the crucial link—the eyewitness accountants—between urban northerners and
the action at the fronts. During the war, New York newspapers employed
large pools of correspondents to follow and gather the latest events in the
South, pushing the professional reporter "closer to the center of national
consciousness," a trend that continued after the war as well.[3] Readers came
to trade their view of journalists as combative, low-class characters for an
image of them as adventurous, reliable storytellers and chroniclers of important events.

The newspaperman's bad reputation improved more dramatically as
journalism itself evolved in the 1880s and 1890s, until reporting emerged as
a profession that well-educated young people considered seriously for themselves. As one writer proudly noted in 1893, the "day of the long-haired,
unkempt, wild-eyed journalistic genius" who "dashed off a brilliant jeu-
d'esprit on Monday" and "spent the rest of the week drinking and talking
about it, has vanished far into the dim distance."[4] If the "old" reporter had
been drunk and uneducated, the "new" reporter, according to stereotype,
was younger, "more energetic and ambitious, college-educated, and usually sober," as "self-respecting and industrious" as "men of similar age in
any of the professions."[5] Some of these new reporters harbored literary
aspirations and viewed the newspaper office as the first step toward a literary life, but others looked to new journalism itself as an exciting career
path, a place to sell stories as inventive and imaginative as fiction—and to
sell them to a vast reading audience, at that. Even if a reporter had no
desire to fictionalize (or to fictionalize further) the stories he created on
the job, his occupation provided license to witness "real life," or in Jacob
Riis's words, the "great human drama" unfolding in the city streets, "the
tumult of passions" and "a human heroism that redeems all the rest."[6]
Drawn by such drama, fine young men (and some fine young women)
strove to break into the confines of the newspaper office (not an easy task
in urban centers) and to make a name there.[7]

The profession may have been opening to "respectable" job candidates, but actual working conditions for most journalists were far from comfortable or genteel. New York reporters, who enjoyed the highest pay rate in the nation, still earned only between fifteen and sixty dollars a week, depending on their popularity.[8] Reporters worked more hours per week than most professionals and many craftsmen; in New York they handled up to fourteen or fifteen story assignments a day. Moreover, positions on urban newspapers were notoriously unstable, as ruthless "hiring and firing system[s]" kept reporters and editors alike "in fear of their jobs."[9] Many people were eager to find positions on papers, and managing editors capitalized on the economics. Pulitzer, for example, frequently hired two men for each job, to compete openly for it. Not surprisingly, nasty office politics dominated the *World,* breeding an environment of suspicion and sabotage.

Nevertheless, a number of reporters achieved the ultimate success. They became heroes to the thousands of readers who picked up papers like the *World, Sun,* or *Journal* every day, and as the headlines trumpeting Nellie Bly's work suggest, several papers in turn loudly announced the reporters' presence on their staffs. What made journalists like Bly so admirable to their readers was their ability to be, in fact, both authors and characters. The public came to believe that great reporters did not merely write breathtaking stories. Rather, the most popular writers made names for themselves within their stories. Indeed, such author-characters as Bly and Richard Harding Davis owed their fame to their ability "to transcend normal news channels through participation in the news event or by a breathtaking 'stunt,'" as is evident in each of the case studies presented in this study.[10]

Perhaps no other reporter of the 1890s filled the author/character role as well as Davis, who worked for the *New York Sun* and *New York Journal* before signing with *Harper's Weekly.* Davis's career defined a standard by which a new journalist could become the active participant in news making (a point I take up in some detail in chapter 4). He was also one of his generation's most widely read authors of both fiction and nonfiction, and "his impact upon the values of the upper-class reading public is difficult to overestimate."[11] The son of Clarke Davis (managing editor of the *Philadelphia Inquirer*) and the now more famous Rebecca Harding Davis (who spent twenty years writing features for the *New York Tribune*), young Richard found his first jobs on Philadelphia papers in the late 1880s after attending Lehigh for a phenomenally unsuccessful two years.[12]

It was at Lehigh that Davis introduced what was to become his signature practice: in the school paper and literary magazine, the *Lehigh Burr,* he published stories that starred a dapper young hero who was based rather transparently on Davis himself. Later, at the *Philadelphia Record* and the *Philadelphia Press,* Davis both amazed and irritated his coworkers by uncovering the gritty underbelly of urban life while wielding a natty walking stick and dressed as though he were headed to afternoon tea. But he established a modest following after posing as a ruffian to expose a thief's den of iniquity, thus becoming arguably the first reporter to "go undercover."[13] Bit by bit, Davis polished the trademark style he had introduced at Lehigh. To him a news story was finally little more than a story—an imaginative creation—with a cast of characters whom the reporter could join with a quick change of costume, and whom the reporter simultaneously created in the pages of the newspaper. Whether visiting condemned murderers in prison, profiling leading actors, or struggling with the aftermath of the Johnstown flood, Davis sought out melodrama and natural excitement and then served it up eloquently to newspaper readers.

Not achieving quite the dramatic display or widespread fame he desired during his three years in Philadelphia, Davis moved in 1889 to New York, where he landed a job at the *Evening Sun,* the risqué sibling of the more respectable morning edition.[14] Davis was an instant hit. Walking to the office on his very first day of work, he had the good fortune to recognize and help capture a famous con artist by posing as a naïve visitor to the city, trapping the villain perpetrating a swindle, and handing him over to the police. Davis then rushed on to the *Sun* offices to compose the encounter as "a yarn of adventure with Richard himself as the protagonist."[15] Writing in third person, Davis related how he played the role of gullible newcomer by agreeing to bet a thousand dollars on a seemingly sure business deal. Stringing the swindler along, Davis searched in vain for a policeman before finally taking the matter quite literally into his own hands:

> He crossed the street again, seized [the swindler] by the collar and remarked that this thing had gone far enough. The prisoner slipped out of his overcoat but Reporter Davis seized him round the neck

and held on until Policeman Lyna came along and took the bunco
sharp to the Oak Street Station.[16]

This, then, was the Davis formula, one that other aspiring new journalists
reproduced religiously. Whenever possible, the reporter should help make
the news. He should never shirk from danger or adventure. He should
take an active role in solving crimes. At the same time, he should never be
anything other than a proper gentleman, for the "absurdly chivalrous"
Davis "advocated," if nothing else, "a proper attention to the old-world
notions of decency, morality, and manners."[17]

It wasn't long until Davis himself showed up not only in his stories for
the *Evening Sun* but also as a character in his own fiction. Like many
reporters, Davis used his newspaper work as a springboard for purely
imaginative stories. Journalists, after all, did not find it burdensome to
convert news stories that looked like fiction into fiction that looked like
news stories. Davis's phenomenal fictional success—all but forgotten today—began with tales first serialized and then published together as
Gallegher and Other Stories. The collection's title story inaugurated a new
genre of story called "newspaper fiction," featuring "tough characters"
who "behave in the most sentimental fashion, all for the love of the paper."[18] These stories, resting (as realist fiction did itself) somewhere between newspaper articles and purely imaginative writing, were an instant
success.[19] "Gallegher: A Newspaper Story," for instance, recounts the adventure of an office boy for a Philadelphia daily, a crime-obsessed young
man who has learned everything on the streets—"not a very good school
in itself, but one that turns out very knowing scholars." Gallegher, we are
assured, "had attended both morning and evening sessions."[20] With careful observation and uncanny knowledge of the criminal mind, Gallegher
escorts the police to a notorious killer and leads his newspaper to a scoop
on the news. A series of adventures featuring illegal prizefighting and
frenzied cab chases pave the way for Gallegher's triumphant delivery of
the news to his editor—just, of course, before the presses start rolling.
Davis quickly followed his debut collection with a series of stories starring Courtlandt Van Bibber, "an affable, handsome, debonair bachelor," a
thinly disguised and "idealized portrait of Davis" himself.[21] Rather than
an office boy, Van Bibber is a cool sophisticate who, like Davis, functions
comfortably in any range of activities and roles, from sentimentally re-

uniting an orphaned stage actress with her long-lost society father to hosting posh dinner parties at Delmonico's.

In life and in art, Davis captured the desire of many young Americans for action, masculinity, and manners. His early work and characters (both self-created and fictional) epitomize the fashion in which reporters could break down barriers between life and art. Journalism and fiction, reality and artificiality had become utterly entwined for Davis and other authors—and readers—by the end of the century. If Davis showed up in his own stories, he took his authorship a step farther and animated his own characters in real life, finally *becoming* Courtlandt Van Bibber and other heroes of his. His own name "became synonymous with the word 'gentleman'"—or perhaps more precisely, "gentleman adventurer."[22] His splendid combination of both swashbuckler and delightful tea guest, all wrapped up in one finely appointed package of chiseled good looks, established Davis as the hero of the day. "College boys and their sisters posted sketches of Davis" and of his fictional heroes on their walls—and the real-life hero and fictional hero were "impossible to distinguish."[23] Davis represented to his young admirers the most appealing aspects of new journalism. In this career a cultivated person could gain fame and fortune traveling "all about the world as a special correspondent . . . falling into and surviving one ridiculously dangerous adventure after another, and then returning home to write about them all."[24] Moreover, a man could even reinvent himself as an improvement on a fictional hero.[25]

This focus on invention, however, served as a target for critics when they cast disapproving eyes toward new journalism and the growing ranks of fame-hungry reporters. Young Americans may have aspired to be the next Richard Harding Davis or Nellie Bly, but some commentators feared the influence such celebrity-seeking would have on the rising generation. As chapter 5 demonstrates, the movement toward standardizing the profession—and away from the very self-creation Bly and Davis perfected—went far to devalue the capital held by new journalism. Until that standardization in the early twentieth century, however, a famous journalist could write himself into his own stories, either as a Davis-brand swashbuckler or, in the case of Julian Ralph in the next chapter, as the critical narrator of a modern tragedy.

CHAPTER THREE

A Front Seat to Lizzie Borden

Julian Ralph, Literary Journalism, and the Construction of Criminal Fact

> Fact and fiction have furnished many extraordinary examples of crime that have shocked the feelings and staggered the reason of men, but I think no one of them has ever surpassed in its mystery the case you are now considering.
> —Andrew Jennings, defense attorney for Lizzie Borden

Introduction

In 1878 thousands of American readers devoured a thrilling new novel, *The Leavenworth Case: A Lawyer's Story,* written by a previously unknown author, Anna Katharine Green. Her murder mystery tells the gripping tale of female cousins whose wealthy uncle and guardian has been found shot in his study. Circumstantial evidence quickly points to one of the cousins, although characters in the novel (along, most probably, with Green's readers) reject as "dreadful" and "horrible" the idea that a woman could commit such a deed.[1] The protagonist of the story, a young lawyer named Mr. Raymond, joins city detective Ebeneezer Gryce and a stealthy cross-dressing investigator named Q, along with a cast of other mysterious characters, to clear the accused cousin's name, uncover hidden romances, and prove that indeed the butler had done it.

The Leavenworth Case, although a fairly obscure novel today, stands as a watershed in the history of fictional crime narratives, because of its incredible success as one of the first full-length detective novels written in America.[2] Easily among the top best-sellers in the nineteenth-century American literary marketplace, this "overnight sensation" sold more than 750,000 copies between 1878 and 1894. In 1903 Green's publishers announced they "had worn out two sets of plates" producing new editions.[3] Readers were particularly delighted by the novel's verisimilitude—it reproduced floor plans, news headlines, newspaper articles, and incriminating letters, facsimiles of which were tipped into the bindings of the first edition to extend the realism. It seemed almost as if a real crime had been appropriately sanitized of actual blood and then dramatized for genteel readers in the comfort and safety of their parlors. Buoyed by her sudden success, Anna Katharine Green ultimately produced a long list of detection and mystery titles, including two separate series, which introduced a "spinster sleuth" named Amelia Butterworth and a girl detective named Violet Strange. She also encouraged new audiences for *The Leavenworth Case* by staging the novel as a play in 1892, the very year the American reading public was swept away by yet another murder mystery that brought crime into the comfort and safety of their parlors—the mystery of Lizzie Andrew Borden.

In a sensational reworking of Anna Katharine Green's *Leavenworth Case*—the situations were eerily similar in the slaying of relatives within locked rooms—Borden was accused of murdering her father and stepmother with an ax one torrid day in August 1892.[4] The murder of Abby Borden took place in the Borden home in Fall River, Massachusetts, around nine o'clock in the morning while Lizzie was allegedly either in the barn or in the backyard (her story changed with each telling). Sometime within the next ninety minutes, Andrew Borden arrived home for a midmorning nap. He never woke up. With the Borden maid conveniently tucked away in her third-floor garret taking a nap of her own, Lizzie, as she later told investigators, stumbled upon her father's mutilated corpse in the dining room. Because no one else had been home, and because Andrew Borden was well known for his almost pathological determination to keep doors and windows locked both day and night, overwhelming evidence seemed to point to Lizzie's guilt.

After countless newspaper stories detailed the gruesome murders and provided documentary "reproductions" similar to those in Green's novel (a particular favorite being floor plans clearly indicating where the victims had been hacked down), Borden came to trial in June 1893 amid nearly unprecedented public scrutiny and media frenzy. For months, citizens in New England, across North America, and in Europe devoured the details of the murder and debated the facts and fictions of the case. Even Anna Katharine Green herself offered her expert opinion in regional newspapers.[5] As a glance at any 1890s paper suggests, reports of crime and murder—even parricide—were familiar to readers, especially in the papers of the new journalism. For complex social reasons, however, the case of Lizzie Borden garnered incredible attention.[6] By the time court convened to judge the case of Lizzie Andrew Borden, national newspapers stood poised to guide readers step by vicarious step through the unfolding legal process and to turn the case into as intriguing a story of mystery and murder as anything Anna Katharine Green could have imagined.

By the 1890s crime reportage had become something of an art form, dovetailing with novels like Green's, a "new" genre but already one of the most popular segments of the literary marketplace. Practitioners of new journalism recognized that murder mysteries, perhaps more than any other kind of narrative, demanded treatment that probed beyond the bare outline of fact. Real murder cases—with their inherent drama, spectacle, suspense, climax, and dénouement—could be as exciting—even more so—than the latest fictional rage if reporters fashioned the stories into emblematic tales rife with the emerging conventions of fictional crime stories.[7]

While countless late nineteenth-century American reporters blended the facts of crime with popular fictive techniques in their depiction of murder cases, one of the most skilled and respected masters of this hybrid form was Julian Ralph, who wrote for Charles Dana's *New York Sun* from 1875 to 1895. Although Ralph lacks the twentieth-century critical fame that such figures as Mark Twain and Stephen Crane now enjoy, he was nevertheless a widely known author of both nonfiction and fiction, and for two decades he perfected a distinctive journalistic style that earned him recognition and a loyal public following despite the *Sun*'s lack of bylines. Ralph's rich career offers multiple entry points into an investigation of late nineteenth-century literary and journalistic intersections, but among his most compelling work is the series of articles he wrote from New Bedford, Massachusetts, where the trial of Lizzie Borden for murder was convened.[8]

This chapter will examine how Ralph constructed this murder mystery for the *New York Sun* and how his newspaper stories reworked and reframed fictional detective tales, the popularity of which surged in the 1890s. It opens with a historical overview of the *Sun,* the paper that encouraged reporters to practice a literary style of journalism, before turning to Ralph's dispatches from the Borden trial. Unlike the previous chapters, which pose the newspaper as a "corporate author," the focus here is on the work of one reporter, using his articles as a pathway to the practices in one of the less commonly recognized—but extremely important—newspapers of the 1890s. This journalistic work corresponds with the genre of mystery and detective fiction, which developed hand in hand with mass-market journalism.

Julian Ralph's work serves as a particularly powerful example for this investigation, since he found in the Borden trial a story more intriguing than fiction, given the trial's status within "the real." However, though Ralph drew upon literary culture in his reportage, as did the writers for the *Journal* and the *World* in my other case studies, he also sought a storytelling more subdued and critical than that found in those newspapers. Reading this particular segment of Ralph's writing, then, allows insight into the intersections among documenting and storytelling, representing and symbolizing, and subjectivity and objectivity, as one famous reporter used the trial as a venue for dramatic reporting and cultural critique alike. Similarly, the dispatches demonstrate how reporters and editors of the 1890s recognized the potential market for a blurring of fictional and factual techniques, self-consciously assessed the news as a marketable literary invention, and valued the critical power inherent in a "literary" form of journalism.[9]

Charles Dana's Sun: *Literary Reporting and an "Old" New Journalism*

When Lizzie Borden came to trial, Ralph's editor, Charles Dana, recognized a most unusually sensational legal case. He had no choice but to send his ace reporter to Massachusetts, for his readers would be eager for dispatches from the old whaling town. Dana also realized he faced enormous journalistic competition from the other New York editors, particularly Pulitzer, and from such Boston papers as the *Globe*. For all these papers, the Borden case was to be a crucible, a testbed for the comparative and competitive advantages of contrasting journalistic ideals and styles.

Interestingly, the *Sun* is not often considered in the same journalistic class as the *World* and the *Journal;* indeed, the latter newspapers took pains to differentiate themselves from the *Sun* and to label it stodgy and antiquated. Nonetheless, the *Sun* is included in this study because it served, undeniably, both as inspiration for and variant of the aesthetic Pulitzer and Hearst practiced more graphically. Built solidly on the idea that news articles were first and foremost stories with potentially lively plots and characters, the paper proclaimed its mission to capture the interest of all classes of readers with thrilling and often sensational articles, and then to bring those readers into an appreciation of finer styles of writing and egalitarian political ideas.[10] In the spirit of his direct predecessor, Benjamin Day of the penny-press decades, Dana had fashioned his paper on the principles of unbridled excitement, manufactured news, and lurid stories, principles Pulitzer and Hearst took to extremes in the 1890s. Even though its mass popularity peaked just before the 1890s, the *Sun* still functioned as an influential player within the marketplace of new journalism, even as it served as a point of comparison with its neighbors on New York's Newspaper Row.

Born in 1819, Charles Dana as a young man developed interests in Transcendentalism, social reform, and communal projects; those interests led to his residence at Brook Farm from 1841 to 1846. Later, Dana accepted a job as city editor of Horace Greeley's *New York Tribune,* a position he held until 1862, when he resigned after a bitter dispute with Greeley about Dana's increasingly incendiary antislavery editorial tone. After serving as assistant secretary of war for the Union during the Civil War, Dana edited the *Chicago Tribune* before purchasing the *New York Sun* in 1868. The *Sun* had continued its 1830s commitment to a working-class audience, drawing its readership almost entirely from Democratic New Yorkers. Somehow, however, Dana, ironically relying on the capital of Republican stockholders, transformed the *Sun* into the most successful city newspaper of the 1870s and 1880s without alienating either his Democratic readers or his more conservative stockholders. Always insistent on political independence, Dana divorced his paper from strict party affiliations and blended the convictions about workers' rights he had nurtured during his Brook Farm years with his permeating senses of good humor, literary quality, and pragmatic politics.

Like Pulitzer and Hearst, Dana valued a fusion of storytelling and newstelling. Frank O'Brien, an early news historian, gushed that Dana

> smote the rock of humanity, and abundant streams of literature rushed forth. . . . He believed that all the information, the philosophy, and the humour of the world could be conveyed through the type of a daily newspaper as surely as and much more broadly than they had

been conveyed through the various mediums of the old newspapers, the encyclopedias, the novels, the pulpit, and the lecture platform.[11]

Dana supported narrative that encompassed and blended fact and fiction, information and impression, seeking not to reproduce reality "objectively" but to reveal humanity itself to the nineteenth-century reader. Indeed, the editor coined the term "human interest story" to describe the vital component of his paper that appropriated an imaginative writer's techniques to bring life to newsworthy facts. It was the fusion of journalism with "the literary quality that made the trifle live" in Dana's paper.[12] To Dana, the lifeless alternative to this style was mere verbiage:

> Suppose you tell all the truths of science in a way that bores the reader; what is the good? The truths don't stay in the mind, and nobody thinks any the better of you because you have told the truth tediously. The reporter must give his story in such a way that you know he feels its qualities and events and is interested in them.[13]

For Dana, presenting the news as a literary form meant that the audience would be able to participate in a realism beautifully transformed upon the page.

Despite Dana's convictions about a lively and literary style, the *Sun,* one of the most popular newspapers of the 1870s and early 1880s, faced financial difficulties during the later 1880s and 1890s. In the last years of the century, the paper that had set the pace for new forms of journalism and that had inspired a young Pulitzer found itself outmoded and caught between two stylistic extremes: the emerging "objective style," typified by such information-heavy papers as the *New York Times* and *Post,* and the even more sensational style of new journalism championed by Hearst and Pulitzer, the latter of whom Dana hated and referred to viciously as "Jew-seph Pulitzer." In his conviction that the newspaper operated within a larger literary culture, Dana was not so different from Pulitzer and Hearst. But his vision of literature ultimately differed from theirs. Though like them he spoke to a working-class audience, he eschewed the most self-aggrandizing melodrama of the *World* and the *Journal,* as well as even more pulpy newspapers like the *Boston Globe.* Instead, Dana encouraged a "higher" literary style from his reporters. A "remarkable number" of *Sun* employees, including Julian Ralph, "at some point in their careers won at least passing fame as writers," and the basic "atmosphere at the paper was unusually hospitable for those who wanted to try their hand at something beyond the daily assignments."[14] The paper's Sunday editions even ran sketches and short stories written by *Sun* staff members alongside fiction from such established authors as James, Harte, Stevenson, and Kipling.

A brief comparison of the stories that introduced the Borden murders in various newspapers does much to clarify some of the critical differences between the *Sun* and other urban papers, even as it emphasizes the fundamental stylistic similarities between the *Sun* and its more famous kin, the *New York World*. On August 6, just two days after the murders, the *Sun* reported that the mystery was deepening and that the Borden sisters were prime suspects, spicing up its reporting by adding a small illustration, some-

The *New York Sun* reported on early developments in the investigation of the Borden murders by adopting such typical new journalism techniques as illustrations and detailed headlines. *New York Sun*, August 6, 1892.

In its reportage about the Borden murders, the *New York World* entertained its readers with eye-catching headlines and detailed illustrations. *New York World,* August 6, 1892.

thing not seen frequently in this paper. The *World* on the 6th used larger typeface for its grabbing headlines, more illustration, and a telling literary comparison with Poe, asserting that "The Mystery of the Rue Morgue Was Simple by Comparison with This One of Fall River." Using more extreme sensationalism and catering to the basest of emotions, the *Boston Globe* of August 5 fairly screamed in a half-page headline that "TWELVE CUTS Were on the Heads of Each of the Slain" and that "Their Heads" had been "Smashed With a Hatchet." Finally, opposing the *Globe's* shrill sensation and even the tempered sensation of the *Sun* and *World* was the *New York Post,* with its "informational style," which would become the example of standardized, "objective" writing after new journalism over-played its own fictionalizing.

, 1892—TEN PAGES.   PRICE TWO CENTS

'OW FOR THE NEW DEAL!

inent was formally opened yesterday and, according to a deal between Liberals and Conservatives, thur Wellesley Pool was unanimously re-elected speaker of the Commons. But a new deal itor; John Bull will give to Salisbury a hand that will make the Tory chieftain anything to Gladstone, a hand that will make the Grand Old Man premier; and to Erin, every lover opes, a hand that will make her the proud possessor of Home Rule.

TWELVE CUTS

Were on the Heads of Each of the Slain.

Old Man Was First One Killed.

Mrs. Borden Sought to Escape Death.

Their Heads Smashed With a Hatchet

No Clue as Yet to This Most Atrocious and Brutal Crime.

Victims Not Known to Have Had Enemies.

Fall River Terribly Excited Over the Slaughter.

WALL RIVER, Aug. 4.—Andrew J. Borden, 70 years old, and his wife, Addie D., were murdered and horribly mutilated at their own home, at 92 2d, about 11 o'clock this morning.

TURNED AGAIN.	CHARGED WITH MURDER.	HE WASN'T AFRAID.
Restored to Sight wo Hours.	Frank Gallineaux Under Arrest at Tombs.	Nor was Gov. Tillman Looking for Trouble.
Again Faded from the John Wesley.	Alleged that He Struck Thomas Holland With a Hammer.	Col. Orr Wanted to Know if He was the Liar Referred To.
to See Again Unless ary is Permanent.	In Defence Says that in a Quarrel His Antagonist Fell.	Almost a Riot at a Campaign Meeting in Union, S. C.

Readers of the *Boston Globe* waded through eight layers of headline to reach the most sensationalistic news about the murders of Andrew and Abby Borden. *Boston Daily Globe,* August 5, 1892.

Read side by side, this sampling of articles highlights the stylistic range of responses to the Borden murders. On one end of the narrative spectrum were the garish theatrics of the *Boston Globe,* a paper riddled with enticing illustrations and heavy with provocative, layered headlines—a visual and textual style most closely analogous with today's tabloid journalism. On the other end of the spectrum lay the *New York Post,* which stripped not only the murder mystery of accompanying illustration but also the story itself of its most compelling dramatic intrigue. The *Post* did print news of the Borden murders on the August 5 front page, but the paper's editors dropped the story within a day. The *Post's* readers were apparently much more interested in economic, political, and yachting news, as the stories surrounding the brief, bland account of the Fall River murders suggest. The new journalism of both Dana and Pulitzer lodged somewhere in between the *Globe* and the *Post*. The difference between the two was essentially a matter of degree, both in terms of the amount of illustration used and in the size and language of the headlines. Both the *World* and the *Sun* offered a narrative designed to draw readers into the excitement unfolding in Fall River. They animated the dramatis personae, introducing a widening cast of possible suspects, potential witnesses, shocked neighbors, and puzzled police authorities. While they both mentioned and briefly described the gruesome nature of the crimes, neither the *Sun* nor the *World* lingered over the horrific blood and gore splattering the walls of the Borden household, as the *Globe* did.

consisted of Sir William Vernon Harcourt, Lord George Francis Hamilton, First Lord of the Admiralty; Sir Michael Hicks-Beach, President of the Board of Trade; Right Honorable Henry Matthews, the Home Secretary, and Right Honorable Edward Stanhope, Secretary of State for War. James Keir Hardie, the labor representative of the South Division of West Ham, appeared in the House wearing a cloth cap, which he failed to remove during the oath-taking. The Speaker, noticing it, at once called him to order, and he reluctantly doffed his cap. With 670 members to take their places and be sworn, some days must be occupied with the indispensable formalities. Until the arrival of the "fighting time," old Parliamentary hands will feel small interest in the proceedings. There is a growing feeling among all parties that, having regard to the arduous work involved by the general election and considering the period of the year, it is eminently desirable to accelerate proceedings as much as possible, in order to make September a holiday month.

JAEGER SENTENCED.

Ten Years' Penal Servitude for Rothschilds' Defaulting Cashier.

BERLIN, August 5.—Rudolph Jaeger, who for seventeen years was chief cashier in the banking house of the Rothschilds at Frankfort, and who in April last was found to be a defaulter, was to-day convicted and sentenced at Frankfort to ten years' penal servitude. Jaeger's stealings were estimated at over 1,500,000 marks. When arrested he was found to have in his possession nearly this amount.

THE COWES REGATTAS.

Meteor and Irene in the Closing Race—L'Esperance the Winner.

COWES, August 5.—Emperor William this morning cruised on the Solent for a half hour

report at the next session of Congress. Chairman Oates of the sub-committee was prepared to report, but the majority of his sub-committee declined to adopt his report.

THE FALL RIVER MURDER.

No Trace Yet Found of the Person Who Committed the Crime.

FALL RIVER, Mass., August 5.—After a most thorough and persistent search, no trace has been found of the murderer of Mr. and Mrs. Andrew J. Borden. Four policemen are on guard at the house and have been patrolling the neighbourhood since the affair was made public. A few very near relatives are allowed to enter. Emma, the daughter, who was visiting in the vicinity of New Bedford when the murder took place, is at home to-day and has charge of the house. Her sister Lizzie is not in a much better state than she was yesterday when she discovered her father dead. The funeral will take place to-morrow morning at eleven o'clock and will be strictly private. The strict watch that has been kept over Morse was even more strictly kept to-day than over. It appears to be the desire of the police to make no arrests until after the funeral. An advertisement will appear in to-night's local papers signed by Emma and Lizzie Borden offering $5,000 reward for the arrest and conviction of the murderer.

NEW BEDFORD, Mass., August 5.—John W Morse, who is suspected of knowing something about the murder of Andrew J. Borden and his wife at Fall River, made his home with Isaac C. Davis at South Dartmouth. He came from Hastings, Ia., and has lived in Mr. Davis's family for about a year. Members of the Davis family say he left South Dartmouth last Thursday for Fall River for the purpose of purchasing a head of cattle for Mr. Davis. He was expected home last night. They give him an excellent name and do not believe that he is in any way connected with the murder.

and Wisconsin case, and holds that a certain be the only basis of apportionment, that persons of color not taxed cannot be included in the Senate representation. A are so included the act is void for that r The opinion shows the inequality of the p tion in the Senate districts and the gross di ty between the population in the city and try districts; also the disparity of district between Monroe and Albany and other ties.

The Court holds that the inequalities grows as to the Senate and Assembly di that it is manifest that the discretion Legislature was exceeded, and therefor act is void.

THE GOELET CUP RACE.

Yachts Sailing for Cups over the Island Course at Newport.

NEWPORT, August 5.—The weather f Goelet cup race this morning was very sq and the start was delayed by a heavy thu storm. It was not until half-past eleven o' that the yachts went down to the sta point, which was off Brenton's Reef ship. The judge's steamer, went down and took up her po were to cross in their race for the cups, are valued at $1,000 and $500 respectively schooners and sloops. The Club steamer boats were off the lightship waiting for boats to get away.

The entries closed on board of Ilsena at o'clock this morning, and were as follows Schooners—Constellation, Alcaea, Ma Lasca, Alert, Mayflower, Atlantic, Mar rite, Iroquois, and Quickstep. Sloops—Gracie, Ventura, Wasp, Sapor Harpoon, and Gloriana.

Never since the races for these cups established was there such a fine list of yac ers entered, and the promise o race was never better. Lasca

The *New York Post* catered to readers whose interests lay more in yacht races and Congressional investigations than in sensationalistic murder cases, as evidenced by its somber, limited report about the Borden crimes. *New York Post,* August 6, 1892.

Yet, despite their fundamental narrative similarities, the *Sun* differed from other forms of new journalism in one central respect—Dana refused to commercialize his paper. While Pulitzer and Hearst actively courted advertisers, Dana kept his daily short, with minimal advertising, believing that the only way to maintain a paper's integrity was to indebt it neither to advertisers nor to a particular political party. He also avoided using enormous headlines and splashy illustrations, which of course became normative for new journalism. Dana feared that the readers whose culture he hoped ultimately to uplift would be anesthetized by such elements. But Dana's became an uncomfortable—and ultimately unprofitable—position to champion as newer, more commercialized, and less idealistic forms of new journalism grew increasingly forceful in the literary marketplace.

Julian Ralph: Special Correspondent to the Lizzie Borden Trial

If the *Sun* was setting in the 1890s, Julian Ralph's name continued to rise before the reading public.[15] Ralph's work on the Borden trial exemplified the *Sun*'s aesthetic ideal. Throughout his career, Ralph fused fictive tones and techniques with factual reportage.[16] Like other new journalists, Ralph underlined the subjective realities in his work, sketching rich stories behind the "who," "what," "where," "when," and "how" of daily events. Dismissing stringent divisions between factual and fictive forms, Ralph argued in his memoir, *The Making of a Journalist,* that "newspaper methods, when sublimated, reach far towards the realms of genius," an insight that Dickens, Boswell, and even Plutarch would have understood.[17] Such news writing depicted the "human, pathetic, picturesque, humorous, or peculiar"—it was journalism that "provided illustration to illuminate facts."[18]

By 1893 the forty-year-old Ralph had, like many of his colleagues, established a broad reputation as both a journalist and an imaginative writer. In addition to publishing short stories, novels, and travel books, he had signed on with *Harper's Weekly,* a position that finally earned him a byline, another new convention Dana impatiently dismissed. Ralph continued to accept special assignments from Dana, however, and Borden's trial was precisely the kind of spectacular event on which the *Sun* and other papers deployed their biggest guns. Indeed, the trial was a veritable media magnet. Special telegraph facilities were established in New Bedford, along with at least eight new Western Union lines. Major urban newspapers sent entourages of stenographers and telegraph operators to speed the production of the news. The Associated Press relayed the latest news across the nation, and Paul Julius Reuter's new agency kept a rapt European audience up to date.[19] Among this information-hungry collection of local, national, and international correspondents and news illustrators assembled in New Bedford Ralph earned a place of respect and importance. He enjoyed a front-row seat for the courtroom proceedings and kept his chair close to Borden's own for two weeks. As his trial dispatches reveal, he understood the value of this seat. It gave him a vantage point, an approximate position from which he could not only present the progress of the arguments but construct the trial as a narrative that dramatized the specific case of Lizzie Borden, critiqued a voyeuristic American culture, and examined the habits of readers caught up in the facts and fictions of crime detection.

For Ralph, the facts of the trial were readily apparent—an elderly husband and wife had been brutally hacked to death in broad daylight in their tightly locked home on a busy city street. The only people home with the victims that day had been Andrew's thirty-two-year-old daughter Lizzie and the Bordens' Irish maid. These were the facts. But for Ralph the subtext—the narrative beneath the facts—offered the real story. The case invited commentary on middle-class mores and gender conceptions, and it demanded a careful fusion of factual and fictional techniques. Moreover, where other reporters might make the substance of their stories sensational and gory, Ralph, in contrast, sought a story through careful detection and subtle development of character—precisely, as the latter part of this chapter argues, in the way that the "new" genre of detective stories for middle- and high-brow readers involved, principally, an intellectualized "scientific detection" rather than mere blood and guts.[20]

Ralph's competition, including reporters for the *Boston Globe* and, to a lesser extent, the *New York World,* oversensationalized the case's most horrific aspects by lingering over bloody hatchets and crushed skulls. Such papers reveled in the lurid side of the case, turning it into an amusement to be consumed voyeuristically and digested without critical perspective. This news became a literature as escapist in nature as cheap crime novels. Ralph's work stood apart from these versions of the story, because his dispatches insisted equally on journalistic facts, literary color, and social interrogation. Ralph sought the "truths" of the case, but at the same time he wanted to use his more intellectualized, literary style to interrogate the symbolic or "soft truths" of the case and the assumptions about the suspect made in and out of the courtroom. Although the majority of his correspondence consisted of transcribing the day's proceedings, Ralph carefully framed those proceedings with his own descriptions and stage settings. In this way, he transformed the Borden trial into a commentary on womanhood and on "the late nineteenth-century family as a guarantor of social balance," ultimately calling into question the subjects, objects, construction, and consumption of crime reportage.[21]

Ralph's main tasks in reporting the trial both factually and fictively included establishing its underlying social significance and humanizing the protagonist, Lizzie Borden, in a drama enacted before a national and international audience. For months some Americans had listened to rumors about the callousness of this strange woman, while many more had steadfastly defended her innocence. Thus, when Ralph sent his first dispatch into print, he grappled with the polarization already framing Borden as well as with the hefty cultural implications he read in the case:

> Miss Lizzie Andrew Borden is by far the most interesting prisoner New England has ever had. . . . She is either the most injured of innocents or the blackest of monsters. She either hacked her father and stepmother to pieces with the furious brutality of the ape in Poe's story of the Rue Morgue or some other person did it and she suffers the double torture of losing her parents and of being wrongfully accused of their murder. It is almost impossible to believe that she is guilty, and yet it is equally difficult to understand how any one else could have worked such fearful havoc in the house in which she was stirring.[22]

In his use of a most familiar literary reference from Poe, Ralph set the crime in nearly epic proportions. Here was not merely the case of a woman accused of parricide. Rather, the very nature of innocence and guilt—and the difficulty of determining the truth—stood on trial in the New Bedford courtroom, with unsettling consequences either way the case fell. From his opening paragraph Ralph set the stage for a pivotal social drama, but he also strove to personalize its tragic heroine. This woman, he reminded his readers, was "no Medusa or Gorgon. There is nothing wicked, criminal, or hard in her features."[23] Ralph's point here was not to presume Borden's guilt or innocence. Rather, he aimed to remind his readers of the human element involved in crime and to undermine the possibility that readers would demonize the accused and transform her into a stock fictional villain. Moreover, by making reference to Poe's famous short story—already heralded as progenitor of a *type* of story—Ralph reminded his audience of the most amazing elements of the case, elements that had already been used famously by Poe, as well as Anna Katherine Green. The crimes were as bloody and brutal as those Poe imagined, and, like those of the Rue Morgue, they occurred within a locked home. The crimes of Fall River, that is, echoed what were becoming standard, formulaic conventions for detective stories as the genre developed.

Operating under this lofty agenda, Ralph deepened Borden's persona with each new article. The defense attorney had remarked that he had "read many cases in books, in newspapers and in fiction—in novels—and I have never heard of a case as remarkable as this."[24] Ralph aimed to make it as remarkable a case to his readers as well. Each morning he moved close to Borden and examined her face, speculated on her mood, and tried to read her as a "human barometer" for how the story would unfold that day. Thus at one point, when the evidence turned against Borden, Ralph observed, "her face was blue, and her skin moist with an unwholesome, shining dampness."[25] The next day, during more favorable testimony, "she held her head up, looked at everything out of bright eyes, moved her chair about, and shifted herself in it, quite like anyone else."[26]

Ralph's reading of Borden drew her more fully as a character yet, paradoxically, demonstrated that she could not be understood as a stock fictional villain. After Borden fainted in court, for instance, Ralph speculated:

> The fact is, Lizzie Borden had not been regarded as quite human until her poor nerves gave way. This happened so suddenly and was so startling after ten months of her monotonous stolidity that people went wild with conjectures. They also became wild to get in the court room, and when the doors were opened the room filled up like a teacup under running water.[27]

Ralph's simile asked his readers to identify their own attitudes toward real criminal characters through a set of carefully constructed juxtapositions. He highlighted Borden's strain in maintaining self-control and then contrasted the mobbish and almost feral reaction of a crowd wild with expectations of sensation. The implication in the description is clear: the New Bedford audience—and by extension the reading public, metaphorically

devouring Borden as a dehumanized object every day—was complicit in
"fictionalizing" this modern American tragedy and in refusing to allow the
subtle realities of the case to emerge.

Witnessing Borden's position vis-à-vis her courtroom audience, Ralph
recognized the need to dispense with a misleading veil of unembroidered
factuality. While his compassion for Borden grew stronger with each chapter in his story, he also manipulated her character in order to ponder more
generalized problems facing some American women. Paradoxically, he constructed her as a narrative object to undercut the risk of her objectification
by the reading audience. Ralph, in other words, rejected an easy, stock
characterization of Borden as a monster criminal, yet he simultaneously
constructed her as another stock character garnered from his reading of
American fiction and history: the late nineteenth-century Puritan daughter, a figure who attracts "public attention to a peculiar phase of life in New
England—a wretched phase of it" in which "crime seems to attend . . . as
relentlessly as the knife of a surgeon is aimed at a cancerous growth."[28]
America harbored an unacknowledged social problem, Ralph implied. An
entire class of women had been dispossessed and possibly even driven to
criminality; Borden, innocent or not, illuminated the pronounced discomfort of Americans toward the old-maid figure. Indeed, "the daughters of a
class of well-to-do New England men" should be pitied, for the "men who
seem never to have money enough no matter how rich they become, whose
homes are little more cheerful than jails," ultimately nurtured conditions
where "women folk had, from a human point of view, better be dead than
to be born to these fortunes."[29] The case revealed to Ralph, fundamentally,
something disquieting about the very nature of Borden's life and, by extension, the lives of other American women in similar social situations.

With the motif of the Puritan daughter, Ralph transformed the story
of Lizzie Borden as a specific, live person into a story about how America
reacted to self-possessed, unmarried women. Also, he drew what seemed
to him obvious links between this New England crime and one from
history. Only a few months earlier, the Salem witchcraft trials of 1692, one
of New England's signature events, had returned to the consciousness of
Americans, just as the nation commemorated its bicentennial. Ralph repeatedly outlined connections between the two events by casting the
courtroom characters in the roles of famous literary and historical figures. He opened his trial dispatches, for instance, with the suggestion that
"before a stern and grim-looking bench of Judges as ever sat in Puritan

New England of old, Miss Lizzie Andrew Borden was put on trial for her life."[30] As a result, everyone talks "of Hester Prynne" and "of other women whose fearful experiences are suggested by this girl's misery."[31] Here, Ralph self-consciously manipulated well-known fictional characters and historical memory to rewrite American legends and to dramatize the fervor and tension swirling around New Bedford.

The witch-hunting attitude still abounded, he speculated, noticing the hostility that a core group of women in the courtroom cast in Borden's direction, in an image that recalled the opening of *The Scarlet Letter:* "These women are more refined looking, more gentle and sweet of face than the prisoner, and yet they are cruel hearted and come to gloat over the lone old maid."[32] Even more frightening to Ralph was the women's blood-thirsty assumption of Borden's guilt: "They look as sweet and fair and soft natured as so many fallow deer, but when any one speaks to them of the trial they say, 'Oh, I do hope they will hang her.'"[33] Appearance and reality clashed for Ralph, and in depicting these peripheral characters—stock figures themselves—he insisted that his reading public recognize the calloused attitudes surrounding and shaping the story. Indeed, these trial watchers seemed interested in Borden in the same way they would be interested in a character within a purely imaginative work. Their concern was not about what happened to a fellow human being; it was about reaching a thrilling, dramatic climax to the mystery.

Ralph spent the two-week trial worrying over a culture that would promote rabid hostility toward another human without critiquing those emotions, and he strove to expose this attitude to his audience through his casting of Borden in the role of a virginal, isolated, dispossessed woman—the arguably innocent damsel in distress. Engaging the natural drama inherent in any trial, Ralph used his courtroom seat to sketch out character and theme in detail, just as the characters and themes of a serialized novel deepen with each new installment. The image—and maddening excitement—of the Puritan daughter carried Ralph well into the last day of the trial, when he triumphantly proclaimed the outcome of the modern witch hunt:

The suspected witch was in the dock, the fagots had been piled all around her, the cords that were to tie her to the stake were the same that had cut into her flesh and her spirits for ten months, and only an hour before she was set scot-free the hard-headed District Attorney was flourishing an unlighted torch before the audience. But it took only an hour for the jury to decide that witches are out of fashion in Massachusetts and that no one is to be executed there on suspicion and on parrot-like police testimony.[34]

Ralph waged war on the issue of presumed criminality in late nineteenth-century American society, and society, at least in this instance, capitulated. The worries he expressed so constantly about determining innocence or guilt in a sanguinary environment found happy resolution in the court-room, leaving Ralph to hope that his audience would continue to interrogate its relationship to American crime on a more personalized basis.[35]

Reporter as Character: Self-Reference and the Business of Constructing the News

Ralph manipulated such fictive elements as character and theme in order to frame his narrative as social critique. Refusing the most extreme melodrama, he sought an alternative storytelling that would not reduce "the social complexity of crime-related situations" and ignore "the more profound social and political aspects of crime."[36] Tellingly, Ralph recognized that to convey how suspected women are framed, he needed to admit frankly that news narratives are themselves framed. The news, in other words, is invariably produced out of subjective reality—it is in some way always a "fictive" construct. Ralph made no claims to calmly assured truthfulness by using a deceptively authoritative voice. Nor did he explode the case's novelty through a shrill, even hysterical voice. Rather, Ralph cast his signifying voice into the courtroom narrative repetitively, insisting that his audience identify these reports as the product of an industry that creates scenes for public consumption and entertainment, not as the product of factually verifiable reality—something that would in theory remove the need for critical questioning. In this way, Ralph reminded readers that the newspaper in their hands was not a divine proclamation of truth, nor was it a wholly imaginative work. Rather, it was the commodity of a modern enterprise in the business of constructing and commercializing the news, and in some ways also of constructing and commercializing criminality.

Ralph asked his readers to witness the business of news making at first hand when he sketched the crowd of reporters in the courtroom. Here he employed a vivid simile: "On one side of the room sat six rows of reporters, bending over their pads and looking like a writing class in school."[37] More personally, he periodically reminded the audience of his physical proximity to the defendant: next to Borden "is THE SUN correspondent, and the correspondents of the other New York papers sit all along on the same line"[38]—the criminal suspect, in other words, and others whose profession it was to characterize her in newsprint shared space in a verbally constructed reality. Borden was finally only what the reporters said she was. Later, Ralph asserted that "only the correspondent of THE SUN and the deputy sheriff" could see behind the fan that obscured Borden's face from her other observers.[39] Of all the writers in the courtroom, Ralph alone held the privileged view behind the veil and, by extension, the deeper sympathy missed by others who lacked his vantage point. Ralph here trod the line between adopting an "objective" third-person narrative voice (he refers to himself only as "THE SUN correspondent") and assuming a fictive, first-person stance. Writing authoritatively, he injected his subjective presence into the text to remind a news-hungry audience that just as the narrator of a novel filters events through his or her own perspective, so the newspaper reporter serves as the narrative lens through which the public consumes news.

As the trial closed, Ralph even included exchanges of dialogue between his correspondent character and the New Bedford townspeople, reinforcing his study of how crime reaches the reading public. As the town restlessly awaited closing arguments, for example, the correspondent discussed the evidence with some unidentified (possibly even imagined?) New Bedford natives, and here Ralph's writing drew deliberately upon fictive techniques:

> There is a great deal of speculation here about what the prisoner will do if she is acquitted, as every one here thinks she will be. . . . "What'll Lizzie do?" [the natives] ask. "Why, she'll just go ter home and settle down and live plain and economical like and save money and die a snug old maid. She's got sand, she has, and there can't anybody frighten her out of doing what she wants to."[40]

Later in the same article, Ralph relayed more commentary from a New Bedford native regarding the sequestered jury:

> "The hull thing allus reminds me of the way we used to shanghai sailors when the whaling business was at its height, afore the war,"

said an old boatman to THE SUN correspondent to-day. "We used to get them drunk and make them sign articles when they did not know what they was doin' and then we used to row them out to a schooner that laid off in the stream. When we got them aboard the schooner we used to fill them up with more rum and chuck them down in the fo'castle and lock them in. . . . When the ship was ready we filled the men up again with forty-rod bug juice and loaded them on the whaler. They jinerally woke up and come to their selves when they was a couple of days out to the ocean."[41]

Fundamentally, these passages, with their representation of Yankee dialect and attitude, illustrated the local color and human interest that Ralph and Charles Dana both favored. The sketches of townspeople interacting with the correspondent populated a scene of interesting characters, working-class idioms, and local tall tales. But in Ralph's hands the scenes grew from simple sketches into more powerful fictive devices, contributing to his cultural examination of the trial. The townspeople consuming the trial news became representative of a larger reading public consuming the townspeople themselves as news. The conversations with locals were significant, in other words, because through them Ralph once again broadened the trial to illuminate news construction, public consumption, and self-reflection. The *Sun* correspondent himself represented one level of observer and consumer. He in turn described other local observers and consumers of modern crime. The pattern extended to the wider reading public—Americans reading these dispatches through Ralph also consumed the news, consumed Lizzie Borden, and consumed the public nature of crime itself. Ralph's self-referentiality demanded that the reader remind herself of these sources and layers of "reality."[42] Ralph refused to marginalize the newsworthy object into a "spectacle separate from his observed persona, so that the reader, who identifies with the journalist"—as well as, in this case, with Borden—would not "remain 'safe and separate.'"[43] Closing the gap "between subject and object" meant, then, avoiding "the universalizing ideology of the individual who asserts the truth of the world from a representative viewpoint."[44]

Throughout the courtroom drama, Ralph narrowed that critical gap by establishing his own persona as a character in the drama, both as conversant with locals and as virtual confidant with the mysterious defendant herself. When the jury finally delivered its verdict, he closed the gap further by casting his representations in tactile terms. Hearing a "not guilty" verdict pronounced, Borden fell "quicker than ever an ox fell in the stock yards of Chicago" (not, granted, a particularly flattering image), and "her forehead crashed against the heavy walnut rail of the dock so as to shake the reporter of THE SUN who sat next to her, twelve feet away, leaning on the rail."[45] Ralph once again placed himself near the center of the drama, engrossed enough with the story's climax to be leaning forward expectantly in his chair, intimate enough to feel, quite literally, the physical reaction of the acquitted woman. He finally redeemed that intimate investment most profitably when he visited Borden herself in her lawyer's chambers after the trial. The door, barred except to those "to whom she was indebted for friendship," opened for Ralph, along with his audience, and when Borden "heard that a man who was present represented THE SUN she rose from her chair and gripped the correspondent's hand with as hearty a grasp as ever woman bestowed upon him. 'I thank you,' said she. 'I thank you very much.'"[46]

After acting more as narrator than mere observer and tutoring his consuming public on Lizzie Borden's humanity, her symbolism as the New England old maid, and her unenviable position as a cultural commodity, Ralph finally granted his audience what it most hungered for in the news— direct interview and physical contact with the exonerated (and until then silenced) criminal, the mythologized and demonized—and now vindicated and humanized—heroine of his drama. Borden and Ralph's readers were finally united by the revelation that she and the newspaper audience shared the appreciation of Ralph's journalism. If Ralph was at all successful as a literary journalist, the reader of his dispatches left the New Bedford courtroom armed with more than just a titillating chapter in the story. Rather, the reader absorbed reportage made critical by its very narrative strategies.

Crime in the Literary Marketplace: Detective Stories and a "Better" Class of Readers

Julian Ralph's dispatches from Lizzie Borden's trial for murder read as a literary construction that intertwines factual and fictional mysteries. Yet though the Borden trial stands out in the history of American crime, sensational stories about murder had been popular and profitable in the literary marketplace long before 1892, and they had melded the "real" with the "imaginary" for at least a century. Americans in the late seventeenth through late eighteenth centuries had delighted in hearing execution sermons and reading corresponding pamphlets, which by the end of the eighteenth century traded an emphasis on morality for a stress on entertainment. By the dawn of the nineteenth century, writers and readers had "organized" their responses to murder "within a set of narrative conventions" we might identify as "Gothic."[47] That is, crimes were presented not as sermons but as stories that deliberately blurred the lines between illusion and reality.

This trend of fictionalizing the facts behind crime in street literature and pamphlets continued in following decades, finding a welcome outlet in the penny press of the early nineteenth century. One of the most famous crimes of the 1830s, to name just one example, involved the murder of a New York prostitute named Helen Jewett, whose accused killer was a young clerk from a respectable family. James Gordon Bennett's *New York Herald* joined other penny papers in liberally describing the sordid details of the case, pausing at the bloodstained crime scene and lingering over suggestively rumpled bedclothes. Bennett's account of the murder worked in a way essentially similar to sentimental novels of the 1830s that used the subtitle "A True Story" to imply actuality. Here was a narrative that took as much license as a purely imaginative work, complete with claims to truth embodied in its appearance in a newspaper.[48]

More directly, in 1845 the *National Police Gazette* built a business around mingling information and poetic license, especially in its most "prized feature," the "serialized criminal biographies" that led off each edition of the weekly paper.[49] These stylized biographies cast real criminals as formulaic types—something Ralph obviously had in mind when he stressed Borden's innocence and humanity. Nevertheless, the *National Police Gazette* repeatedly insisted on its own commitment to factuality, despite the serial's obvious stress on richly embroidered sensationalism. An 1847 poem neatly summarizes this blend of solid fact and titillating entertainment:

> What mischiefs dire! What murders black!
> What corpses lie upon your track!
> What fiendish rapes! What beastly acts
> Stand 'ranged in rows of stubborn facts![50]

By massaging those "stubborn facts" with the tools of the imagination, a writer could grow even the briefest court accounts into marvelous stories of black murder and human beastliness. Any skilled reporter could combine "dialect, impolite language, colloquialisms, slang, puns, and folklore" with "lavish descriptions and detail" to bring the most trivial crimes to life as stories.[51]

Predictably, crime novels and short stories took as their starting points real cases that had already appeared in newspapers. Indeed, penny papers like the *Herald* and the *National Police Gazette* (as well as Benjamin Day's *New York Sun*) were largely responsible for the immensely popular and inexpensive crime-based novels of the early and middle nineteenth century. George Lippard, for instance, based his epic *The Quaker City: A Romance of Philadelphia Life, Mystery, and Crime* (1843) on an actual case of seduction and captivity he had covered as a reporter for the Philadelphia penny paper *Spirit of the Times.* Similarly, Poe, widely credited with creating the American detective story, modeled "The Murders in the Rue Morgue" (1841) and "The Mystery of Marie Rogêt" (1842) on cases that the New York papers had covered extensively. In "The Mystery of Marie Rogêt" (one of many fictionalizations about the real-life Mary Rogers) he even offered solutions, via the voice of C. Auguste Dupin, to the unsolved murder of a beautiful young woman found dead in the Hudson River. In yet another of Poe's attempts to integrate his fiction into an immediate and potentially profitable journalistic context, Dupin literally reads the "evidence" he has gathered from New York penny papers in order to "solve" the mystery.[52]

These journalistic crime narratives—and the novels and stories both inspired by what had been reported in the papers and inspiring reportage itself—had always offered a lucrative business opportunity for writers, and business continued to thrive in the 1890s. But the last decades of the nineteenth century also brought popularity to detective narratives for new classes of readers, specifically those that had traditionally regarded crime stories as coarse. Modern scholars lack a reliable gauge for determining precisely which people or groups of people read penny papers and the *National Police Gazette,* but clearly middle- and upper-class Americans were not expected to do so. Six-penny papers, with their sober reliance on business and politics, were, at least apparently, meant for educated, genteel readers. The "elite" papers of antebellum America considered their offerings to be in stark contrast to those of the penny papers. In the parallel plane of fiction, *The Quaker City,* to cite one example, might have been the most profitable novel before the *Uncle Tom's Cabin* phenomenon, selling in excess of sixty thousand copies within its first year alone, but "better classes" of readers certainly did not read it openly. Genteel critics pilloried it routinely; one reviewer even called it "the most immoral work of the age."[53]

By the 1890s many newspapers—as demonstrated vividly by the *Boston Globe* coverage of the Borden murders—continued to write crime narratives in the screaming, lurid style of the old penny papers, penny dreadfuls, and "horrid fiction."[54] With their shocking headlines, illustrations, and descriptions, much late nineteenth-century journalism turned fact into melodrama and catered to the most basic of human reactions—"disgust or sympathy"—by crafting stock heroes and villains.[55] New venues also emerged for cheap crime literature, such as the *Nick Carter Weekly* (1891), a story-paper series that detailed the exploits of a super-sleuth. Another newcomer was the fictional detective story within more respectable, mainstream newspapers, as epitomized by Nellie Bly's *The Mystery of Central Park*. Research based on the contents of the Borden house suggests that Lizzie herself might even have enjoyed these periodical offerings, which occasionally stressed "themes of domestic violence," sensation, sexual "repression," and murder.[56]

As a genteel woman, Lizzie Borden might also have enjoyed mysteries "better suited" for her class, for Anna Katharine Green's work epitomized a new kind of criminal detection story directed toward more refined tastes. Green's *Leavenworth Case* attracted the interest of wealthier and better educated audiences to the mystery genre, lifting the stigma previously attached to crime fiction. Green's novel was only the beginning. By the late 1880s the genre's doors had been blown open to respectable readers, thanks in no small part to Arthur Conan Doyle, who began publishing his Sherlock Holmes stories in the British *Strand* magazine in 1887. By 1890 stories of the great British detective had reached American audiences through the pages of *Lippincott's Magazine,* and two of Doyle's novels, *The Sign of the Four* and *A Study in Scarlet,* were also top sellers in the United States in 1890.[57] Within three years the Holmes vogue "simply swept the country" and furthered the "production of good detective stories" for polite society.[58] By the time Andrew and Abby Borden met their untimely demises, detective stories for middle- and high-brow readers had become an "immense commercial success" within the literary marketplace.[59] They merged vocabularies of sensation with vocabularies of "scientific" rationalism, so that intellectual detectives functioned "within an internally logical and rigorously efficient plot, in spite of any bizarre premises upon which it might be based."[60]

In the final years of the century, Americans of all classes were fascinated with mystery, murder, and mayhem; homicide became a central point "in a variety of popular genres," including factual stories, fictional stories, and stories somewhere in between.[61] Crime fiction and nonfiction continued to function as tightly interwoven strands within the same cloth; detective and mystery stories used details from real-life crimes and reporters narrated real-life crimes using conventions borrowed from fiction. Furthermore, echoing the movement of stories about crime out of the hands of "vulgar" readers and into the hands of "respectable" readers, both fictional and nonfictional narratives of the 1890s located violence and murder not only in dark alleys and sordid settings, as they had in the past, but "in middle-class homes or minds," opening readers to the most unsettling realization that "society may be morally corrupt to its roots."[62] No longer were killers, either in reality or in the imagination, "psychotic outsiders or social imposters," as had been supposed in the past.[63] Now, as Green's *Leavenworth Case* suggested and as Borden's trial implied to some readers, they could "belong to the community they assault[ed]."[64]

One murder story that took up this very issue and that resonates with the Borden case was Mary E. Wilkins Freeman's "The Long Arm." In 1894 newspaper syndicator Irving Bacheller encouraged Freeman to enter a detective story contest he was promoting. Freeman's work was first published in Bacheller-syndicated newspapers across the nation before a separate volume published "The Long Arm" beside other contest winners. Modeled explicitly on the Borden murder case, Freeman's story used the new conventions of the mystery to "solve" the real-life murder in fiction. Freeman appropriated the same conventions that Ralph manipulated to present the clues (via daily trial transcripts) to his readers and encourage them to solve the murder mystery themselves. "The Long Arm," like the Borden case, is a "locked-room mystery" in which a spinster has been accused of killing her elderly, widower father. The story opens after the protagonist, Sarah Fairbanks, has been acquitted of the crime. Not content to rest until the crime is solved, however, Fairbanks vows to "make an exhaustive examination of the house, such as no officer in the case has yet made, in the hope of finding a clue. Every room I propose to divide into square yards, by line and measure, and every one of these square yards I will study as if it were a problem in algebra."[65]

In this declaration, Fairbanks not only highlights the very analytical process Ralph encouraged in his readers but provides what Borden's neighbors so earnestly desired after the trial: she takes an active role in searching for answers, and she allows her voice to be heard through the story's first-person narration. Like Borden, Fairbanks was not "allowed to make [a] full and frank statement" of innocence or guilt while on trial.[66] Now freed, she resolves to "affirm neither my innocence nor my guilt. I will present the facts of the case as impartially and as coolly as if I had nothing at stake. I will let all who read this judge me as they will."[67] After several ambiguous pages implying that Fairbanks could in fact have killed her father, Freeman reveals the real murderer—another spinster who was enraged about the upcoming engagement between her longtime female companion and Mr. Fairbanks.[68]

As "The Long Arm" so neatly suggests, the Borden case arrived at a key moment both in terms of literary culture and in terms of middle-class culture generally. Literature of crime and detection was moving away from a market primarily of supposedly coarser readers, being openly consumed instead by genteel classes and infused with discourses of rationality. However, as Freeman's story implies, the reality of middle- and upper-class crime became more frightening when it placed at risk traditional assumptions about gender and the sanctity of the home.

Leaving the Story Behind: Literature, Journalism, and New(s) Celebrities

If Julian Ralph's days with the *Sun* were numbered after his meeting with Lizzie Borden, he nevertheless left behind a collection of stories that have continued to enjoy fame. Popular historians of the Borden case cite Ralph's work among the most laudable, lyrical, and balanced of the contemporary news narratives.[69] But Ralph and Borden remain yoked in yet another, perhaps more essential way. Both of their names were commodified in subsequent years: Borden's by folk history and by a literary market that still, in the early twenty-first century, produces fictive work from her predicament; and Ralph's by a print market in which he actively engaged because it would offer an opportunity to advance both his literary and his journalistic fame.

As early as October 1892, with the publication of Edward Stratemeyer's *Dash Dare on His Mettle* (a dime novel churned out a mere six weeks after the Borden murders), and 1895, with the publication of Freeman's prize-winning "The Long Arm," fiction writers turned to what they considered the unsolved mystery of what had happened in that modest Fall River home one hot day in August 1892, contorted it under the power of folklore and gossip, and kept it alive in the minds of American readers.[70] It was a fame Borden loathed, for rather obvious reasons. Though hordes of Americans had supported Borden through her trial, the tide of public opinion quickly turned against her. Following a rather incriminating inquest appearance in August 1892, she maintained her silence, displeasing many supporters who had expected her to speak publicly about her version of the events—as one would expect at the heroic conclusion of any good mystery novel. A number of newspapers began publishing disapproving stories about Borden, including the *Providence Journal* (which had led anti-Borden forces during the trial as well) and the *Fall River Globe* (which published a raging anti-Borden article every year on the anniversary of the murders).[71] Most likely the inaccurate and infamous rhyme, "Lizzie Borden took an axe / And gave her mother forty whacks. / When she saw what she had done, / She gave her father forty-one," was already in circulation by the end of the century.[72]

Borden's post-trial behavior only accelerated her descent into dark legend. Seeming to flaunt her newly inherited wealth, she purchased an ornate Victorian house, which she named Maplecroft and where she lived with her sister Emma, in the most fashionable of Fall River's neighborhoods. She threw spectacular parties to which she invited no local residents—not that many friends remained—and played hostess to a shocking parade of actors and actresses, a practice that eventually drove the prudish and deeply disapproving Emma away for good. Though in 1905 she reportedly toyed with becoming a playwright, she ultimately lived out her life intentionally avoiding anything but her own entertainment, exchanging the Christian charity work she had reputedly enjoyed before the murders for a life of revelry. A much-discussed affair with famous actress Nance O'Neil—who was, appropriately enough, "the star of a Boston stock company who specialized in tragic roles"—fell apart after condemnatory gossip among Fall River residents, and afterward Borden increasingly preferred anonymity and seclusion.[73] She died in 1927, leaving large portions of her million-dollar estate to, among other concerns, the "perpetual care of my father's lot in Oak Grove Cemetery" and the Animal Rescue League of Fall River.[74]

For his part, Ralph's fame grew with the rising cult of reporter celebrities. He published an impressive number of book-length works, many of which, including the Jacob Riis–like *People We Pass: Stories of Life Among the Masses of New York City* (1896), blended fictional techniques with the working-class realities he had encountered as an urban reporter.[75] Briefly attracted by the fame and income that William Randolph Hearst offered to the best reporters when he lured them away from other papers to work on the *New York Journal,* Ralph served as that paper's London correspondent in 1896 and 1897. He also joined a parade of reporters intent on gaining "authentic experience" by covering wars, first the Greco-Turkish War of 1897 and then the Boer War of 1899.

An anecdote from Ralph's waning days lends poignant closure to the reporter's experiments with literature and journalism. In 1902, as Ralph lay dying of stomach cancer in Vermont, the *New York Times* and the *Springfield (Mass.) Union* entered into a "genteel literary dispute" regarding the ties between literature and journalism.[76] When the *Times,* exemplifying the claim that literature and journalism clearly differed, insisted that "Julian Ralph is not a literary man," Ralph "sent off a bemused reply" suggesting he did not know "whether he should be pleased or distraught" about the assertion.[77] As biographer Lancaster observes, the *Times* remark clearly "had touched a nerve." More than insulting the pride of an ill man, the comment underscores growing tensions over how new journalism had influenced the profession, and over the question of whether journalism really was literary, and vice versa. It was a "genteel dispute" in which Ralph, like other journalists who sought colorful ways of narrating the news, had participated during the waning years of his career. It was a dispute that—viewed from the vantage of coverage of the Borden trial—ultimately provides texture to the framing of the news into a new aesthetic in the late nineteenth century.

Read as texts that together create a whole story, Julian Ralph's dispatches from Lizzie Borden's trial point suggestively to issues that go far beyond the current events of 1893. The reports illuminate how Ralph and Dana's "old" new journalism effectively engaged fictive techniques to humanize, critique, and extend the potentially depersonalized journalistic moment into something simultaneously culturally bound and aesthetic. The articles also complicate the search for boundaries between fact and fiction in narrating the news. S. Elizabeth Bird suggests students of journalism history—and students of literary history—need to resituate their assumptions about fact and fiction, objectivity and subjectivity, a project upon which Ralph himself seemed intent. Objective forms, or "chronicles," Bird writes, mark out the cultural boundaries of what is and is not deviant. Yet alongside the chronicle is the "story," and it is only through story that the teller and audience truly confront, in human terms, these boundaries. A story informs, but it also aims to engage the reader at an emotional level. While the chronicle defines cultural boundaries, the story dramatizes them and makes them live.[78]

Although mainstream American newspapers ultimately came to favor the chronicle as the standard for reportage in the twentieth century (a standard already embraced by the *New York Post,* as seen earlier in this chapter), Ralph insisted that the news required both chronicle and story, "fact" and "fiction," interacting fluidly in an ongoing project of social investigation. Ralph's writing, which insisted on the subjectivity inevitably lying behind the authoritative reportorial voice, problematized both the development of an "objective voice" and the commercialism associated with new journalism. Ralph drew up the literary conventions already popular among his reading audience—the careful analysis of clues, the depth of character, the teasing out of mystery—in order to create a factual account made richer and more vivid precisely because it was framed fictionally. Yet, paradoxically, Ralph's careful construction of the story grew out of his anxiety that Lizzie Borden might be read *only* fictionally, that she might be turned into an imaginative construct. In his delicate balance between fact and fiction, Ralph finally offered an ironic critique of easy characterization and unthinking consumption of the news story, all the while rejecting the adequacy of "the facts" alone. But, as chapter 4 will illustrate, Ralph's was a stance that ultimately came under attack from the most strident of the new journalists, William Randolph Hearst.

True Women and New Women

Lizzie Borden and Gender Anxieties in
Late Nineteenth-Century America

It does seem so dreadful to accuse a man of a crime. But a woman! And such a woman! I cannot listen to it; it is horrible.
—Anna Katharine Green, *The Leavenworth Mystery*

The late nineteenth century was, if nothing else, a period of intense social instability. Thousands of Americans moved from rural to urban settings; immigrants from Eastern European and Asian nations poured into the United States; volatility within the nation's economy, transformed under the melting powers of wide-scale industrialization and severe economic depressions in 1873–77 and 1893, temporarily devastated American ways of life. The question of women's place in society yielded yet another area of instability, and each of the central case studies examined here reveals national anxieties about gender and femininity. Nellie Bly, with her seemingly fearless pluck and her venturing into "masculine" lands, careers, and attitudes, represented the new opportunities women were forging for themselves. On the other hand, as introduced in the next chapter, Evangelina Cisneros depicted an idealized femininity built, essentially, on good breeding. Where Bly was apparently feisty enough to rescue herself had she ever been taken captive in Cuba, Cisneros was represented as a spirited but ultimately defenseless woman more comfortable in lace and linen than in sturdy traveling tweeds.

The press's framing of Lizzie Borden, however, offers perhaps the richest example of how middle- and upper-class gender was constructed and contested in the 1890s. One reason the trial drew marked responses from reading audiences was that it brought together conflicting attitudes about how women of Borden's society would and would not behave. Just as Jack the Ripper was immortalized during this same period in English society in part because of the social tensions he embodied, Borden stood not merely as an accused murderer but as "the catalyst for a series of psychological and social reactions," particularly about gender and crime.[1] Many twentieth-century scholars of Borden history contend she was acquitted because, quite simply, her peers considered a woman of her social standing incapable of committing murder. From the beginning of the century, newspapers and novels had typically depicted female criminals as belonging almost exclusively to socially lower classes. Women's criminal depravity had almost invariably been linked to both economic and moral poverty.

Upper- and middle-class white American women of the nineteenth century were both plagued and protected by powerful ideals perpetuated by magazines, religious doctrine, genteel literature, and the law itself. These ideals, now loosely organized under the label of "true womanhood," maintained that women were the one constant, guiding force in a dangerously fickle world. True women upheld "four cardinal virtues"—including "piety, purity, submissiveness, and domesticity"—that tied them to the home, seemingly the place where they longed to be, and left the public spaces of action and power to men.[2] Women's influence rested in their ability to maintain homes filled with cheer, comfort, and piety, forces that would theoretically educate and inspire their husbands and the boys they reared to be virtuous, responsible leaders.

Though these ideals had of course never been achievable for all women—most notably working-class women and women of color—by the end of the century they increasingly came under attack as women sought lives outside the home, in athletic arenas, in the workplace, and on political stages. Fresh ideals emerged, including that of the "new woman," so named by British author Sarah Grand in 1894. In its most strident form, the new woman was "critical of the social conventions that hindered her personal freedom and stymied her intellectual development."[3] Denouncing the system that granted privilege to men based on their gender rather than on their merit, the new woman called for equality in education and in opportunity.

For critics of the American new woman, she symbolized someone who was at best irresponsibly radical and at worst not even a woman. This was a woman who, critics argued, "was particularly vulnerable to the temptation of materialism," because she "longed for social prestige and luxury rather than expanded opportunities to serve her family and community."[4] What had the world come to when wifehood, motherhood, and the home no longer mattered to those who were supposed to cherish them most? Here must be a reprehensible new breed of human. As one anonymous poet attempting in 1894 to define new womanhood quipped:

> She flouts Love's caresses
> Reforms ladies' dresses
> And scorns the Man-Monster's tirade;
> She seems scarcely human
> This mannish New Woman
> This Queen of the Blushless Brigade.[5]

Although social realities are always more complex than labels like "true woman" and "new woman" suggest, Lizzie Borden was trapped in a gendered battle that can be understood under these labels. In theory and appearance, she embodied the tenets of true womanhood, devoting her life to her father (having apparently given up the possibility of marriage and a husband), cloistering herself at home, and working sweetly and piously in her equally sweet and pious volunteer work. The reality of her situation, however, was quite different, a point that both the prosecution and defense teams fought to suppress in divergent ways. The crime Borden was accused of, with its "'masculine' motive (money and independence) and its 'masculine' weapon, raised all sorts of anxious questions that cluster about the difficult issue of woman's place."[6] Here was a spinster caught within the rigid boundaries of genteel femininity at a time when women of her class and generation were starting to redefine themselves publicly. True women "cheerfully" denied themselves independence in economic and living situations, yet Borden's behavior, if we assume she did in fact kill her father and stepmother, suggested she craved both.[7] True women selflessly committed themselves to their fathers, husbands, and sons, but again Borden's violent behavior betrayed her ultimate dissatisfaction with this presumption.

Andrew Borden had been a notorious miser, both in terms of affection and money. Described by most acquaintances as cold and heartless, he forbade almost all forms of entertainment in his house; his daughters and wife could nurture no outside relationships, not even invite friends to call. A capitalist more intent on the possession of wealth than on the display and enjoyment of it, Andrew Borden denied his daughters access to the family's money, in essence chaining them to a joyless house that they considered far beneath them economically and socially.[8] Moreover, Andrew Borden had begun to transfer some of his daughters' inheritances to their hated stepmother, to whom they coldly referred only as "Mrs. Borden," although she had married their father when they were young children.[9]

If modern readers recognize here the psychological and economic factors that sometimes serve as motives for crime, regardless of gender and class, the idea that genteel women could be driven by such greed was unthinkable in Borden's time, a point that worked in her favor at the trial. Greed—like violence, "lust, and gratuitous cruelty"—was considered a particularly masculine malady, the antithesis of what true womanhood symbolized.[10] Well before Borden's case, the "rhetoric of true femininity" had been an ultimate defense for wealthy white women who faced prosecution.[11] Traditional ideas about gender, as disseminated in newspapers and in fiction, had taught that women who murdered were "naturally 'fiendish'" creatures who "violate[d] every principle of woman's 'nature.'"[12] As they do today, newspapers provided the narratives that audiences wanted to read and believe in, and the fact that the nineteenth-century press depicted "women who kill" as "insane or demoniacal" suggests that that is in fact what readers believed.[13] Satisfying society's need to categorize and marginalize female killers, newspapers and early detective fiction both created a wide gap indeed between criminal women and genteel ladies. If nothing else, Lizzie Borden was a lady. Therefore, by the logic extended to its natural end, Borden must be acquitted and the physical evidence against her—a spot of blood on her dress (which she had hurriedly burned), a stained hatchet in the cellar, the absence of her footprints in the barn (where she insisted she had been during the time of the murders)—must be explained away. Anything else posed too great a risk to an entire gendered and classed epistemology, and threatened the male jurors judging Borden. For if Borden was in fact found guilty, "the jurors' daughters could be similarly capable" of patricide, a concept too frightening for anyone to contemplate seriously.[14] Furthermore, if a lady could be guilty, an unfathomable social leveling must take place, suggesting that well-heeled women might be as capable of violence and general moral debasement as, for instance, "the working-class Irish-Catholic."[15]

In later years fiction writers attempted to negotiate some of these frightening possibilities, and one of the most fascinating outcomes of the trial was a subgenre of mystery and detective stories that explored the very character traits Borden exemplified, a type Julian Ralph cogently recognized himself when he painted Borden as representative of "the daughters of a class of well-to-do New England men" whose "homes are little more cheerful than jails."[16] If in 1878 Anna Katharine Green's fictional unmarried cousins had been absolved of all wrongdoing in *The Leavenworth Case,* fifteen or twenty years later female characters would not enjoy that privilege so readily. Several stories about single or spinster women appeared around the turn of the century, many of which were written by women, and these fictions "serve[d] as a barometer of disequilibrating social and economic change" centered on gendered issues.[17] About 10 percent of American women born between 1865 and 1895—a demographic that included Borden—never married. While unmarried women have never enjoyed significant levels of respect in society, by the turn of the nineteenth century dominant attitudes toward spinsters had evolved from pity to distrust and even fear. Some spinsters, like Borden herself, were locked in a state of perpetual pseudo-childhood, remaining under their fathers' watchful eyes and trapped in their family homes. Others cast off the prescribed roles of daughter, wife, and mother, choosing instead solitude, the company of other women, and financial independence.[18]

Some of the "spinster" mysteries in the late nineteenth and early twentieth centuries, like Mary E. Wilkins Freeman's "The Long Arm," took as their explicit starting point the details of the Borden murders. Other stories, like George Ira Brett's "Murder at Jex Farm," presented purely imaginary wealthy female murderers.[19] Some of the fiction continued to portray women as "the anchor of stability in the family and the administrator of class identity," teaching other characters and readers "how to be morally middle class and responsibly genteel."[20] Yet other stories—and sometimes even the stories that seemed to portray women as stable and "true"—introduced the possibility of female violence within the home. The homes of middle- and upper-class, single, white women became places "where fierce emotions and libidinal impulses run just beneath the veneer of gentility," factors undeniably present in the Borden household.[21] One writer who dealt with this class of spinster extensively was Mary Roberts Rinehart, who produced more best-selling novels between 1895 and 1944 than any other American author. Her stories explored "jealousy, rivalry, and deceit among near relations" and depicted women "who seem fully capable of killing members of their own families."[22] At the same time, Rinehart's spinster was threatening in a different fashion, in that she represented "a figure of freedom and an enabling persona of authorship, a woman in control of her sexuality, her bank account, and her narrative."[23]

Lizzie Borden strove to maintain similar control of her own story, sexuality, and money. Had she aspired to be a new woman, her family and community most probably would not have granted her opportunity to write this role for herself. While her father was alive, Borden was denied an education and a career. Her only occupations included Sunday School teaching and volunteer work in the Christian Endeavor Society and the Ladies Fruit and Flower Mission. Even after the major obstacles to Borden's freedom, namely Andrew and Abby Borden, were removed, the upper classes of Fall River—which had been supportive of Lizzie during the trial—turned on her and imposed new social restrictions when she failed to voice her own innocence (as the heroines of genteel detective novels invariably did). Borden's peers grew convinced that a woman of her status could in fact be guilty, a point seemingly verified by the way she spent her inheritance and by her relationships with theatrical men and women.

Lizzie Borden's trial for murder, the legal and journalistic narratives that defined it, and the genres of literature inspired by it typified the vexing fears about evolving gender constructions that Americans faced with increasing frequency in subsequent years. Trials, newspaper stories, and fictional works inevitably "make explicit prevailing ideologies by providing opposing narratives."[24] These narratives of Borden's womanhood ultimately reveal the stories her culture wanted and expected to hear, by upholding traditional representations of class and gender.

CHAPTER FOUR

The Evangelina Cisneros Romance, Medievalist Fiction, and Journalism That Acts

> He should have been born in the active days of knights-errant—to have had nothing more serious to do than to ride abroad with a blue ribbon fastened to the point of his lance, and with the spirit to unhorse any one who objected to its color, to the claims of superiority of the noble lady who had tied it there.
> —Richard Harding Davis, *The Princess Aline*

Introduction

In 1889, reporters for a saucy San Francisco paper, the *Examiner,* thrilled readers with breathless accounts describing how a small fishing boat had capsized off Point Bonita in San Francisco Bay, drowning four men and leaving one clinging precariously to offshore rocks as waves "dashe[d] over him and he begged in the name of God for help."[1] Members of the lifesaving station, deciding that conditions were too risky and that the man was doomed anyway, elected to do nothing to aid him. The publisher of the *Examiner,* however, unable to imagine "a human being left to perish in that manner"—and doubtless recognizing the public relations potential inherent in the situation—chartered a tugboat "to send out to Point Bonita to attempt a rescue," manning the boat with two of his own fearless reporters.[2] The rescue was successful, and the next day the *Examiner* proclaimed in enormous headlines that its brave reporters had done "the work of the life-saving station." Sneering at the "farcical service" of the lifeguards, the *Examiner* emphasized that the journalists had "dashed into the sea" to save the man while "the lifeboat men and the tug men had not been able to do anything for him."[3] Here, an *Examiner* article boasted the following day, was a story more moving for readers than anything else in print. It proudly observed that

> copies of the EXAMINER containing the thrilling account of the rescue were sold almost as fast as they could be printed. On the cable cars, lingering on doorsteps, in parlors, boudoirs, business offices, on the ferry-boats, in the hotel lobbies, everywhere, people were seen poring over the full-page account of the cry in the night, the naked man on the rock, the powerless people on shore, . . . and the triumphant carrying of the line to the benumbed castaway by the EXAMINER's young men.[4]

Clearly, the *Examiner* was offering its thrilled audience something more than mere reportage, something more than a dry recounting of the day's facts. This was "talking and acting" journalism; it was journalism that *made* part of the story itself by enacting a rescue and by, quite literally, determining and writing the plot. In the process the *Examiner* had made the story all the more amazing and enjoyable for readers.

Owned by the young and brash William Randolph Hearst, the *San Francisco Examiner* had been a gift from his father, a silver magnate who had acquired it as payment for an unrelated business deal. Eagerly picking up this paper, the political organ his father had ceded, young Hearst transformed the way news was narrated on the West Coast by adopting the methods of his onetime hero, Joseph Pulitzer, and then magnifying them tenfold. If Pulitzer's New York paper was sensational, Hearst's was sensational in the extreme. If Pulitzer's paper employed surprisingly fresh layouts and techniques, Hearst demanded his to be even fresher and more eye-catching.

While Hearst had modeled his San Francisco paper on Pulitzer's, he was not content to remain on the West Coast, quietly producing his own version of the *World*. Soon, he invaded New York as new owner of the faltering *Journal* and engaged Pulitzer in a ferocious head-to-head battle for the hearts and imaginations of East Coast readers. The publishers' infamous competition spawned the most notorious era in late nineteenth- and early twentieth-century newspaper history—that of "yellow journalism."[5] The competition between Pulitzer and Hearst also inspired some of the most outrageous amalgamations of fact and fiction evident in 1890s newspapers, including one of the greatest romances of the late nineteenth century.

In the middle of 1897, as the United States inched toward conflict with Spain over colonial control of Cuba, one sensational event served as a rallying point for Americans intent on war. A young Cuban woman named Evangelina Cisneros[6] was imprisoned in Havana and charged with conspiracy to assassinate a Spanish official. Hearst, however, dumbfounded that such a lovely specimen could be guilty of treasonous crimes, concocted a more emotionally laden version of the story for his rapt readers: suggesting that Cisneros was held captive because she had chastely refused the advances of a Spanish colonel.

Had the Cisneros story been limited to reportage about her imprisonment, whatever its cause, it might have served as little more than a passing example of alleged Spanish atrocities against Cuban women on the eve of the Spanish-American War. But the story is pertinent today because of the way actuality collided with fictionality in Hearst's *Journal*. The case serves as a prime example of how Hearst's reporters manufactured the news and framed it fictionally in order to transform traditional newspapers, which wrote *about* the news, into a "journalism that *acts*," as Hearst himself put it, a journalism that constructed the news and believable—if ultimately suspect—stories.[7]

In the case of the *Journal's* reportage about the imprisoned Cisneros, the construction of news depended upon the manipulation of fictional modes. Readers at the turn of the century approached the *Journal* confident they would find thrilling stories told by people who spoke from experience—they would encounter expert, eyewitness accounts of crimes, scandals, accidents, and all things sensational (all mediated, of course, through a reporter's colorful pen). What makes the *Journal* writings "literary" is the manner in which they self-consciously merged fictional vocabularies with vocabularies of "the real." In this case, reporters for Hearst's *Journal* promptly turned Cisneros into a cause célèbre, portraying her as a virginal heroine transmogrified from the pages of a medievalist romance novel and held in the fearsome grip of a diabolical Spanish overlord. In other words, Hearst's writers blended the apparent facts of the news with specific literary vocabularies, creating a metafiction that *Journal* readers consumed voraciously. Hearst acknowledged a specific motive for creating this metafiction of

Evangelina Cisneros: he wanted his readers and the government to act, just as his was "the journalism that acts." That is, he wanted to free Cisneros from her Havana jail cell, and he wanted to sell more newspapers as a highly desirable by-product of that political action.[8] Hearst recognized that the way to motivate readers—and in turn the government—to act toward the same goal was to make Cisneros's story real to them, something achievable by narrating the facts of the case within a literary frame so that the truth could be stranger (and even better) than fiction.

This case study is positioned as "the Evangelina Cisneros *romance,*" for *Journal* editors capitalized on a literary vogue (the medievalist romance), incorporated it into the news, and rewrote the news as a real romance.[9] This chapter will first survey Hearst's articulations of new journalism, then turn to the Cisneros romance itself, using it to foreground the literary context of the medievalist romance. What emerges from this example of new journalism is evidence that newspaper writers manipulated romantic discourse to construct a literature that wrapped itself in fictional cloaks even as it proclaimed factuality and that deliberately blurred lines between fact and fiction, realism and romance, to manufacture once again a journalism that acted—and to create an entertainment that rivaled the most imaginative of texts.

Willie Hearst's Newer, More Active Journalism

William Randolph Hearst came to journalism somewhat casually. Within fifteen years of taking up the profession, however, he had built a veritable publishing empire of eight newspapers and two magazines located in five major American cities and claiming a readership of three million.[10] The only child of self-made millionaire George Hearst, from childhood William had displayed a flair for "showmanship and sensation," taking particular joy in melodramatic theater; indeed, "he could project himself into any drama and shed copious tears with the heroine."[11] Certainly, Hearst fostered his propensity toward drama in his role of newspaper publisher.

After George Hearst acquired the *San Francisco Examiner* in 1880, the paper served as a rather uninspired political organ for the local Democratic Party until, by 1885, twenty-two-year-old William fell in love with Pulitzer's *World* and longed to try new journalism himself. Begging his father to release the paper to him, he vowed to improve the techniques that had made Pulitzer's publication so profitable. The New York editor, Hearst argued, had proved newspapers should no longer tie themselves down politically. Rather, the *World,* "undoubtedly the best paper" in the nation, appealed "to the people" and depended "for its success upon enterprise, energy, and a certain startling originality."[12] Here were precisely the traits Hearst could bring to West Coast journalism. Outlining a specific agenda to persuade his father, Hearst detailed how he would recruit energetic young reporters and advertisers; how he would improve the illustrations, exchanging the current "nauseat[ing]" ones for those that could "stimulate the imagination"; and how he would make all these changes at once, jolting complacent San Francisco newspaper readers awake and creating "a revolution in the sleepy journalism of the Pacific slope."[13] "We must be alarmingly enterprising and we must be startlingly original," William urged his father. "We must be honest and fearless."[14] The promised result, young Hearst predicted, would yield an increase in circulation by ten thousand readers within the year.

George Hearst, not so easily convinced, delayed transferring ownership of the *Examiner* until 1886, when William was expelled from Harvard because of plummeting academic achievement—not to mention a series of tasteless pranks, which culminated in his sending monogrammed chamber pots to his professors. By the next year, after he was elected to the U.S. Senate, George Hearst finally turned responsibility of the *Examiner* over to his son, with the hope that William would finally settle down and make something serious of himself, and of the paper too. The father's hopes were rather spectacularly fulfilled. As he had predicted to his father, Hearst stunned San Franciscans with his radical journalistic style. Mimicking what he had learned watching Pulitzer and studying the *World's* technique, Hearst served a rich stew of shocking exposés, screaming headlines, endless extra editions, luridly detailed illustrations, and intense front-page stories calculated to "startle, amaze, or stupefy" his audience.[15] The paper pressed Hearst's natural love for theatrics into play and granted him the venue to order stories that "built up suspense that carried on from day to day like a serial thriller" and manufacture pieces "that could be spun out from day-to-day in a circulation-building sensation," just as Pulitzer had achieved with the Nellie Bly trip.[16] Practicing a policy of "excitement fortissimo," the *Examiner* specialized in what one editor called "the gee-whiz emotion"—Hearst lectured his reporters that "any issue the front page of which failed to elicit a 'Gee Whiz!' from its readers was a failure, whereas the second page ought to bring forth a 'Holy Moses!' and the third an astounded 'God Almighty!'"[17]

Hearst may have modeled his journalism on Pulitzer's, but while news making was at heart an act of social responsibility for Pulitzer, for Hearst it was finally not much more than one grand theatrical event, "a glorious lark," as one of his biographers describes it.[18] He reveled in hoaxes as much as Benjamin Day of the 1830s *New York Sun* had, and he made few distinctions between news that actually occurred and news that was entirely fabricated (though his editorials consistently swore upon the bibles of truth and accuracy). While some of the stories in earlier issues of Hearst's *Examiner* "tend[ed] toward objectivity," by the early 1890s outright falsification was being openly supported by editorial policy.[19] In essence, a Hearst biographer writes, the publisher was

> an inventor, a producer, an arranger. The news that actually happened was too dull for him, and besides it was also available to the other papers. He lived in a childlike dream world, imagining wonderful stories and then going out and creating them, so that the line between fact and fancy was apt to be fuzzy.[20]

For stories that were not utter inventions, Hearst nevertheless insisted his reporters actively develop the "plot" and, if necessary, insert themselves into their work as "the heroes and heroines of a morality play within a play."[21] In such instances as the *Examiner's* rescue of men stranded at Point Bonita, which opens this chapter, its aid for towns blockaded by a flooded Sacramento River, and its reporters' tireless trek toward a train snowbound in the Sierra Nevada Mountains, Hearst's paper did not merely report on what had already happened. Rather, writers involved themselves in the action and then trumpeted their paper's admirable qualities in the next day's headlines.[22] Hearst explained the philosophy in an October 1897 editorial: "*Examiner* reporters are everywhere; they are the first to see everything, and the first to perceive the true meaning of what they see. Whether a child is to be found, an eloping girl to be brought home, or a murder to be traced, one of our staff is sure to give the sleepy detectives their first pointers."[23] Hearst, however, played at manufacturing news and fashioning a "journalism that acts" on the West Coast only as a precursor to his ultimate dream: to take his garish journalism to New York to meet Joseph Pulitzer's *World* on its own turf and defeat it in what would be his greatest story ever.

In late 1895 Hearst's dream seemed closer to fulfillment when he purchased the faltering *Journal*, a New York City Democratic Party paper once owned, strangely enough, by Pulitzer's brother Albert. Almost immediately, Hearst declared war on what he called "old journalism" and, more specifically, on Pulitzer himself. Unsatisfied with how far his rival had taken newspaper innovations, Hearst declared that his ever newer journalism was writing that "does things" while the "old journalism" (into which category he derisively cast the *World* and the *Sun,* along with such stodgy dailies as the *Post* and the *Times*) ineffectually made "editorial protests against such disturbing competition."[24] Old journalism, which Hearst accused of partnering with big business and conservative politics, "was asleep—as soundly as Rip Van Winkle after his nip of schnapps."[25] As a consequence, these newspapers missed such vital happenings as coverage of the casualties of a shipwreck, snowstorms wreaking havoc in the Northeast, and even the declaration of the Greco-Turkish War. While other newspapers took "the dignified course of sitting still and doing nothing," the *Journal* championed "intelligent activity," for "the business of a newspaper is to tell the story of a day's human life—its joys, sorrows, hopes, aims, struggles, progress, failures, successes, sins."[26] "Nothing should be omitted," Hearst gushed, "that may touch with power the sources of creative energy in other men."[27]

Bravado aside, Hearst realized Pulitzer—and, to a fading degree, Dana—already held New York readers in firm grip with his stories of sin and sensation. So Hearst unleashed his most cut-throat strategies, first dropping the price of his daily to one penny and forcing Pulitzer into a heated price war; then ballooning the new journalism standards of broad headlines, detailed illustrations, sensational focus, and breezy prose to clownlike proportions; and finally stealing away Pulitzer's and Dana's best reporters and editors and hiring other writers, like Richard Harding Davis, who brought their fame and celebrity to the *Journal,* especially once Hearst had splashed their names in huge fonts across headlines.[28] Indeed, Hearst strategically nurtured the professionalization of authorship by hiring not only dedicated and unknown newspaper reporters but also well-known fiction writers to be reporters, helping to turn journalists into a most celebrated class.[29]

Hiring celebrity writers and making celebrities of writers served to strengthen the newspaper's role as a stage for entertainment rather than politics or business. Even more than the *World* or the *Sun* before it, the *Journal* specialized in news as a series of *stories* actively formulated by the best writers America had to offer. For instance, Hearst concocted countless articles involving stunts, including a transcontinental bicycle relay between *Journal* and *Examiner* offices that spotlighted the trendiest form of transportation and echoed the travel trick Pulitzer had initiated with Nellie Bly. In another, more sensational example, Hearst employed a "murder squad" of detective reporters who wrote their own real-life murder mysteries in lurid fashion and who offered solutions to mysteries even the police seemed unable to crack. When the *Journal's* "murder squad" found the murderer of Willie Guldensuppe, a New York masseuse who had been dismembered and sunk in the East River, Hearst crowed in an editorial that "the Journal, as usual, ACTS while the representatives of ancient journalism sit idly by and wait for something to turn up."[30]

No other story, however, offered quite the same potential for excitement as the story unfolding in Cuba before and during the Spanish-American War.[31] With conflict brewing in the Caribbean during 1897 and the early part of 1898, Hearst realized that the island offered a thrilling supply of heart-rending tales about desperate insurgents and "women victims of Spanish cruelty."[32] Cuba became his "major theme" of 1897, a place where he could build

> a daily scenario of the Cuban conflict which had little relation to fact but was as exciting to the mass mind in much the same way as a cliff-hanging continued story, and in its stark delineation of a struggle between villain and hero, its depiction of the Spaniards as cowardly knaves and Cubans as noble, long-suffering victims of outrage. In the Hearst press the typical Spaniard emerged as a monster of cruelty that raped Cuban women, tortured and murdered their husbands and children, then burned their houses.[33]

The conflict in Cuba between the insurgents and their colonial rulers was not, for Hearst, a complex of political and historical issues. It was instead a grand and melodramatic story, supplying its own ready cast of characters. Making no attempt to discern truth from falsehood, fact from fiction, the *Journal* published story after unauthenticated story of fierce battles, daring exploits, and—Hearst's favorite—Spanish atrocities against innocent Cuban maidens.

Starring: Evangelina Cisneros and Charles Duval (a.k.a. Karl Decker)

A sketch of Cisneros's imprisonment and ultimate rescue illustrates how the *Journal* loaded romantic conventions onto its own story.[34] Before her imprisonment Cisneros had been living with and caring for her father, a Cuban separatist under house arrest at a Caribbean penal colony. Early in 1897, Cisneros was herself arrested for attempted murder and sent to a Havana prison. Spanish authorities claimed that she and her lover had plotted to assassinate the colonel commanding the penal colony. When a *Journal* reporter touring the Havana prison discovered the beautiful Cisneros awaiting trial, however, the "facts about her arrest were altered," either "through the imaginative efforts" of the reporter or the designing efforts of Cisneros herself.[35] Soon the story blossomed in the pages of the *Journal* into a tale casting Cisneros as a falsely imprisoned maiden who had bravely defended "her chastity against the lustful advances" of the Spanish colonel.[36]

The *Journal* published several "revisions" to this plot before finally settling on one sporting the "correct" romantic formulae. On August 17, 1897, for instance, the paper reported that Cisneros had been falsely imprisoned when debased women rioted at the penal colony where she and her father lived. In this version, she was swept up accidentally in a mass arrest of women and sent to the Havana prison. The next day, however, the *Journal* insisted that Cisneros had been imprisoned because the "vile negresses" at the penal colony had rioted.[37] Hating her aristocratic blood, they had implicated her as a participant in the melee and ensured she was arrested with them. The August 19, 1897, story saw yet another revision. Now the paper reported that the riot at the penal colony occurred because all the other prisoners protested the Spanish colonel's sexual advances. Yet on August 22, 1897, the *Journal* claimed Cisneros was unjustly imprisoned "simply because of the blood that flows in her veins" and because "the innocent girl was rescued by her friends from the lustful Spanish military governor."[38] Finally, the August 23, 1897, *Journal* published a plot for Cisneros that crammed as many romantic conventions into the reportage as possible. The maiden had been wrongly imprisoned in Havana when she herself attempted to defend her honor against the sexual advances of the penal colony's Spanish colonel. According to the *Journal,* the Spanish government (and Hearst's main newspaper competitors, as well) subsequently attempted to besmirch the innocent Cisneros's character by circulating the false information that she had plotted to kill the colonel.[39]

With this most desperate tale finally in place, Hearst became "producer, director and stage manager for the greatest of journalistic melodramas," a sob story about "a wronged girl in the clutches of the decadent Spanish Empire."[40] Seeking both greater American presence in Cuba and some sensational news to boost circulation, he astutely told his managing editors that the story of Cisneros would "do more to open the eyes of the country" to the plight of Cuba "than a thousand editorials or political speeches."[41] Hearst was right. The paper introduced Cisneros to American readers by providing the testimonies of former Havana prisoners who swore they had seen Cisneros rudely treated, though she was a "fairy-like little Cuban maiden" and even more lovely than any "fairy princess" of fiction.[42] Alas, this fairy princess was locked in a jail "past description" and worse than any dungeon perilous, a place, according to the *Journal,* of "hideous squalor," "querulous cries," "stagnant gutter[s]," and a "horrible death-rate."[43] Here the maiden was kept among murderers and other "animal-like" (and darker-skinned) women.

Other *Journal* reporters picked up the motifs of the romantic novel and continued to tell the story within this discourse, whether or not they had concrete facts to add. One reporter's imagination, for instance, transformed Havana into a melodramatic scene of dark suspense, a stage perfectly set for intrigue and adventure, with

> the heavy stone walls, the dingy tile roofs, the fearsome inhabitants,
> . . . the swarm of soldiers and police, and vigilance of martial law,
> the dark scarred walls of Moro Castle over the bay, the frowning
> forts, the sentinels with bayonets ever fixed on their rifles, the dreadful
> atmosphere full of suspicion, treachery and terror.[44]

It was on this treacherous stage that Cisneros was wasting away, fighting off smallpox, consumption, "a touch of fever," and "general debility."[45] What had the civilized world come to, the *Journal* implored, when this innocent heroine—a veritable martyr and "Cuban Joan of Arc"—was left to rot in such a dungeon?

With this question blasting the front pages by August 17, the *Journal's* reportage sparked a national effort on Cisneros's behalf and urged the country toward a duel with the evil master who threatened America's chivalric and martial ideals. Cuba's democratic neighbor could not sit idly by while womanhood was deflowered. Such inaction would offend the nation's proclaimed vigor and virility. Mass meetings, organized largely by women's clubs, convened across America. A petition drive began, led off with the signatures of such emissaries as Julia Ward Howe, Mrs. Ulysses S. Grant, Mrs. Jefferson Davis, and even President McKinley's mother. Countless telegrams of protest buzzed overseas to the Queen of Spain, while other telegrams begged the pope to aid the "girl martyr."[46]

The excitement of this modern-day romance lasted through August 1897 and into early September before public interest waned. Recognizing that his chance to force action, and to stimulate record circulation, was passing, Hearst dispatched reporter Karl Decker—whose rather striking pen name was "Charles Duval"—to Cuba in order to act where the government, Queen, and pope had not. Decker's mission: to break Hearst's innocent maiden out of her squalid jail cell and ride off with her on a white steed—or at least put her on a steamer bound for the United States.

News of the daring prison break thrilled readers when they picked up their papers on October 8, 1897. Once Decker and Cisneros were safe in New York a few days later, they detailed for a smitten audience how the fabulous rescue had proceeded.[47] By sheer luck, or so it seemed, the house across the street from Cisneros's jail cell had been available for rent. From here, Decker and two Cuban accomplices had suspended a warped twelve-foot plank between the house roof and the cell window, some thirty-five breathtaking feet above the stony ground. Working feverishly under fear of discovery for two nights, Decker had hacked through the cell's bars until he could gather the grateful Cisneros in his arms and help her crawl back across the chasm to the refuge of the house. Falling safely into freedom, Decker related, the maiden had given "a little moan and dropped to the floor" in relief.[48]

But the dangers had been far from over. Three days later, Decker— "keeping the needs of the *Journal's* romancers in mind"—had disguised Cisneros in men's clothing and smuggled her to the United States, directly under the nose of the chief of police himself, who was searching out-

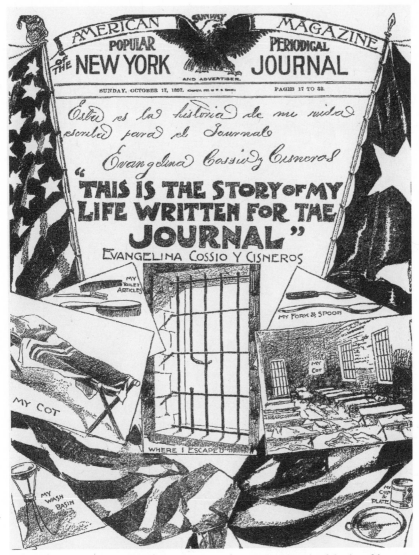

Evangelina Cisneros thrilled American readers with the colorful tale of her escape from Spanish captivity—and her rescue by "the journalism that acts." *New York Journal,* October 17, 1897.

bound ships for the famous escapee.[49] Then, reworking the tale of Robin Hood's incognito presence at King John's archery contest, the *Journal* purported to have arranged a banquet on board the freedom ship, which Spanish detectives attended. Despite such flirtations with danger, Decker safely whisked Cisneros to New York, where she met with fanfare, parades, a

THE DAYS OF KNIGHT ERRANTRY ARE STILL WITH US.

A comic for the *New York Journal* encapsulates the medievalist ideal epitomized by Hearst's newspaper in its chivalric rescue of Evangelina Cisneros. *New York Journal,* October 18, 1897.

new wardrobe, and immediate American citizenship (all conveniently arranged and financed, of course, by the *Journal*).[50] Secure at last in America, Cisneros easily switched from her role of brave heroine, willing to aid her rescuers with courageous verve, to the role of soft, gentle heroine, eager to partake in "universal" feminine behaviors. One could, after all, tell from the "unusual excitement," trembling hands, and "color in her olive cheeks" as she shopped for new dresses that "Miss Cisneros is as much woman as she is patriot."[51] At long last, Cisneros, the "passive victim, the fragile flower of Cuban womanhood rescued from rapacious Spanish jailers," could revel in the glory of "a virile white knight of the American press"—the *Journal*.[52]

Actually, the process by which Cisneros was broken out of prison was far less adventurous, and the very need for such a break was questionable to begin with. The prison guards, bribed from the ever-ample *Journal* coffers, were "conscientiously looking the other way" during the escape, and Cisneros might have walked out of the prison with impunity.[53] In addition, the barred window through which Decker sawed was dilapidated and loose enough to pull free without cutting. Nevertheless, the elaborate plot involving prison guards, sawed-through window bars, and an escape on a rickety plank over a thirty-five-foot chasm served its purpose, for it "provide[d] the prison personnel with a plausible alibi," and, more importantly, it made for great reading.[54] Huck Finn and Tom Sawyer's needless "rescue" of captive Jim at the end of *Huckleberry Finn* (1885)—itself a spoof on medievalist melodrama—inevitably comes to mind. The truths that reporters bent and placed within the adventure story framework underscore the extent to which writers used fictional elements in creating the Cisneros story.

Accordingly, the *Journal* and other national newspapers spared no verbiage in linking the rescue with the most romantic of models. "The Days of Knight Errantry Are Still with Us," one headline proclaimed.[55] Karl Decker, a "veritable knight errant," was the "Modern d'Artagnan." The adventure outranked "the deeds of the heroes of the yellow-back novels," and the story easily served as "the most chivalric exploit of modern *Journalism*."[56] One reporter crowed, "Behold in the American jail-breakers the emissaries of modern journalism—knights whose chivalry is worthy [of] the golden days of old Spain, when her real castles now so gloomy were in their glory."[57] An editorial argued that although the action had been illegal and might even cause international trouble, "if innocent maidens are still imprisoned by tyrants, the knight errant is yet needed."[58]

Another editorial decreed: "The easy liberation of Miss Cisneros by Yankee determinism and chivalry is a curious lesson to the once chivalrous Spain, now ruled by a young woman."[59] "No novel, full of gallants in slashed doublets, was ever more dramatic than this."[60]

In his articles, journalist Murat Halstead linked the story extensively to the literary genre, insisting that in this "true romance" of "chivalrous conduct," "fine touches" of drama were evident that "only a newspaper expert could have dreamed [up]."[61] Everywhere Halstead looked he saw not simply journalism but sheer poetry: "There has never been written a more enchanting description of the surpassing beauty of a moonlight night in the tropics than that which is strung like a pearl in the *Journal* story of the rescue."[62] That description seemed "put on the stage by some master of realistic art," a skilled author who could build suspense masterfully by portraying the rescuers giving up "the sawing of a bar of iron at the window because it rang like a fire alarm!"[63]

A book-length edition of the stories—complete with bewitching photographs of Cisneros and an introduction by Julian Hawthorne, son of the nineteenth century's romancer par excellence—soon followed.[64] Here the romantic framing continued; indeed, one could now sit down in a soft chair and consume the tale as one would a novel, and Hawthorne's introduction made this comparison explicit. "We are indeed accustomed to finding truth stranger than fiction," Hawthorne asserted, "but it is a new sensation to find it also more romantic—more in the fashion of . . . the Goth fairy-tales of Medaeval ages."[65] Indeed, perhaps the Spaniards themselves would one day "bring themselves to admit that the story of Karl Decker and Evangelina Cisneros can fitly take its place beside the most brilliant and moving of their ancient chronicles of daring."[66] Hawthorne, setting the stage for Decker's suspense chapters and Cisneros's captivity chapters, emphasized the story's fictive elements, the story's "setting and background," its "dramatis personae," its "dash, intrigue, and cumulative interest," all of which proved "almost ideally perfect" for romance.[67]

Actuality fit perfectly into the "required" elements of romance, and "as in the old Romances, there is no uncertainty as to which way our sympathies should turn."[68] What made the *Journal's* action so laudable was that it fulfilled its part of the romance formula so predictably. A newspaper, after all, had never before been expected to "act." The "old" journalism would alert Americans to the situation and then rest assured that it had done its public duty. But for the purposes of this grand story, mere reportage would be like "some puissant prince of fairy legend," impotently alerting an "ogre to the situation and asking him to make changes"—hardly the stuff of which good romance or martial idealism is made.[69] Rather, the *Journal* understood its American duty to go beyond the point where "the realistic novelist would end his narrative" and to turn fact into metafiction by acting.[70] Indeed, "the proprietors of the *Journal* would rather make a good thing real than debate whether or not so good a thing as Evangelina's rescue would be a probable incident," as a mere novelist would do.[71]

Hawthorne's assertion that the story unraveled with intentional, if ironic, artistry could not have been more correct. For the *Journal* had linked the Cisneros story with a popular fictional genre, the medievalist romance. The romantic elements spurred American readers to action because they made the supposed facts of the case digestible and understandable, yet thrilling in the way a novel could be thrilling. If the most admirable characters in medieval romances were those who braved dangers and acted upon convictions, Hearst had created the ultimate heroes and heroine—Decker, Cisneros, and especially the *Journal*—for the ultimate romance. Simultaneously and paradoxically, the framing of the story with fictional elements reinforced not the adequacy or importance of literature but the triumph of the real over the imaginary. Here was the stuff of real life, looking an awful lot like the stuff of imagination—yet readers could not forget it *was* real, or so the *Journal* said, and thus even more impressive than romance.[72]

Romantic Revival in the Age of Realism

Thinking about Hearst's Cuban stories in terms of melodramatic suspense and stock "villainous" and "heroic" characters is appropriate, given the literary context in which they were produced.[73] Though literary historians often associate the 1890s with naturalism and realism in the United States, in fact the most widely published and universally read genre in the American market was the historical romance. In the 1890s "historical romances full of heroic exploits flooded American magazines and bookstores," appearing in cheap magazines and paperback books but also in "quality monthlies" and more expensive volumes.[74] At least half of all best sellers between 1894 and 1902 were "novels of high romance," in some 600,000 to 750,000 copies.[75] Such novels as Anthony Hope's *The Prisoner of Zenda* (1894), Mark Twain's *Personal Recollections of Joan of Arc*

(1896), Charles Major's *When Knighthood Was in Flower* (1898), and Marion Crawford's *Via Crucis* (1899) offered readers countless "tales of knights in days of yore," filled with "aggressive, courtly, dashing" heroes and "timid, staunch, beautiful" heroines.[76] Indeed, Frank Luther Mott calls the 1890s a "romantic parade," characterized by "men handsome, booted and spurred, with rapiers in hand, long cloaks floating in the breeze; the women gentle but clearly courageous, in taffeta and lace, and beautiful enough to move any red-blooded man to give his life in their defense."[77]

However, if romances seemingly offered escape from everyday life, they simultaneously strove to "jolt modern readers into . . . effective action in the present."[78] Fiction was only part of a widespread interest in medievalism in the United States, which was evident as well in, for example, architecture, visual arts, and philosophy.[79] Somewhat paradoxically, medievalism, with its "romantic" literary sheen, served as part of the broader push toward "the real thing" in American culture. Convinced that modern life had promoted "impotence and spiritual sterility," Americans sought "'authentic' alternatives" to these debilitating psychic states.[80] Such leaders as Teddy Roosevelt, for instance, "feared that modern life was rotting the old American virtues out of the generation, softening their bodies, their character, and their willpower."[81] One antidote involved commitment to a "modern form of chivalry," a "knightly code that emphasized duty, honor, and a willingness to make sacrifices for a good cause."[82] Genuine connection with real life would occur by focusing not on the "bewildering range of . . . social problems" but on the idealized principles "supposedly embodied in medieval or Oriental cultures."[83] Many American writers, then, sought not to focus on the sordid realities of everyday existence but to "hold up their mirror to [the] heroic nature" so evident in their view of medieval life.[84]

This effort toward "authentic experience" is evident in such realist texts as that describing Nellie Bly's trip around the world and the great naturalist works of Crane, Norris, London, and others.[85] But "authentic experience" also fueled the romantic revival of the late nineteenth century. The medieval hero and heroine provided ideal models for readers, and their tales "personified wholeness of purpose and intensity of experience."[86] Romance hinted at how rich American culture could be if readers eschewed decadent trivialities and cast off their ennui, centering instead upon an ethic of strenuous behavior, or what T. J. Jackson Lears calls "the contemplation of medieval willfulness."[87] Thus, historical romance was not a literature of "encrusted convention and pale idealism" but a literature of "fierce emotions and manly actions—of 'real life.'"[88]

Against this romantic backdrop shone new journalism, itself a literature of "real life" and willful action. Editors marketed new journalism as the reading material of choice for a modern age. In general, they criticized much fiction—especially the overly "artistic" type—as too far removed from the pressing concerns of modern society, too out of touch with "the real thing." Publishers like Hearst implied that historical romance might be enjoyable, but only the news could be both romantic and real, both fictional and factual. The news, in other words, rivaled the pleasure one felt while reading good fiction, yet it was ultimately better than fiction because it was real, or so the *Journal* claimed.[89]

In addition, some of the best-known reporters of 1890s America, including Richard Harding Davis, seemed as if bred to fit the mold of fictional romantic hero. Here were men "who would be accepted in the drawing rooms of the effete rich" yet "who could carry the principles of gentlemanliness into the most brutal situations and show that Americans, through birth and training, were adequate to them."[90] The reporter could fulfill the yearning for authentic and adventurous experience that informed so many romances and that drove American society more generally, as well.

The Evangelina Cisneros story as conveyed in the *Journal* offered precisely the means by which readers could enjoy both realism and romance and by which they could vicariously live out the ideals of adventure and activism prevalent in popular fiction. By responding to the romantic motifs and calls to arms presented in the *Journal* after Cisneros was imprisoned, readers could participate in an "authentic experience" and engage in chivalric enterprise by crusading on a Cuban woman's behalf. If the lesson to be drawn from romantic literature was that modern Americans could model themselves on fictional, martial ideals, the *Journal* led the way with its example of action in this modern tale about a damsel in distress and her American knight in shining armor.

Conclusion

The serialized story in this case of new journalism—including the news accounts that stood in place of Cisneros's own voice while she was imprisoned, the initial reports of her rescue written by various *Journal* reporters, and finally the stories narrated by Decker and Cisneros themselves—were treated as subsequent chapters in a single, romantic news-novel. *Journal* reporters self-consciously drew upon the most compelling and thrilling conventions of the wildly popular medievalist fictions circulating in the literary marketplace. Crafting their news stories to fit the most apposite literary examples of heroism and adventure, they framed their rescue of the Cuban maiden in terms that both confirmed and challenged the offerings of imaginative literature. Journalism became in the reporters' hands not a chronicle of things that had happened but a force in creating reality itself. Moreover, journalism was transformed into a force of action and energy—it became the entity that quite literally brought static fictional icons to life. Here was a tale providing direct example of legendary heroism enacted in the modern world, an example in which readers could themselves participate by protesting against Spain and, of course, by purchasing the *Journal*. That tale was finally, *Journal* writers emphasized, far more thrilling than any crowding the booksellers' shelves because of its foothold in reality itself.

Ironically, if Hearst faced one problem with his modern romance, it was that the story was too good, its conclusion too "happily ever after." The *Journal* and American swashbuckling ideals "won" in this rendition of a familiar plot, essentially halting progress toward military confrontation—with its attendant circulation-building stories—that Hearst ultimately desired. As if aware of the irony of its victory, the *Journal* abruptly dropped both Decker and Cisneros once their newsworthiness wore out. Decker continued a career in journalism, but as late as 1933 he was still complaining about his unpaid expense account. Cisneros—the newly minted American who had gushed in the pages of the *Journal*, "America is nothing but one big party! . . . I love it! I love it!"—soon married one of her Cuban rescuers and returned to her native land.[91]

The Cisneros romance did have longer-term—and more deleterious—effects. As Joyce Milton asserts, its "campaign helped to sell the American public on a false image of Cuba" as a "pale-skinned, upper-class virgin waiting breathlessly for a broad-shouldered American to rescue her and make her his."[92] Doubtless this journalistic literature, poised as it was between the romantic and the real, achieved its fundamental goal of prompting action, but it also turned fact into a fiction, a fiction made all the more problematic to the most critical of readers because of its implied status as truth. If Hearst was selling a story about the journalistic enactment of honor, valor, and courage, he was also constructing a secondary tale about race, imperialism, and expansionism. What was "real" in these dual stories, and what was pure construct? It hardly mattered to anyone other than some critics and of course to Hearst's enraged competitors, outsmarted at their own games by an upstart western millionaire. For its part, the largest portion of the American reading public simply embraced the narrative wave, enjoying the aesthetic that could so thoroughly subsume popular fiction and reconfigure it in a form even more relevant to their pressing modern concerns. If fellow editors and publishers looked on with a mixture of disdain and jealously, several more years and countless more romances would pass before the fictionalizing excesses of new journalism led to radical changes in the way news stories were seen fit to print.

Captive Cubans, International Impulses, and New Journalism

> You know, when I was not thinking how much I myself owed to
> the American people, I seemed to see through all the cheering and
> the music and the brilliant lights, the real, the grand future of Cuba.
> —Evangelina Cisneros, *The Story of Evangelina Cisneros*

One of the essential developments of 1890s American culture involved a
fundamental shift in the country's paradigmatic foreign policy. During
her travels around the world in 1889 and 1890, Nellie Bly had noticed that
people of other nations lacked an understanding of America's vast scale.
One ship's captain, she noted, observed how many foreigners believed
"the United States is one little island, with a few houses on it." The captain continued: "Once there was delivered at my house . . . in Hoboken,
a letter from Germany, addressed to, 'CAPTAIN ALBERS, FIRST HOUSE IN
AMERICA.'"[1] Bly might not have made these observations seven or eight
years later. Having opened the decade fixed on a policy of isolation, by
1898 the nation had transformed itself into an international powerhouse
and a colonialist presence as politicians moved the nation closer to the
affairs of other countries.

The growing crisis in Cuba in the late 1890s became the linchpin for
that shift, and although the news stories of Bly and even Lizzie Borden
demonstrate to some degree concerns about "foreign-ness" and international affairs,[2] the case of Evangelina Cisneros represents most clearly

how America's leaders and readers redefined the nation in terms of its new, international role. In addition to its romantic conventions, the *Journal's* narrative about Cisneros used the vocabulary of yet another literary genre to tell the story in a cross-cultural discourse, one nicely parallel to medievalist romances of the 1890s—the captivity narrative. Even a brief examination of how captivity functioned as a motif in the *Journal's* Cisneros story provides insight into how Americans viewed other nations as potential new frontiers once American isolationism and continental expansionism both ended at the close of the nineteenth century.

From the seventeenth through nineteenth centuries and beyond, captivity narratives served as staples in the American literary diet. First formulated to convey colonialist ideology and theological instruction in the late seventeenth century, the narratives took the forms of anti-Indian, anti-Catholic, and anti-French propaganda in the middle eighteenth and early nineteenth centuries. It was at this time also that the narratives grew "literary" as writers injected romance, "melodrama, and sensibility" into the tales, rendering them ever more fictional.[3] Increasingly, the narratives' "chief concern" became "neither accuracy of sensation nor fidelity to the hard facts of frontier life but rather the salability" of a "hybrid" mode of writing rife with "formulaic expectations and proscriptions."[4]

The result of such commercialization was an "almost inevitable step from narrative excesses for the purposes of propaganda to excesses in the interest of sensation and titillation, from promoting hatred to eliciting horror, from inspiring patriotism to encouraging sales, from chauvinism to commercialism."[5] Some literary historians point to Ann Eliza Bleeker's *History of Maria Kittle* (1797) as the first clearly fictionalized captivity narrative, and many other best-selling novels—notably *The Quaker City* (1843) and *The Awful Exposures of Maria Monk* (1836)—joined *Maria Kittle* in manipulating and fictionalizing captivity as a major plot vehicle, though they still maintained claims to actuality. In the 1860s, Erastus Beadle began to sell a series of formulaic dime westerns that would extend the fictionalization of the genre, the first of which was Edward Sylvester Ellis's *Seth Jones; or, The Captives of the Frontier* (1860).

By the 1890s, the formula of captivity and redemption appeared frequently within the historical romances that had become so popular, the very genre in which the Evangelina Cisneros romance was framed.[6] Two of the most popular novels of the decade, for instance, revolve around captivity motifs. Anthony Hope's *The Prisoner of Zenda* (1894) narrates the tale of Englishman Rudolph Rassendyll, who travels to the fictional king-dom of Ruritania, land of his ancestors, on a pleasure tour. Arriving in time for the coronation of his kinsman as the new king, Rassendyll dis-covers with surprise that he is the spit and image of the crown prince. When the prince is unable to attend his own coronation—having been drugged by his evil brother, Black Michael—Rassendyll steps into his cousin's place, receives the crown, and spends the rest of the novel plot-ting the rescue of the rightful regent from behind Black Michael's dun-geon wall. Similarly, Charles Major's *When Knighthood Was in Flower* (1898) portrays Mary Tudor as the captive of her older brother Henry VIII, who has locked her in his castle to prevent her elopement with a gallant but common-born knight.

The journalistic story of Evangelina Cisneros is, in light of these nar-ratives, interesting in terms of genre, but the tale of the captive Cuban also reveals more general attitudes about territorial captivity in the late nineteenth century. The recent Indian wars in the western United States had fulfilled a variety of literal and figurative expansionist needs and also produced an array of captivity narratives. The battle of the Little Big Horn in 1876, the Colorado Ute War in 1879–80, and the surrender of Chief Geronimo in 1886 had inspired literatures of captivity and rescue. However, the romance of the western frontier associated with the wars and their attendant narratives was already becoming a thing of the past by the end of the century. The assassination of Chief Sitting Bull (1881) and the massacre of Native Americans at Wounded Knee, South Dakota (1891), marked the effective end of the Indian wars and the possible end of a literary tradition.

Similarly, the 1890 census officially declared the frontier closed, and three years later Frederick Jackson Turner reflected on the psychological and national import of that declaration in his famous Frontier Thesis. Ameri-cans longed for new territories to conquer, either psychologically or physi-cally, new spaces in which to take captives and to be taken captive by a native other. The territorial bounty of the Spanish-American War—Puerto Rico, the Philippines, Hawaii,[7] Cuba—was converted into this frontier, spawning the Cisneros narrative, just as the frontier of the North Ameri-can continent had spawned Indian captivity narratives in earlier eras.

Medievalist romances of the late nineteenth century, like the Cisneros narrative, merged with "the quest for authentic experience" and "acceler-ated the spread of militarism" and of American-style imperialism, a point made evident as Hearst and other influential Americans increasingly advocated armed intervention in Cuba.[8] Moreover, because the iconography of medieval knighthood symbolized virtuous martial action in the American imagination, it provided "a tough-minded rationale for force in foreign relations." Many medievalist texts, including the *Journal*'s, constructed this subtext to encourage an active, forceful response to foreign problems.[9] Frank Norris's 1902 essay "The Frontier Gone at Last" provides but one illustration of how writers and critics merged a medieval mindset with modern military action. Americans should turn to the Middle Ages, Norris suggested, to envision the nation's potential. Just as his Anglo-Saxon forebears had sought their own frontier, "peeking and prying at the Western horizon, trying to reach it, to run it down," so modern Americans—being as martial and regal as the Anglo-Saxons—should "peek and pry" westward.[10] The Spanish-American War had opened not only Cuba and a new kind of "Westering" (as John Steinbeck put it three decades later) but the Far East as well, "pushing the Frontier before it."[11] The *Journal*'s own captivity narrative, then, was cogent reminder of what many other medievalist romances of the 1890s also suggested—that America's most familiar frontiers may have closed, but new territories lay in wait to rescue from darker forces.

In order to fit "foreign" figures like Evangelina Cisneros into the familiar framework of the frontier tradition, *Journal* editors adopted her within a certain class of American womanhood long before she took her actual oath of citizenship in October 1897. In the August 1897 articles, for instance, Cisneros appeared as a light-skinned lady with the most delicate of features. One reporter described Cisneros as "young, beautiful, and cultured," not some "Amazon to take the chances of war like a soldier; she is little more than a child in years, delicate and educated."[12] Another passage studied Cisneros's aristocratic genealogy, noting that she was "born to wealth, . . . nurtured and reared as carefully as the daintiest maid on Fifth Avenue. She had maids to braid her dark hair, a coachman to drive her carriage. She was a beauty, an heiress." Indeed, "her uncle was a marquis, her mother a handsome aristocrat."[13]

The presentation of Cisneros in such genteel terms familiarized her for mainstream American audiences, diverting attention away from her nationality and Catholic religion and, instead, toward her compatibility with white, Anglo-Saxon, Protestant Americans. The conversion of Cisneros from an overtly "ethnic" and colonized heroine into a romantic captive stepping straight from a formula book served as ironic proof to readers that Cuba and its citizens (at least those of the "better" classes) were already practically American and therefore ready for the taking—or redeeming back into the nation (a point reinforced when Cisneros was granted immediate U.S. citizenship). Michelle Burnham points out that as captivity narratives evolved, they forged an emotional connection between the (rescued) captive, who relates her story, and the audience, which consumes the narrative. We see this connection in the Cisneros captivity as it portrayed Cisneros as the "daintiest maid on Fifth Avenue" and as it toyed with the idea of territorial annexation, for the narrative "constructed and reinforced a binary division between captive and captor that is based on cultural, national, or racial difference."[14] In the vacuum created by this cultural and national difference, the portrait of Cisneros as an Anglicized captive merged the national category of "Cuban" with that of "American." The *Journal* justified America's "rescue" of Cisneros; by extension, Cisneros represented Cuba itself, an island waiting for America's "rescue" as well.[15]

This attitude of international rescue leaves perhaps the most disturbing legacy of the Cisneros affair. With bold strokes the *Journal* turned a complicated problem about foreign affairs into a formulaic narrative, one with a history that provoked predictable responses in American readers. The *Journal*'s story, with its prescription of captivity and redemption, animated the image of the "poor and defenseless foreigner," an image that would guide the nation's course for international affairs—with frequently devastating results—throughout the next hundred years.

CHAPTER FIVE

From There to Here

Cooke, Conventions, Conclusions

> The time has come to redraw the line between journalism and fiction. . . . The writer of fiction must invent. The journalist must not invent.
>
> —John Hersey, "The Legend on the License"

Creating Jimmy's World

On a Sunday morning in September 1980, readers of the *Washington Post* were riveted by "Jimmy's World," the tragic, searing tale of an eight-year-old "third-generation heroin addict" whose "sandy hair" and "velvety brown eyes" juxtaposed eerily with the "needle marks freckling the baby-smooth skin of his thin brown arms."[1] "Jimmy," the story indicated, was the pseudonym of a real boy living in Washington, D.C. Every day, amid the "human collage" of people drifting into Jimmy's house, someone—usually his mother's live-in boyfriend—"plung[ed] a needle" into the boy's "bony arm, sending the fourth grader into a hypnotic nod," all with his mother's silent consent. The story brought to life the motif of the young innocent struggling within a "world of hard drugs, fast money and the good life" that he believed "both can bring."

"Jimmy's World" illustrated in graphic detail the statistics Washingtonians had already heard over and again: that "heroin has become a part of life, . . . affecting thousands of teen-agers and adults who feel cut off from the world around them, and filtering down to untold numbers of children . . . who are bored with school and battered by life." Regular readers were already well aware of heroin's horrors, but this story went far beyond the familiar. It showed, unequivocally, that heroin was no longer a problem for older adolescents and adults alone; it was destroying the lives of young children. Extensive quotations in Jimmy's own words animated overworn facts about the rising number of drug addicts in the city, his voice providing sadly literal commentary on the loss of innocence.

Most tragic and shocking of all, however, was the story's conclusion. At "the end of the evening of strange questions" posed by the visiting reporter, "Jimmy slowly changes into a different child. . . . He is twisting uncomfortably in his chair one minute, irritatingly raising and lowering a vinyl window blind the next." The mother's boyfriend instructs the child to "be cool" while his heroin cooks, and then, in a move that left stunned newspaper readers gasping, the boyfriend

> grabs Jimmy's left arm just above the elbow, his massive hand tightly encircling the child's small limb. The needle slides into the boy's soft skin like a straw pushed into the center of a freshly baked cake. Liquid ebbs out of the syringe, replaced by bright red blood. The blood is then reinjected into the child.
>
> Jimmy has closed his eyes during the whole procedure, but now he opens them, looking around the room. He climbs into a rocking chair and sits, his head dipping and snapping upright again, in what addicts call "the nod."

The awful depiction of a child thus abused launched the nation's capital into something of a panic. In a modern rendition of the public outcry inspired by the Evangelina Cisneros story, Jimmy's tale "struck at Washington's Heart." Readers bombarded the *Post* with their outrage, lit up the paper's switchboard "like a space launch control room," and inundated the mailroom with letters to the editor and offers to help. When the *Post* refused to disclose the child's real name (the article, readers were told, had been written under promises of confidentiality), the city threatened to subpoena the reporter's notes. The chief of police opened a "mammoth citywide search" for the boy, and Mayor Marion Barry demanded that the city enlist "all schools, social services, and police contacts" to rescue Jimmy from his hellish captivity.[2]

As the boy's story spread nationally and abroad, pressure to locate Jimmy grew. Soon Mayor Barry assured the excited public that he and his administrators had located Jimmy but that "the boy and his mother [had] 'gone into hiding' to avoid being taken into custody." He had gathered this information, he said, from a Howard University psychiatrist who had "known the family for some time."[3] Retracting his threat to subpoena the *Post,* Barry announced, "I don't need the *Washington Post* to tell me where he is. . . . [W]e already know."[4] Indeed, the mayor's spokesman asserted (much to the police department's surprise), "city officials had actually visited a house in which they believed the family lived."[5]

To his embarrassment, Barry's spokesman was forced to recant his confident assertions the next day, admitting that any disclosures about Jimmy's whereabouts were "premature."[6] For seventeen days the police searched unsuccessfully for the hapless boy. Finally, Barry called off the search, limply explaining that "the boy's life would be endangered if the heroin dealers and users who frequented his home thought the boy might talk to authorities."[7] Other *Post* reporters, intending to interview more child addicts for follow-up stories, were equally unsuccessful in locating either Jimmy or similarly afflicted youngsters. For that matter, even the author of "Jimmy's World," pressured by some of her coworkers to show them Jimmy's house, could not locate the subject of her story again.

But none of that particularly mattered at the time. "Jimmy's World" was the result of months of labor by twenty-six-year-old reporter Janet Cooke. Employed by the *Post* for only nine months, Cooke had impressed editors with her ability to craft moving stories in graceful prose, whatever the subject matter. One of her early pieces, for instance, described a seemingly peaceful neighborhood in which three elderly people had been bludgeoned to death and suggested that "the setting could have been the work of Currier and Ives. The shower of sunlight. The crisp chill in the air. . . . But fear hung like misplaced tinsel over Oakwood Street."[8] Another story envisioned a civil rights meeting "in a hot, packed basement of a Baptist church" in regenerative terms as it "push[ed] its way into the early spring atmosphere as defiantly as the first crocuses that poked through the hardened soil outside."[9] With such lyrical style at her disposal, Cooke seemed destined for success at the newspaper. She had the ability to lend an air of poetry to her news stories, and she likewise seemed to bring an impressive young confidence to the *Post* offices. Indeed, as the paper's ombudsman later observed, "when she walked, she pranced. When she smiled, she dazzled."[10]

With the completion of "Jimmy's World," Cooke had presented her editors and readers alike with her professional calling card, a tragic masterpiece rendered in lyric prose. The product of two hours of taped interviews and 145 pages of handwritten notes, the story had taken center stage in Cooke's life during its creation. She had devoted her life to it; she confided to her editors that she had even received death threats from the boyfriend of Jimmy's mother. The payoff, however, was precisely what the ambitious young reporter desired, for Jimmy's story launched Cooke from her entry-level reporting job on the "ghettoized" "District Weekly" section of the newspaper into a more coveted spot on the "Metro."

It seemed most fitting, after the initial furor surrounding "Jimmy's World" subsided, that Cooke's work should be rewarded. So it was no surprise when, in April 1981, editors and employees of the *Washington Post* learned that Janet Cooke had received the Pulitzer Prize in feature writing for her captivating story.

That development brought Cooke's meteoric rise among the ranks of modern journalists down in a sensational and fiery crash. When the prizes were announced, the Associated Press released a biographical sketch of Cooke based on information she had included on a standard *Post* personnel form. Cooke's former employers at the *Toledo Blade,* however, realized that the AP's information about her educational background contradicted facts she had provided the *Blade* years earlier. A call from Toledo to New York opened floodgates that would wash away the foundation of "Jimmy's World," carrying Janet Cooke and her Pulitzer Prize along in the sludgy tide. The Pulitzer committee's biography, it was soon discovered, not only contradicted the *Toledo Blade*'s information but also the résumé Cooke had submitted to the *Post* when she applied for her job there in 1979. Cooke had embroidered at least two layers of false credentials atop the résumé she had used at the *Blade,* a résumé that was itself loaded with misrepresentation.

Alarmed, and fueled by doubts some of Cooke's colleagues had harbored since "Jimmy's World" appeared months earlier, editors at the *Post* converged on the young reporter, eventually forcing her to admit she had fabricated extensive portions of her résumé. Fearing the worst, executive editor Ben Bradley told Cooke she had twenty-four hours to prove the factual basis of her prizewinning story. As managing editors pored over Cooke's voluminous notes, unsuccessfully seeking any "indication that she had actually interviewed a child using heroin," Cooke went out with a city editor to "find" Jimmy.[11] As in October when another reporter had asked her to identify Jimmy's house, Cooke, however, seemed entirely unfamiliar with the young boy's supposed neighborhood. Indeed, as the accompanying reporter noted later, "It didn't take long to see that she didn't know the area. It's one of the toughest sections in town. I know it well. She said she didn't see the house. I asked her if it was to the right of us, the left of us, or had we passed it. She didn't know."[12] Several more hours of intense interrogation followed until finally, late at night, Cooke confessed that, like her résumé, Jimmy was "a fabrication." "I did so much work on it," she sobbed to her interrogators, "but it's a composite."[13] Without further delay, Cooke resigned and returned her Pulitzer Prize, leaving the *Post* to struggle with the aftermath of her fabulous story.[14]

Professional reaction to Cooke and her "composite" was swift and definitive. Commentators and fellow reporters expressed shock and dismay that a journalist would dare invent such a story, that she would presume to pass off a "fiction" as fact. Countless articles referred to Cooke as a "liar," a "fake," a "fraud." Others referred to her work as a "hoax," implying that Cooke's chicanery had been callous and intentional.[15] Journalism great James Michener proclaimed "one of the saddest weeks in the history of American journalism" and charged that Cooke, ignoring all the "great traditions" of the nation's press, had "knocked down the central pillar of her profession—integrity."[16]

Several editors blamed Cooke's sin on another scandalous "new journalism," that of the 1960s and 1970s, which championed composite characters, invented dialogue, and the "innermost thoughts of subjects in a combination that can blur the line between fact and fiction."[17] Like their nineteenth-century predecessors, "new" journalists of the twentieth century wrote stories that could be either imaginative or actual without indicating "where one ends and the other begins . . . in the belief that such a free-wheeling approach allows the writer to arrive at the larger truth of his story, the truth beyond the truth."[18] Deeply alarmed by this "free-wheeling," traditional journalists had attacked Truman Capote, Joan Didion, Tom Wolfe, Norman Mailer, and others for upsetting the commonly accepted boundaries between fiction and nonfiction in such works as *In Cold Blood* (1965), *The Right Stuff* (1979), and *The Executioner's Song* (1979).[19] These writers "called attention to their own voices" with bravado and "self-consciously returned character, motivation, and voice" to reportage.[20] Mainstream editors and reporters charged that "new" journalists played fast and loose with the facts, and critics attributed the upsetting phenomenon to the era's general social confusion and artistic experimentation. This "amalgam of impressions, personal feelings, social biases and imaginative and manipulative uses of fictional techniques," most journalists agreed, did not belong in any self-respecting newspaper.[21]

Sadly, while professional reporters and critics spotlighted the unforgivable sin of genre-crossing in the newspaper, the nation turned its attention away from the terrible truth Cooke had attempted—however problematically—to illuminate: that young children were being sucked into the deathtrap of drug abuse. Numerous other articles by various *Washington Post* reporters had already made the same basic claim about childhood heroin use.[22] Cooke's article had tried to animate the issue by use of a "composite character" (or so Cooke herself later claimed), but once the Pulitzer scandal broke, follow-up articles failed to remind readers of the central problem it had addressed.[23] Much more attention was paid to Cooke and her professional crime. Cooke's breach of standards seemed a convenient escape valve for people who were, perhaps, reluctant to face the reality that young children could be—and doubtless were—addicted to drugs. Readers and critics could focus their energies instead on the more comfortable topic of journalistic ethics. Once Cooke admitted to one "fiction," protestors easily discounted the entirety of her message. If Cooke had lied about an actual little boy named Jimmy, then she probably also lied about the very issue of childhood drug abuse. Despite the inclusion, then, of solid statistics and verified sources in "Jimmy's World," and despite Cooke's later insistence that Jimmy was in fact a composite character (a claim supported in part by the attempts of one drug counselor to put Cooke in touch with a very young addict), readers and critics easily dismissed the larger truth Cooke may have been attempting to illustrate.[24]

How could it be, only a few decades after Joseph Pulitzer, Charles Dana, and William Randolph Hearst flourished with their various forms of the first "new journalism," that an American reporter could find herself pilloried and stripped of her profession's greatest honor (one endowed, most ironically, by one of the authors of the original new journalism)?[25] How did the use of composite characters—or for that matter, wholly fictionalized characters—to illustrate a point or tell a story evolve from a mainstream journalistic standard to a device of tricksters, liars, and frauds? How did the dance between journalism and literature get from there to here?

Perhaps more than anything, the Cooke fiasco was the inevitable result of two genres that grew increasingly divergent in the early twentieth century. Both journalism and imaginative writing became more strictly defined under the force of professional conventions and new ideas about fictional artistry. During the first decades of the twentieth century, journalists identified themselves as social scientists, concentrated more wholly on the undeniable facts of a story, and trained their students to write about those facts in a spare fashion. Simultaneously, imaginative writers distinguished their art as an "autonomous object," independent of "the external world"; they concentrated on the "deeper" story of humanity and created poetry that was itself, ironically, "informational" in nature.[26] Literary production and newspaper narratives were still tied together in the aftermath of nineteenth-century new journalism, but the stories journalists and fiction writers told about themselves and their respective crafts eventually came to signify difference, not commonality. It was a paradigm of difference that made the conditions of Janet Cooke's untimely demise possible, if not probable.

The remainder of this chapter attempts to explain how news narrative got "from there to here," surveys the criticism lobbed against new journalism, and outlines the efforts of such conservative papers as the *New York Times* to standardize an informational style of writing. It then examines a parallel metamorphosis in American literature by considering conservative critics' ultimate discomfort with new journalism and arguing that such criticism bolstered the emergence of a modernist aesthetic that proclaimed a spare, imagistic poetry—rather than journalism or pseudo-journalism—as the "real thing."[27] Together, these shifts in journalistic and literary practice provide a closing frame for explaining the shift in journalistic standards and for explaining as well the public and professional outcry against Janet Cooke.

Institutionalizing the Facts: Press Criticism and the Demise of New Journalism

In large degree responding to new journalism's excesses during the Spanish-American War of 1898 (Hearst, for example, was not shy about claiming responsibility for the war, proudly asking in his masthead, "How do you like the *Journal*'s war?"), critics of the popular press grew more vocal after the 1890s and pressed for stabilizing influences and professional standards on Newspaper Row. Outspoken critic E. L. Godkin, editor of the conservative *Nation* (a weekly publication of the *New York Post*), referred to new journalism as "juvenile intelligence for boys and girls."[28] W. I. Thomas agreed, sneering that new journalism catered to the "essentially childish," "popular mind."[29] Another critic lamented that with their great "tide of filth," newspapers had become little more than "the common sewer for public and private immorality," a place to revel in the "sins, the crimes, the misfortunes, and the weaknesses of our poor humanity."[30]

Critics were outraged by new journalism's tendency to fictionalize and invent, practices they considered morally and epistemologically dangerous. Newspapers functioned as a form of public record. If the facticity of these public documents was only a veil, how could one finally determine what was real? Where did the authoritative line between invention and reality lie? Furthermore, if news supplanted fiction, how could society justify the prestige it had bestowed upon imaginative writing? Recognizing the close relationship between new journalism and literary realism, some conservative critics also called realistic fiction "dangerous," because "it disguised that it was fiction when it passed off the events it portrayed as facts."[31] How much more dangerous, then, when the news disguised its fictionality under the pretext of factuality and thereby further confused distinctions? Too many newspaper stories read, after all, like *stories,* and many critics of journalism felt such stories crowded out "significant news" in favor of light entertainment and literal storytelling.[32] Increasingly, conservative newspaper editors and social commentators decried the aesthetic impulses of new journalism, which led not only to highly amusing stories but also—more egregiously—to outright falsification. To manufacture news in any degree, wrote one critic, was unforgivable, for

> the "faking" of news can never be harmless. Even though the fictitious touches in an apparently innocent human interest or "feature" story may be recognized by most readers, yet the effect is harmful. . . . [D]eliberate falsification of news for any purpose, good or bad, must be regarded as an indefensible violation of the fundamental purpose of the press to serve as a wholesome, upbuilding influence.[33]

In the spirit of "the artist and caricaturist," agreed another critic, new journalism "perverts facts and manufactures stories purporting to be true."[34] This manufacturing was inherently disruptive, for "when masses of fiction are systematically presented to us as truth, our view of the world must be frightfully out of focus."[35]

The condemnation of new journalism's aesthetic had undertones of class-based attack. Some critics, often the same ones who criticized the democratic gestures of realism in literature, openly assailed the equalizing tendencies of new journalism, fearing that it would "drive out the ideas and serious discussion" seemingly inherent in more elite papers and fiction, and fretting that "these new papers" provided a vulgar immigrant audience with "frightening political power."[36] "This," Charles Dudley Warner sniffed, "is the penalty of cultivating the ability to read in advance of the taste to discriminate."[37] America was now home to a huge population of readers that "though lettered, is childish," and to this group of readers new journalism gave "endless stories, both real and make-believe."[38] Americans—especially immigrant, working-class, and impoverished citizens—needed to learn to be "moral enough, clean enough, intelligent enough or refined enough to prefer a real 'news' paper and a decent paper to the 'fake' paper and the unclean."[39] Fueled by such anxieties and prejudices, critics set out to ensure that "serious" papers—those which in theory never sacrificed information for sheer drama—became the industry standard for mainstream twentieth-century journalism.[40]

For most critics, the antidote to the unwholesome, disruptive, and artificial influence of new journalism was an educational curriculum that imposed desirable professional standards on young reporters and upheld a rigid line between literature (or "invention") and journalism (or "fact"). They designated the college classroom as the site for that curriculum; it was here, in the shift toward college-based professionalism, that mainstream newspaper standards and practices changed once more, this time from an "entertainment model" to an "information model" of news delivery. Critics had complained about lax journalistic standards for decades, but those complaints did not change actual policy and practice until reporters began to attend college as a first step in their career paths.[41]

The first university-level courses in journalism were developed in the 1870s, and by the early years of the twentieth century increasing numbers of urban editors considered an undergraduate degree necessary for entrance into and advancement within the profession.[42] When professors in the early twentieth century indoctrinated aspiring reporters in "proper" conduct, they taught them to craft stories free of fictional elements. A rising generation of journalists learned to collect news as scientifically as possible; to privilege hard news (i.e., news about government and economics) over soft news (i.e., sensational and human-interest stories); and to seek public uplift and intellectual merit in their writing.[43] Specifically, as the first dean of the University of Missouri's School of Journalism declared in 1910, reporters were to abolish "fakes, falsehoods, scandal mongering, acting as private detective, and coloring of the news to give a false interpretation."[44] The authors of a 1912 journalism textbook explained that university training "outlines a code of journalistic ethics that leaves out of consideration the questionable practices of the charlatan reporter and refuses to indorse [*sic*] the sensational methods of the 'yellow press.'"[45] Teachers of journalism, the textbook continued, should "indicate in the student's mind, unceasingly and uncompromisingly, the principle that the reporter's business is to get the facts" and warn that if a student "undertakes to 'fake' a story, the offense entails summary dismissal from the class and loss of credit."[46] Almost universally, students of the new professional schools of journalism in America learned to follow an information model of news reporting and to eschew the vivid storytelling—and outright fabrication—that had made new journalism so successful in earlier decades.[47]

The most tangible outcome of professionalism was the acceptance of this informational reportage as the industry standard within the first two decades of the twentieth century, a move that effectively undermined the cultural status new journalism had previously enjoyed. New journalism's dramatic stories had been wildly successful during the final decade of the nineteenth century, but when, after the Spanish-American War, critics expressed outrage about how papers merged fact and fiction, more "objective" forms of reportage gained social footing, mainstream acceptance, and eventually solid profits.[48] As the first years of the twentieth century passed, Americans came to view "newspapers which stress[ed] information" as "more reliable than 'story' papers"—and they began to prize that reliability above the dramatic storytelling they had enjoyed in nineteenth-century papers.[49] These information-based papers, initially associated with educated and genteel readers, waged a "moral war" against what they saw as the grossest sins of new journalism: its tendency to manufacture the news as if it were a work of fiction, its focus on celebrity, its battles for ever-higher circulation figures, its blatant appeal to the working and immigrant classes, and its "debasing" of public taste.[50]

Beginning in the late 1890s, the *New York Times* emerged as the golden child of informational reportage. The *Times* marketed itself as the premier example of respectable news delivery, quickly establishing a standard by which other newspapers were judged. After Adolph Ochs purchased the struggling paper in 1896, wealthy readers—and those who aspired to wealth—took up the daily, attracted by its "conservatism, decency, and accuracy."[51] The *Times* did not waste space on inspired revisions of travel adventures, carefully detailed constructions of murder trials, or breathtaking yarns of damsels in distress. Rather, as Ochs asserted in his statement of editorial mission:

> It will be my earnest aim that the *New York Times* give the news, all the news, in concise and attractive form, in language that is parliamentary in good society, and give it as early, if not earlier, than it can be learned through any other reliable medium; . . . to make the columns of the *New York Times* a forum for the consideration of all questions of public importance, and to that end to promote intelligent discussion from all shades of opinion.[52]

The *Times* thus separated itself from "low class writing," declared it would offer only "the news that's fit to print," and promised it would "not soil the breakfast cloth" in the process. Not incidentally, the information "fit to print" was most often suitable for business interests and conservative politics. Ochs reported extensively on real-estate transactions, financial markets, and federal and state government. Even the Sunday pages were devoted to "serious" news rather than entertainment. Conspicuously absent from the paper were the stunts, sins, and sensations that had made Pulitzer, Dana, and Hearst—and their reporters—famous. Overall, the *Times* presented articles "for the rational person or the person whose life was orderly," articles "as useful knowledge, not as revelation," and certainly not as story.[53] The most basic subject matter of *Times* articles, in other words, dictated a style that crowded out the colorful aesthetic of new journalism.

An obvious challenge facing the *Times,* however, was that the "rational" and "orderly" audience was not as sizable as the audiences that purchased the *World,* the *Sun,* and the *Journal.* To remedy this problem, Ochs employed some rather savvy marketing strategies to increase circulation and

compete more evenly with established newspapers—soliciting for subscribers and advertisers by telephone, for instance; bombarding "better"
neighborhoods with pamphlets praising the *Times;* and lowering the price
of the newspaper from three cents to one. The results were impressive.
The *Times*'s circulation jumped from nine thousand in 1896 to twenty-
five thousand in 1898, to seventy-five thousand a year later, to 121,000 in
1905, and so on.[54] Rising circulation rates seemed to support Ochs's theory
that people would purchase "a clean newspaper of high and honorable
aims," provided they could afford it.[55]

Eventually, some of the new journalists themselves followed the *Times*'s
more conservative lead, a move that doubtless sped the mainstreaming of
information-model journalism. Charles Dana, increasingly cranky in his
old age, had allied himself with critics of new journalism before his death
in 1897. While Hearst essentially gloried in the criticism, Pulitzer attempted "to walk a line between the sensational and the vulgar" after the
Spanish-American War, "piously" asking "his editors to go after a better
class of readers."[56] "There will be no faking," he ordered his reporters.
"Tone down the worst of divorce, murder, salacious stories. Keep the
tone higher on the first page showcase."[57] Pulitzer's newly found conservatism is evident in his decision to support the professionalization of
journalism and the standardization of news writing through his endowment of Columbia University's School of Journalism. A *World* representative, explaining the purpose of the endowment, pointed out that "newspaper men, who are in many directions the informers and teachers of the
people"—not to mention the shapers of public opinion—"have hitherto
received no special preparation for their delicate and important duties."[58]
The Pulitzer of old may not have found much wrong in that lack of
preparation, provided his writers supplied plenty of color and drama. The
rationale behind the endowment, however, points toward the significant
shifts in journalistic aesthetics that were already underway in the first
decade of the twentieth century and that had already changed the way
Pulitzer practiced his craft.

Yet another development—this one technological—may have supported
the rise of information-model newspapers after the turn of the century.
Even as newspapers shied away from rewriting and improving upon fictional genres, they embraced a new "genre" of news narrative—photojournalism, which functioned in some degree as a substitute for the more
illustrative prose of new journalism. Before photographs were used regu-

larly in newspapers, illustrations appeared as steel engravings or woodcuts based on photographs (or entirely on the artist's imagination).[59] Technology's limitations meant that during the nineteenth century photography was practiced, for the most part, in the studio and was printed only in magazines and weeklies. The invention of handheld cameras and roll film at the end of the century "revolutionized photography," freeing photographers from their studios and sending them into the city streets to record newsworthy events more regularly.[60] For the first time, cameras were malleable enough to be shaped like briefcases or bags, allowing photographers to "make images surreptitiously" and to "illustrate a broader range of news stories" in a more "natural" way.[61] By the first decades of the twentieth century, this portability, along with the development of half-tone printing after the 1880s, allowed editors to rely on actual photographs rather than hand-drawn illustrations. Without question, the added layer of authenticity had great appeal for a public dedicated to "the real thing." Predictably enchanted by technological developments in illustration, readers expressed unquestioning belief in the "infallibility and objectivity" of news delivered photographically.[62]

Photojournalism might have been, then, one of many contributing factors in normalizing information-model journalism. New journalists had painted dramatic scenes with the familiar tools of the novelist: characterization, description, allusion, setting, suspense, and so on. Photojournalism undercut the need for such "verbal photography," for once photographs were printed in newspapers easily and economically, readers were less likely to miss the florid prose that served an illustrative function in new journalism. Novelist Maurice Thompson had earlier suggested that only "photography is realism; everything else is romance"; in the newspaper world this new and improved realism brought "epochal" shifts in knowledge production and "fundamental changes in the way information was gathered and disseminated to the public."[63] The flexibility new journalists had enjoyed in "painting" a story verbally was gradually removed, for after 1900 the photograph became part of the text that told the real story, and (at least in theory) it could not be changed or manipulated the way words could. A pared-down, information-based writing style was fitting accompaniment to this new medium, and photography provided an entirely new way of narrating the news and granting it authority. All that was needed to secure that narration was the outline of fact: who, what, where, when, and why.

The Modernists: Verbal Efficiency and Photographic Poetics

While universities standardized a journalistic curriculum and defined a form of writing distinct from imaginative literature, and while information-model papers defined "the real" in terms of fact-based, non-illustrative prose, literary critics and authors operated on a parallel course to redefine the role of the imagination in a news-hungry society (although, as stated later, artists of the avant-garde ultimately echoed information-model reporting in their own quests for authenticity). Literary critics of the late nineteenth and early twentieth centuries were deeply concerned that the "written word" had become "a commodity, bought and sold like other articles of commerce," and they cast much of the blame for this state of events on the media.[64] Thanks in large part to the utter avalanche of words tripped by the explosion of the newspaper and magazine markets, most readers no longer considered writing the product of artistic genius and inspiration. It was, rather, a skill anyone could learn—a point reinforced by the plethora of "how to" writing manuals published at the turn of the century. Attention to skill over artistry meant that writers who hoped to support themselves by their genius "had to be constantly attuned to the demands of increasingly demanding publishers and a novel-crazed public, and not a smaller group of like-minded readers."[65] Some artists grew increasingly uncomfortable with the idea that a mass audience (the ethnic and social makeup of which was shifting suspiciously) drove the production of literature.

Most noticeably, Henry James and William Dean Howells complained loudly about market-driven writing and the role newspapers played in American reading circles. Both men had worked as newspaper reporters—albeit briefly and unhappily. Howells, the son of a small-town newspaper editor, had served all of one month in 1857 as a journalist in Cincinnati before fleeing to write poetry for the *Ohio State Journal* and composing a campaign biography for Abraham Lincoln, work that landed him a comfortable tenure at the American consulate in Venice during Lincoln's presidency. James's "career" in newspaper journalism lasted a bit longer—he survived a few months of 1875 as Paris correspondent to the *New York Tribune* before he was fired for refusing to submit more timely, less wordy prose.

Fueled by these embittering experiences, both men trained critical eyes on new journalism and struggled to define the essential difference between literary and journalistic realism. They acknowledged that realism, in general, was the democratic language of common people yet insisted that not all "realism" was "real." To Howells, "good art" was nothing less "than the reflection of life," yet good art also required an artful hand. True, newspapers were filled with reflections of life that seemed quite real. These reflections, however, demonstrated "facts far fouler and deadlier than any which fiction could imagine."[66] Clearly, a journalist's realism could not—or should not—be considered naturally "literary." A novelist must first purify foul facts and turn them into something beautiful, an artifice that finally signified something more "real" than what it described.

James, similarly, established clear boundaries between artful realism and the mass-produced realism of newspapers. The realistic novel was "a direct impression of life," he admitted, but that direct impression could not appear in the pages of a newspaper and still be artful.[67] Rather, the process of transfiguring reality into realism required skill greater than the common journalist could manage, for "to 'render' the simplest surface . . . is a very complicated business" best left to great minds: "The deepest quality of a work of art will always be the quality of the mind of the producer. In proportion as that intelligence is fine will the novel, the picture, the statue partake of the substance of beauty and truth."[68] Newspapers, quite in contrast to such beauty and truth, were

> bristling with rude effigies and images, with vociferous "headings," with letterings, with black eruptions of print . . . that affect us positively as the roar of some myriad-faced monster—as the grimaces, the shouts, shrieks and yells, ranging over the whole gamut of ugliness, irrelevance, dissonance, of a mighty manic who has broken loose and who is running amuck through the spheres alike of sense and sound.[69]

James's shrill attack picturing newspaper realism as a beast set loose to devour all that is good and beautiful reveals his ultimate sense of helplessness in the face of a hostile literary marketplace.[70] Noise, hysteria, chaos—James regarded such factors as characteristic of new journalism, and he associated them, by implication, with the monstrous, shouting, ugly, and ultimately irrelevant urban classes to whom new journalism appealed and who themselves upset the sense and sound of James's America. If cheap periodicals represented the "great common-schooled and newspapered democracy" of America, the future looked dim for the nation, for the "literate of the billion will not be literate as we have hitherto known it at its best."[71]

Howells's and James's carefully rendered constructions of realism belie some of the critics' central fears: that the "newspaper and the novel were becoming more alike," that "the roles of the novelist and the reporter were converging," and that important social distinctions between the two were eroding.[72] The authors' attacks against journalism were in essence "an attempt to defend literature's privileged status and the author's prestige in an era when both were threatened by mass-circulation journalism's commodification of writing."[73] What, after all, would distinguish the writer of realistic fiction from the journalist if literature lacked eminence? What would differentiate the artist, striving for the muse, from the reporter, merely churning out words for a steady paycheck? Here was the same problem Poe had faced some sixty years earlier when he struggled to define his own artistic aesthetic against the increasingly commercial aesthetic of the penny press world.[74] The situation seemed exponentially more grave to artists at the turn of the century, compelling cultural conservators to establish "a hierarchy of discourse, with the 'literary' firmly fixed about the 'newsy.'"[75] Reprising Poe's frequently contradictory remarks from the 1830s and 1840s, authors and literary critics of the late nineteenth and early twentieth centuries tried to elucidate their own poetic principles, insisting that a real writer would never descend to the level of common popularity unless absolutely compelled by reason of imminent starvation or by a desire to manipulate the mass mind with a stroke of intellectual genius.

For the next generation—the critics and artists in the first two decades of the twentieth century—the time had come to rescue fiction from "a public whose only literature was the family story paper or the cheap novel."[76] One powerful outcome of these literary rescue efforts surfaced in modernism. This "constellation of related ideas, beliefs, values, and modes of perception" was a reaction against Victorian sentimentality (as well as Howellsian and Jamesian domestic fiction), with "its ideal vision of a stable, peaceful society . . . presided over by a benevolent God and governed by immutable natural laws."[77] Developments in physics, mathematics, philosophy, psychology, and warfare undermined belief in a verifiable, tangible, objective reality governed by natural laws; an international modernist movement grew out of the resulting sense of fragmentation. For such artists as Ezra Pound, T. S. Eliot, and William Carlos Williams, the scenes depicted in romantic fiction, sentimentalized realism—and, for that matter, journalism itself—were not authentic, not finally real. Indeed, modernists argued, objective realism as it had been constructed by earlier writers was itself something of a myth. One could not attain truth simply through the mimetic representation Howells and other novelists championed. Modernists sought a different sense of the real. They endeavored "to know 'reality' in all its depth and complexity," striving, as Harriet Monroe wrote, "for a concrete and immediate realization of life" that was "less vague, less verbose, less eloquent" than the literatures of earlier eras.[78]

Expressing fears that technology and consumer culture had removed all authenticity and depth of experience from life, modernists sought to restore through poetry "not realism, but reality itself."[79] Writing could bridge the "gap between [the] world" and the word, but only if the artist would "cut loose the word from its strict reference" and "treat words as things in themselves, not merely representations of things."[80] Beholding this art—in essence an intense contemplation of "real things"—readers would face actuality in a fashion denied by everyday life. Williams, for instance, argued that his poetry produced not a copy but "a natural object" in and of itself.[81] Poetry stripped down to its essence, to its base reality—that was "the real thing," not some verbose, ultimately unsuccessful attempt to reproduce reality.

Modernists adopted a creed of verbal efficiency, an aesthetic that pointed toward a cultural environment in which both literary and journalistic austerity thrived. With apparent simplicity as a governing tenet, modernist literary manifestoes ultimately echoed the standards adopted by information-model journalists themselves. Ezra Pound, for instance, argued for "straight talk" and "direct treatment of the 'thing' whether subjective or objective," excising "absolutely" any "word that does not contribute to the presentation."[82] In what could almost be a recitation of emerging journalistic standards as defined in newsroom style sheets, Pound in his essays "A Retrospect" and "The Serious Artist" (both 1913) instructed other writers:

> Use no superfluous word, no adjective that does not reveal something.
> Use either no ornament or good ornament.
> Don't be descriptive. . . .
> . . . Good writing is writing that is perfectly controlled, the writer [speaks] with complete clarity and simplicity. He uses the smallest number of words.[83]

Similarly, William Carlos Williams embraced a model of efficiency re-
sembling the new standards of the newspaper world. His writing championed the "values of precision and speed"—a poet on deadline, as it
were.[84] The anthology *Some Imagist Poets* literally laid out the rules by
which Williams and other modernists operated, including directives to
"use the language of common speech, but to employ always the exact
word, not the nearly exact, nor the merely decorative word."[85] Journalistic style sheets and practice manuals (which were published en masse in
the first quarter of the twentieth century), by comparison, "prescribed
high standards of lean, simple, condensed writing" and instructed workers to "avoid the use of adjectives" and other "superfluous" words.[86] "The
facts should be set forth" simply, one manual admonished; "They will
speak for themselves."[87] Another style sheet warned against "trite phrases"
and counseled reporters to "use superlatives sparingly. . . . Find the one
noun to express the idea, the one adjective, if necessary, to qualify it, and
the one verb needed to give it life."[88] Yet another manual assured aspiring
journalists that "a short-breathed sentence is like the crack of a whip. It
arouses jaded intellects to attention."[89]

The parallel between poetic concision and information-model journalism seems all the more appropriate in light of Imagism, a poetic aesthetic built on the ethos of the "verbal image."[90] First championed by
Pound in 1912, Imagism called for poems that stood as "the record of the
'thing'" and operated almost as photographs, presenting "an intellectual
and emotional complex in an instant of time" and removing the need for
lengthy explanation.[91] Pound considered an imagistic poem "a VORTEX,
from which, and through which, and into which, ideas are constantly
rushing."[92] Imagistic poetry was to be more authentic than any previously written since, in Pound's own words, "an image . . . is real because
we know it directly."[93] Consider, for instance, Pound's verse:

"In a Station of the Metro"
The apparition of these faces in the crowd;
Petals on a wet, black bough. [1913][94]

Using spare and hard language, Pound and other Imagists provided snap-
shots of life, ripe with meaning and yet packed with detail. Like photojournalism itself, imagistic poems were meant to suggest almost instanta-
neous meaning, devoid of the commentary and description that had

characterized earlier poetry, as well as earlier journalism. Indeed, the "rules" set out in the anthology *Some Imagist Poets* directed writers to "present an image (hence the name 'Imagist'). We are not a school of painters, but we believe that poetry should render particulars exactly and not deal in vague generalities, however magnificent and sonorous."[95] For modernists and information journalists alike, the most powerful writing consisted only of a bare set of facts, comprising headline ("In a Station of the Metro"), photographic image ("The apparition of these faces"), and caption or explanation ("Petals on a wet, black bough"). If "bad art" was to Pound "inaccurate art . . . that makes false reports" (a word that surely resonates with journalistic narrative), "good art . . . bears true witness" and is "most precise."[96] Good art would simply offer "things as they really are," without editorial comment and without superfluous narration.[97]

The credo of the early modernists suggested a return to the very artistic values Poe had advocated in "The Poetic Principle" in his insistence on economic and frugal writing, which evoked "truth" by being "simple, precise, terse, . . . cool, calm, unimpassioned."[98] Similarly, in their commitment to pared-down writing, modernists and information journalists alike put into practice the ideas behind one of the most influential composition manuals of the twentieth century—William Strunk's *The Elements of Style* (1918), particularly that book's advocacy of the active, declarative, tight aesthetic and its valuation of economy, clarity, and plain diction. Despite these striking similarities, however, the modernists were loath to associate their writing with journalism, for they considered the latter a straight path to mass culture and thus to artistic death. Gertrude Stein admonished the aspiring young Ernest Hemingway to leave the newspaper world if he wished to become a real writer. "If you keep on doing newspaper work you will never see things," she warned; "you will only see words and that will not do, that is of course if you intend to be a writer."[99] Stein was pointing toward news writing as something utterly antithetical to real literature. In the class-based contexts of new journalism, however, we can read another layer of meaning within her remarks. Journalism that strove to dramatize life by re-presenting familiar literary genres and conventions—as the *World, Sun,* and *Journal* did—missed the mark of truly significant writing, for they were far too common, far too attuned to mass culture.

Despite its insistence on difference, however, the modernist aesthetic drew from the same source book as journalism, and once again in the early decades of the twentieth century, a critical dialogue was unfolding between "the literary" and "the journalistic." Even as they labored to divide literature of the masses—a grouping that included, of course, the newspaper—from literature of the elite (which was, after all, the only true literature, in the elite's calculation), the modernists appropriated the forms of an emerging style of journalism. Far from developing and functioning independently of popular narratives, modernism was "irrevocably linked to and penetrated by the dense, complex social formations of a burgeoning mass culture."[100] Though the very process of writing and marketing modernist art reinforced contemporary boundaries between literary and journalistic realms, their stories and aesthetics, even at this divisive time, were intertwined.

Janet Cooke, Revisited

That continued intertwining—and professional and critical attempts to disentangle the newspaper from imaginative writing and vice versa—is finally the story of how we got "from there to here." The anger that Janet Cooke provoked with "Jimmy's World" suggests that in the late twentieth century the mingled paths of literature and journalism were not—indeed, they still are not—well enough known to temper a reading of her actions with historical perspective. Critics, professional journalists, and general readers alike believed in 1981 that Cooke had crossed a universal and eternal formal boundary, not a genre line that in fact had been institutionally created and was relatively new. While she is scarcely alone in fictionalizing a piece of journalism,[101] Janet Cooke has become the ultimate symbol for an unforgivable breach in the journalistic code, for she dared to "invent" when, as journalism great John Hersey declared, "the time ha[d] come to redraw the line between journalism and fiction."[102] As a result, Cooke's name became "shorthand for journalistic villainy" and a "monstrous miscarriage of journalism," and her crime is to this day regarded as the most "spectacular public lie in the most notorious journalistic fraud of our time."[103]

What was overshadowed, however, in the immediate aftermath of the Cooke debacle was the question of why her work (at least part of which was factually verifiable) was "villainy," why her writing was ultimately a "lie." Readers understandably judged Cooke's fabrications within the paradigms of "proper journalism" available to them in the post-Watergate era, where journalism's role as a servant to verifiable fact had become more important than ever before. By those standards, any embroidery of documented information was unforgivable, no matter how elegantly the story pointed toward "softer truths." Such journalistic standards were evident behind the 1981 remarks of Haynes Johnson, a *Washington Post* commentator who recounted the story of the *New York Sun's* 1835 Moon Hoax in order to accentuate how "standards, practices and traditions [had] evolved over the decades" until "one cardinal principle" had been "engraved in the business"—the principle of "believability."[104] In the semiotics of late twentieth-century journalism, "believability" as a "cardinal principle" meant one thing—unadorned factuality. In the semiotics of late nineteenth-century new journalism, however, that term could also (and often did) mean something that only appeared true, something that looked believable, whether or not it was based in actual fact.

Read in the context of the early twenty-first century, Johnson's recounting of history suggests yet another shift in what journalism's "cardinal rules" might mean. New thinking in literary and cultural theory has challenged the premises of such terms as "truth," "falsity," and, for that matter, "believability." Perhaps, then, the time has come, some twenty-three years after Janet Cooke, to unravel—or perhaps, more appropriately, to re-ravel—the histories of journalism and literature and to explore how even the most factually sound news stories "are inherently 'fabrications' and 'constructions.'"[105] Perhaps the time has come to ask seriously some of the more fundamental questions introduced by the Cooke affair and similar scandals. Where, for instance, does the border between "fact" and "fiction" lie within particular social and economic contexts? Where has that border been placed throughout American literary and press history? What are the essential differences between literature and journalism—or are there essential differences? What does the process of narrating the news actually entail if we recognize—as we should—the "interrelationship of institutions"?[106]

As contemporary critical theory suggests, boundaries are never as impenetrable as they would seem. The labels "fact" and "fiction" are the result of genre construction, "the product of interpretive communities whose work is the making of the two categories and explaining how they interrelate."[107] Genre definition is itself the "result of social and symbolic processes that publicize, authorize, and legitimize the reality of a group. The history of journalism is, in part, that of establishing, repairing, and transforming the authoritative base for accounts of 'the way it is.'"[108] The same process of authorization and legitimization is evident as well in the history of literature. Such artists as Howells and James—and the modernists after them—sought to sanction a compositional hierarchy based on ideals of artistry and genius. To view these histories of legitimization as separate phenomena is to ignore the complexity of narrative as an elastic, social process.

Our understanding of American print culture generally—and our knowledge of literary value and journalistic standards—can only deepen through further investigation into the interrelated histories of journalism and literature. By reinforcing the idea that newspapers supply and have always supplied "information" exclusively, traditional literary criticism and American literary histories have essentially disregarded a vast and massively influential collection of writing—an omission with enormous ramifications for the way we view, read, and teach American literature and journalism alike. In 1905, as the battle over journalistic standards raged, commentator Lydia Kingsmill Commander insisted that all Americans— especially those of an educated, thoughtful sort—must pay attention to new journalism, if for no other reason than its enormous circulation. These papers, she observed, "cannot be ignored by anyone who would understand his age and his people."[109] Yet scholars have essentially ignored them and have attempted to write the tale of American literary history without considering the dramatic, imaginative stories that reached readers on a daily basis.

Modern Americans would ill serve themselves by continuing to ignore the historical ligature between literature and journalism, because contemporary news media seem to stand at the cusp of yet another shift in standards. As the turn of the twentieth century brought with it radical changes in journalistic practices, so the turn of the twenty-first century has brought its own changes. If in 1981 the *Washington Post* could still proclaim that the "cardinal principle" of newspapers was "believability," that principle is now under challenge, because the economics, technologies, and politics of publishing and news making have developed so dramatically in recent years. In an era that has seen print media—including, of course, both literature and journalism, widely defined—married to visual media and transformed into a beast of mega-conglomeration beyond the wildest dreams of Hearst and Pulitzer, the thorny issues of drama and information, fiction and fact continue to plague readers and critics.

The ramifications of this beast appeared again most spectacularly in April 2003, when *New York Times* reporter Jayson Blair resigned from that esteemed paper after admitting to at least thirty-eight acts of fabrication and plagiarism over a seven-month period. Some of Blair's most grievous breaches of conduct included plagiarizing a story about a mother whose son was killed in the 2003 Iraq war, inventing quotations from the father of another slain soldier, and fabricating a story of meeting the family of Jessica Lynch, a soldier rescued from captivity in Iraq in an episode that resonates provocatively with the Evangelina Cisneros story.[110] As they had in the Cooke case over twenty years earlier, the majority of critics turned attention and blame toward such scapegoats as Blair's ego and mental instability, the paper's editorial management, newsroom morale, hiring practices, ethical standards, the status of the *Times* as an institution, racial pressures, and so on.[111] The issue generally lost in the furor seems to have been, once more, a frank discussion about the nature of narration, the role fiction has played and continues to play in news making, and the conditions of a complex mass communications marketplace that makes particular journalistic standards possible.

As the *Times*'s executive editor took the fall for the Blair scandal, Boston University professor Renata Adler pointed to a central, yet unexplored, problem at the venerable "gray lady":"The *Times,* as an institution, believes what has been published in its pages."[112] The conviction that the *Times* is an inviolable paper of record, that its pages contain, by definition, nothing but unadulterated fact and unvarnished reality—a belief firmly in place since Adolph Ochs purchased the paper in 1896—is perhaps the ironic enabler of American journalism's latest big scandal. When a newspaper proclaims that it prints fact and fact alone, it removes from its audience the burden of critical perspective—a perspective that could serve as a check for anything other than accuracy and truth within the paper. If reporters and editors still proclaim that a story is by definition true because it has appeared in the *Times,* Ochs's model of "all the news that's fit to print" has turned against itself. Most readers of new journalism realized they might or might not be getting pure fact; they realized their news was being presented as a form of entertainment. That knowledge doubtless allowed some healthy skepticism to enter into their reading practice. In the *New York Times* model of today, skepticism has been deemed unnecessary by the institution's forceful reluctance, if not refusal, to admit that fabrication, widely defined, is more closely aligned with any reportage (its own included) than most journalists and editors would find comfortable. Jayson Blair may be an extreme example of how all news—even the most dully informational—is framed discursively and can be read, in our theoretical age, as a fabrication. What appeared to be premodern in the reading practices of nineteenth-century Americans may turn out, in fact, to be ironically postmodern.

If the histories of journalism and fiction tell us anything, it is that as the expectations of readers change, so do the definitions of genre and the standards for publishing in particular genres. A door that Cooke opened partially in 1981 seems to have been pushed farther open by Jayson Blair in 2003. While pundits fret about the arrogance of the *New York Times* and the racial bias behind the scandal, the incident seems to point more centrally toward the infusion of entertainment back into mainstream print journalism. Increasing numbers of American readers, not to mention television news viewers, seem to recognize the dramatic and imaginative aspects of contemporary American news making, a fact reinforced by a recent journalism handbook that asserts: "When it comes to accuracy, the 'right facts' means . . . coverage that 'rings true' to readers."[113] If these are indeed the implicit standards of modern American journalism, perhaps we are not so far away from the nineteenth century's new journalism after all, and maybe what Jayson Blair and Janet Cooke wrote will not seem so criminal in the end. A new era of journalistic standards has begun to emerge, one that places the narration of news within a web of corporate media and mediated interests, one that openly acknowledges the pressure on editors and reporters "to hype what is often little more than tendentious hearsay in order to present front-page scoops."[114]

Time alone, of course, will determine the outcome of Blair's own journalistic fabrications and answer the question of whether his name will replace Cooke's as the symbol of journalism's most grievous transgression. Time will also determine if American journalism is revealing a shift of industry and reader-based standards, with a more frankly postmodern recognition of the overlying motivation of entertainment imprinted on news organizations, of the increasingly profitable encroachment of fabrication onto fact, and of the theoretically arbitrary designators of "fact" and "fiction" themselves. My goal in making these observations here is not to offer an exhaustive reading of modern American media or the Jayson Blair incident. Rather, no matter the outcome of this contemporary narrative scandal, the history of journalism at one of its most extravagant hours can provide a much-needed historical context in which to place this twenty-first-century phenomenon, as journalism becomes increasingly infused with the narrative practices reminiscent of the late nineteenth century.[115] For new journalism, finally, was not about producing a chronicle of current events. Rather, in its revision of literary conventions, its competition for readers within an overloaded literary marketplace, and its self-conscious manipulation of factual and fictional boundaries, it pushed forward fundamental questions about the very process of narration on a public stage and for a mass audience—questions that seem particularly relevant in the early twenty-first century.

The media events presented in this book are but a sampling of the vast collection of stories in the newspapers that millions of Americans once read and reacted to. The tales of Nellie Bly, Lizzie Borden, and Evangelina Cisneros prove that far from being an entirely ephemeral entity, new journalism in the late nineteenth century stood as its own type of realism and operated under its own set of aesthetics, as it does today. It acted in overt contest with imaginative writing as editors and reporters rewrote such popular tales as the travel adventure, the murder mystery, and the medievalist romance. Countless other genres were similarly rewritten in the pages of late nineteenth-century newspapers. Opening academic doors to these pages will not only enrich our understanding of American writing, the literary marketplace, and the role of narrative at the turn of the century. It will invite us as well into a more informed exploration of how the standards and aesthetics behind fact and fiction continue to function in contemporary America as we narrate the news.

NOTES

Introduction

1. In 1883 Newspaper Row was home to these three newspapers, as well as the *Tribune, Herald, Times, Star, Mail and Express, Commercial Advertiser, Daily News, Evening Telegram, Press, Recorder,* and a number of foreign-language papers.

2. The building itself, a crumbling four-story at Nassau and Frankfurt Streets, had been owned by the Tammany Hall machine since 1811. See Turner, *When Giants Ruled*.

3. The importance of Newspaper Row diminished only after Adolph Ochs purchased the *New York Times* and moved the paper to 7th Avenue and Broadway in 1904—Times Square—thereby establishing a new hub of information and entertainment further north in the city.

4. Arnold, "Up to Easter," 638.

5. Ibid.

6. Schudson, *Discovering the News,* 89.

7. Ibid., 90.

8. Shuman, *Steps into Journalism,* 66.

9. Ibid., 122.

10. Ibid., 123.

11. Dicken-Garcia, *Journalistic Standards in Nineteenth-Century America,* 63.

12. Ibid., 89.

13. Shi, *Facing Facts,* 95; Schudson, *Discovering the News,* 13.

14. Shuman, *Practical Journalism,* 24.

15. Ibid., 7. A striking fictional example might be found in William Dean Howells's Silas Lapham, who dismisses the need for books, having found "about all the reading [he] want[s] in the newspapers" (*The Rise of Silas Lapham,* 89). Lapham plans to fill the library of his new mansion with books of the finest-quality bindings—books that will likely go unread in the face of Lapham's continued preference for the news.

16. Whitman, *Uncollected Poetry and Prose,* 115.

17. Qtd. in Reynolds, *Beneath the American Renaissance,* 4.

18. Howells, *Years of My Youth,* 122; qtd. in Strychacz, *Modernism, Mass Culture, and Professionalism,* 1.

19. De Forest, "The Great American Novel," 27.

20. Boyesen, "Why We Have Got No Great Novelists," 617.

21. Shuman, *Steps into Journalism*, 8.

22. See, for instance, Strychacz, *Modernism, Mass Culture, and Professionalism;* Robertson, *Stephen Crane, Journalism, and the Making of Modern American Literature;* Fishkin, *From Fact to Fiction;* and Frus, *The Politics and Poetics of Journalistic Narrative.* General histories of late nineteenth-century American literature almost exclusively take what I call the "journalism as apprenticeship" line, which argues that writers who were first journalists earned the privilege of "seeing the world" through their jobs, then went on to write about it artistically, leaving their newspaper careers behind. Louis J. Budd ("The American Background") calls newspaper writing "protorealism" and marks the importance of newspaper writing only in terms of the books that were reviewed there. "Journalism as apprenticeship" is also the standard in Fishkin's influential work. Robertson and Strychacz are, to date, notable in their efforts to break this model by presenting literary figures (e.g., Crane, Dreiser) within a cultural discourse of fact and fiction. Yet, beyond the canonical writers, newspapers built a new kind of aesthetic, a form of literary realism unto itself that self-consciously reworked and revised familiar literary conventions and genres.

23. Shuman, *Steps into Journalism*, 66–67.

1. *The* Sun, *the Moon, and Two Balloons*

1. Qtd. in Emery, Emery, and Roberts, eds., *The Press and America*, 100–101.

2. See Zboray, *A Fictive People;* and Schudson, *Discovering the News*, 21.

3. Weber, *Hired Pens*, 18.

4. Whalen, *Edgar Allan Poe and the Masses*, 24.

5. Ibid.

6. Schudson, *Discovering the News*, 18; Emery, Emery, and Roberts, eds., *The Press and America*, 100.

7. "A Case of Conscience," *New York Sun*, August 11, 1835.

8. "New Society," *New York Sun*, August 7, 1835.

9. "Highway Robbery," *New York Sun*, August 14, 1835.

10. Tucher, *Froth and Scum*, 46.

11. Ibid., 52.

12. Ibid., 59.

13. Matthew, "Forms of Hoax in the Tales of Edgar Allan Poe," 2.

14. Srebnick, *The Mysterious Death of Marie Rogers*, 122.

15. Weiner, *The Most Noble of Professions*, 5.

16. The Moon Hoax (a name for Locke's moon stories that was, for obvious reasons, applied after the fact) was first printed in the *New York Sun*, August 25–31, 1835. The *Sun* published a pamphlet collecting the individual articles under one cover in early September; it was published again as a book in subsequent

years. I have taken all Moon Hoax quotations from an 1859 reprint of the articles in book form, noting these references by the author "Locke" rather than by their original date of publication in the *Sun*.

17. Locke, *The Moon Hoax,* 23.

18. Ibid., 25.

19. Ibid., 26.

20. Ibid., 36.

21. Ibid., 37.

22. Ibid., 37–38.

23. Barnum, *The Humbugs of the World,* 194.

24. O'Brien, *The Story of the Sun,* 86. The *Sun's* Moon Hoax also spawned at least two theatrical endeavors, which attempted to capitalize on the newspaper's success. One New York amusement house show, replacing another "current events" show, was entitled "The Lunar Discoveries; a Brilliant Illustration of the Scientific Observation of the Surface of the Moon." Another, entitled "Moonshine, or Lunar Discoveries," was a spoof that included a scene in which the man-bats were blown up "with a combustible bundle of Abolition tracts" (90).

25. Harris, *Humbug,* 75.

26. In addition, Locke may have lifted his "bat-men" from an 1827 melodrama entitled *Peter Wilkins; or, the Flying Islanders.* See Pollin, introduction to *The Imaginary Voyages.*

27. Harris, *Humbug,* 72.

28. O'Brien, *The Story of the Sun,* 87.

29. Day, "The Great Astronomical Discoveries," *New York Sun,* September 16, 1835.

30. Ibid.

31. Harris, *Humbug,* 77. Lang in *The Culture and Commerce of the American Short Story* notes that the tradition of the confidence man—the person who "attempts to manipulate an audience directly for the purpose of personal profit"—was an "American invention" at precisely this time (23).

32. Qtd. in Seavey, introduction, xxii.

33. Qtd. ibid.

34. Poe's original spelling for his story was "Hans Phaall," though he spelled it "Phaal" in his letters. After 1842 he called the story "The Unparalleled Adventure of One Hans Pfaall," and it is this spelling and title that have been adopted by modern editors. The original edition ran in the *Southern Literary Messenger* in June 1835.

35. Thomas and Jackson, *The Poe Log,* 160. The topics of the moon and balloons were closely related in scholarly circles, since many scientists believed if humans were ever to attempt ascension to the moon, they would use one of the many styles of balloons under development.

36. Poe, "The Unparalleled Adventures of One Hans Pfaall," 191–92.

37. Ibid., 182, 233.

38. Ibid., 179.

39. Ibid.

40. Though contemporary reviews of "Hans Pfaall" clearly recognize in it an imaginative rather than a factual-sounding hoax intended to fool readers, some critics nevertheless believe (evidence to the contrary) that readers were convinced of its truthfulness. See Weissbuch, "Edgar Allan Poe," 295; and Pollin, introduction, 372.

41. Ketterer, *New Worlds for Old,* 53. See also Ketterer, "Poe's Usage of the Hoax," 377–385; and Matthew, "Forms of Hoax in the Tales of Edgar Allan Poe," 75.

42. Thomas and Jackson, *The Poe Log,* 161–62.

43. Poe to John P. Kennedy, September 11, 1835, *The Letters of Edgar Allan Poe,* ed. Ostrom, vol. 1, 74.

44. See, for instance, Ketterer, *New Worlds for Old;* Bennett, "Edgar Allan Poe and the Literary Tradition of Lunar Speculation," 137–47; Levine and Levine, eds., *The Short Fiction of Edgar Allan Poe;* Meyers, *Edgar Allan Poe;* Moss, *Poe's Literary Battles;* and Pollin, introduction, for more on Poe's "cribbing." Ironically, given Poe's own practical plagiarism of scientific sources, Ketterer asserts that "undeserved reputation, chicanery, favoritism, and especially plagiarism never failed to provoke Poe's wrath and provided evidence for his belief in human gullibility" (Ketterer, *The Rationale of Deception in Poe,* 56).

45. Thomas and Jackson, *The Poe Log,* 167.

46. Weiner, *The Most Noble of Professions,* 13. Possibly even more galling to Poe, his next published work, *The Narrative of Arthur Gordon Pym,* was credited by some reviewers as another hoax written by Locke (Thomas and Jackson, *The Poe Log,* 249).

47. This theme of the "correct reader" was to be played out first in "The Balloon Hoax," and again in "The Mystery of Marie Rogêt" specifically and in the character of Poe's detective, C. August Dupin, generally.

48. Qtd. in Seavey, introduction, 69.

49. Qtd. ibid., 70.

50. Poe, *The Literati,* 121.

51. Ibid., 122.

52. Ibid.

53. Ibid., 126. Although Day continued to give him plum reporting jobs, Locke stayed with the *Sun* for only a year more. He began his own paper, the *New Era;* but when he tried out another hoax there, predictably, no one was fooled, and the paper soon failed. After short stints editing other papers, including the *Brooklyn Eagle,* he found a position as a customs house official, which he held for the rest of his professional career. See Stovall, "Richard Adams Locke," 309–12.

54. See Scudder, "Poe's 'Balloon-Hoax,'" 179–80. In addition to his book-length work, Mason had published numerous newspaper and magazine articles about ballooning during the 1830s and 1840s. Poe was heavily influenced by Mason's work. As he did when writing "Hans Pfaall," Poe cribbed the descriptions of actual scientific accounts of ballooning and aeronautics. See Wilkinson, "Poe's 'Balloon-Hoax,' Once More," 313–17.

55. Many more balloon accounts followed in the popular press, including the great fictional works by Jules Verne, discussed in chapter 2.

56. Poe, "The Balloon Hoax," 466.

57. Ibid., 473.

58. Brigham, *Poe's Balloon Hoax,* 7.

59. Qtd. ibid., 7.

60. Qtd. in Falk, "Thomas Low Nichols, Poe, and the 'Balloon Hoax,'" 48.

61. Matthew, "Forms of Hoax in the Tales of Edgar Allan Poe," 23.

62. Weiner, *The Most Noble of Professions,* 5.

63. Poe, *Doings of Gotham,* 33.

64. Ibid.

65. Ibid., 34.

66. Poe, *The Works of the Late Edgar Allan Poe,* 88.

67. Certainly not all scholars read "The Poetic Principle" and "Philosophy of Composition" as such. Don P. Pierstorff ("Poe as Satirist," 32–34), for instance, insists "Philosophy" is pure satire, and Dennis Pahl ("De-composing Poe's 'Philosophy,'" 1–25) remarks that Poe's "theoretical" works have "traditionally been discredited as but [more] of the many hoaxes Poe is supposed to have perpetuated against an unsuspecting readership."

68. Pahl, "De-composing Poe's 'Philosophy,'" 9.

69. Ibid., 16.

70. Ibid.

71. Miller, "Poe on the Beat," 149.

72. This same tension comes into play in another of Poe's great "newspaper" stories, "The Mystery of Marie Rôget," in which, according to Richard Fusco, Poe's authorial voice sounds "egotistical, arrogant, and, perhaps, megalomaniac" ("Poe's Revisions of 'The Mystery of Marie Rôget'—A Hoax?" in *Poe at Work,* 97). Poe's detective story might itself serve as an elaborate hoax.

73. Carlson, ed., *A Companion to Poe Studies,* 458.

American Literary Realism and the Cult of the Real Thing

1. Orvell, *The Real Thing,* 35.

2. Ibid., 107.

3. Shi, *Facing Facts,* 94.

4. Vance, *Catalogue of Daguerreotype Panoramic Views in California,* 4.

5. Gilder, "Certain Tendencies in Current Literature," 3.

6. This section does not offer a comprehensive survey of realism in late nineteenth-century America. I wish merely to present some of the central tenets of American realism to provide additional framework through which to read the rest of this book. Shi, Orvell, and Pizer, among many others, offer solid, thorough studies of this genre.

7. Borus, *Writing Realism,* 173.

8. Schudson, *Discovering the News,* 71.

9. James, "The Art of Fiction," 173.

10. Shi, *Facing Facts,* 81.

11. Richardson, *American Literature 1607–1885,* 432.

12. Budd, "The American Background," 35; Pizer, introduction to *The Cambridge Companion to American Realism and Naturalism,* 7.

13. Borus, *Writing Realism,* 4.

14. Howells, *Criticism and Fiction,* 104.

15. Garland, "Productive Conditions of American Literature," 694.

16. Shi, *Facing Facts,* 85.

17. Qtd. in Pizer, ed., *Documents of American Realism and Naturalism,* 7.

18. Qtd. ibid., 12. Nothing was more upsetting to critics than the example of realism and naturalism in Europe (particularly the fiction of Emile Zola), which pushed the envelope of propriety far past Victorian tolerance.

19. Shi, *Facing Facts,* 87.

20. Darrow, "Realism in Literature and Art," 110.

21. Kirkland, "Tolstoi and the Russian Invasion of the Realm of Fiction," 81.

22. Qtd. in Shi, *Facing Facts,* 104. In fact, "taste for the fantastic and impossible" had not died out completely. Romance remained the best-selling fiction during the 1890s, though realism held steady ground and appeared in such culturally influential periodicals as *Harper's Monthly, Atlantic Monthly,* and *Scribner's.* Paradoxically, however, romances of the 1890s operated as a type of realism in themselves, as I discuss in chapter 4.

23. Bell, *The Problem of American Realism,* 32.

24. For good discussions of the professionalization of fiction writing in the late nineteenth century, see Wilson, *The Labor of Words,* and Johanningsmeier, *Fiction and the American Literary Marketplace.*

2. "To Turn a Fiction to a Fact"

1. Kroeger, *Nellie Bly,* 81.

2. Originally serialized as *Le Tour de Monde en 80 Jours* in the Paris newspaper *Le Temps,* November 6, 1872, through December 22, 1872.

3. *Around the World in Eighty Days* was by far Verne's best-selling novel, and the stage version that quickly followed (complete with a "live elephant, snakes, and a locomotive on stage") was also wildly successful, leading to additional "business offers, marriage proposals, and requests for locks of [Verne's] hair" (Lynch, *Jules Verne,* 58). Other travelers had attempted a journey around the world as quickly as possible even before Verne wrote his novel. For instance, Americans William Perry Fogg and George Francis Train had circumnavigated the globe in 1869 and 1870, respectively, and published accounts of their journeys (Fogg's 1872 book was even entitled *Round the World*). Train continued to attempt new records in following decades. After *Around the World in Eighty Days* was published, a

parade of "publicity-seekers" attempted "to reproduce or improve on [Phileas] Fogg's performance," though none had been successful or had traveled with such fanfare (Butcher, introduction to *Around the World in Eighty Days,* viii).

4. Although Verne was a French writer (and though he made little money off the American market because of pirated editions), he serves as a good indicator of American literary tastes. American literature in the nineteenth century did not, of course, begin and end at its own borders, and Verne's extreme popularity in the United States, his steady appearance as a "best seller" in the American literary marketplace, and his frequent serialization in American newspapers and magazines are all highly suggestive of American attitudes and reading practices. One critic argues Verne was so important to American readers because they "found in Verne" their "own obsessions with technology, power, and freedom" (Taves and Michaluk, *The Jules Verne Encyclopedia,* 13). See also Mott, *Golden Multitudes,* and Wadsworth, "Excel-ing the Seaside Library."

5. Swanberg, *Pulitzer,* 58.

6. Ibid.

7. Pulitzer was also driven to leave St. Louis because of more pressing personal problems. He had made significant political enemies in the city; more problematically, his editor, John Cockerill, shot and killed one of these enemies in the *Post-Dispatch* office.

8. When Pulitzer purchased the *World* in 1883 and began selling it for two cents, several other New York dailies already existed, led by Charles Dana's two-cent *Sun,* with the largest circulation at 140,000; James Gordon Bennett Jr.'s three-cent *Herald* with a smaller circulation but a better reputation; Whitelaw Reid's *Tribune* and George Jones's *Times,* four-cent papers with even smaller circulations; and a handful of others, including the *Journal,* a one-cent daily owned by Joseph's brother Albert. See Swanberg, *Pulitzer,* 78–79; and Juergens, *Joseph Pulitzer and the "New York World,"* vii, 7–9).

9. Ibid., viii.

10. Pulitzer, editorial, *New York World,* May 11, 1883.

11. Juergens, *Joseph Pulitzer and the "New York World,"* xii. It would be incorrect to assume only "people of small means and limited prospect" read the *World* (ibid., xiii). One factor in the *World's* success was its appeal to broad audiences, and that surely included high-brow readers as well as working-class audiences. As one *World* editorial put it, "Like everybody else," even Matthew Arnold "buys and reads the newspapers that are racy" (qtd. ibid., 17). Pulitzer himself told reporters they must "always remember the difference between a newspaper made for the million, for the masses, and a paper made for the classes. In using the word masses I do not exclude anybody. I should make a paper that the judges of the Supreme Court . . . would read with enjoyment, but I would not make a paper that only the judges of the Supreme Court and their class can read" (qtd. in Seitz, *Joseph Pulitzer,* 417).

12. Juergens, *Joseph Pulitzer and the "New York World,"* 31.

13. Qtd. ibid.

14. Indeed, Pulitzer, like other editors of new journalism, saw little difference between literature and journalism. He admitted that newspapers are naturally "made to sell," but that did not make them at all different from "the highest work of art and intellect" (qtd. ibid., 69).

15. Qtd. ibid., 233.

16. Qtd. ibid., 85–86.

17. "Around the World," *New York World,* November 14, 1889.

18. Pulitzer essentially gave up his everyday management of the *World* to Cockerill, who had followed him from St. Louis, when illness struck in 1889, leaving Pulitzer with failing eyesight, extreme nervousness, and intense sensitivity to sound. Nevertheless, he was still closely involved in the paper's editorial operations through secretaries and a constant stream of memos to employees.

19. Wilson, *The Labor of Words,* 2.

20. Kroeger, *Nelly Bly,* 145.

21. Women had long been dismissed as a viable work force because many editors, including Charles Dana of the *Sun,* considered them incapable of sufficient accuracy.

22. Schlipp and Murphy, *Great Women of the Press,* 136.

23. Kroeger, *Nellie Bly,* 127.

24. Schriber, *Writing Home,* 33.

25. Bly, *Nellie Bly's Book,* 5. The chapters in this book were originally published as feature articles in the *New York World* under the following titles: "Nellie Bly's Story," February 2, 1890; "The Visit to Verne," February 9, 1890; "On a French Train," February 16, 1890; and "Her Last Chapter," February 23, 1890.

26. "Around the World," *New York World,* November 14, 1889.

27. "Miss Bly's Home-Coming," *New York World,* January 9, 1890.

28. This portrayal is typical within Verne's travel novels, where "in the epic journeys . . . women are usually left at home" (Lynch, *Jules Verne,* 105).

29. Bly, *Nellie Bly's Book,* 52.

30. Wilson, *The Labor of Words,* 17.

31. "On the Other Side," *New York World,* November 22, 1889.

32. Qtd. in Kroeger, *Nellie Bly,* 171.

33. "A Boom for Geography," *New York World,* December 21, 1889.

34. "Nellie Bly Is Off," *New York World,* November 15, 1889.

35. "Around the World," *New York World,* November 14, 1889.

36. "Nellie Bly on Time," *New York World,* December 19, 1889; "Success to Nellie Bly," *New York World,* November 17, 1889.

37. "Nellie Bly Is Off," *New York World,* November 15, 1889.

38. "Miss Bly's Home-Coming," *New York World,* January 8, 1890.

39. "On Time!" *New York World,* January 22, 1890; "Bly Versus Verne," *New York World,* November 16, 1889. The newspaper's framing of fact against a fictional plot reworks Hayden White's theory of histories as "stories" formulated "out of mere chronicles" by means of "emplotment," or an "encodation of the facts contained in the chronicle as components of specific kinds of plot-structures"

("The Historical Text as Literary Artifact," 46). The *World's* story, in other words, is emplotted against Verne's plot structure. See also Schudson's "Why News Is the Way It Is," 109–25.

40. At least two different versions of who initiated the meeting with Verne are in circulation today. Kroeger, basing her conclusions on the memoir of editor Julius Chambers, asserts that the *World* brass immediately "set in motion a plan to arrange a visit between Bly and Verne himself" (*Nellie Bly,* 140). *World* Paris correspondent Robert Sherard concurs, stating the New York office instructed him to arrange a meeting between the two since "it would give a good advertisement to the 'story'" (Sherard, *Twenty Years in Paris,* 314). But Bly's account insists that Verne himself had written the *World's* London correspondent to see if he could meet Bly en route (*Nellie Bly's Book,* 31).

41. "Nellie Meets Verne," *New York World,* November 23, 1889.

42. Ibid.

43. "Nellie Bly's Admirer," *New York World,* December 26, 1889. See also "Verne and His Works," *New York World,* November 23, 1889.

44. "Father Time Outdone," *New York World,* January 26, 1890.

45. All quotations in this paragraph are from Verne, *Around the World in Eighty Days,* 155–58.

46. "A Day More," *New York World,* January 24, 1890.

47. "Flying Home," *New York World,* January 23, 1890.

48. Bly, *Nellie Bly's Book,* 214.

49. Orvell, *The Real Thing,* 107.

50. Though he considered himself essentially an artist rather than merely a popular writer, Verne struggled with his reputation during his lifetime, as he does today largely because of a history of weak translations into English. By 1889 he was increasingly frustrated in his attempts to mark himself as someone other than a popular romancer.

51. Evans, "Literary Intertexts in Jules Verne's 'Voyages Extraordinaires,'" 171.

52. Belloc, "Jules Verne at Home," 206; "Nellie Meets Verne," *New York World,* November 23, 1889.

53. Belloc, "Jules Verne at Home," 207; Jones, "Jules Verne at Home," 665. Evans differentiates "scientific fiction" from the *roman scientifique* based on "the manner in which a sustained scientific discourse is grafted onto a literary one" (Evans, "Science Fiction vs. Scientific Fiction in France," 1–11). A work of scientific fiction "presumes a predominantly pedagogical function" with a primary goal of "implantation of (what is considered to be at the time) factual scientific knowledge." Science fiction, a later development, "utilizes science—or, quite frequently, pseudo-science—for purely fictional purposes" with a primary goal of acting "as a catalyst for plot progression and special effects" (ibid., 1). The didactic goals of Verne's collection of novels entitled *Voyages Extraordinaires* were laid out clearly by his publisher: the novels would "outline all the geographical, geological, physical, and astronomical knowledge amassed by modern science and . . . recount, in an entertaining and picturesque format . . . the history of the uni-

verse" (qtd. in Evans, "Literary Intertexts in Jules Verne's 'Voyages Extraordinaires,'" 172). "Science fiction" as a literary term first appeared in 1851 in England but was not used commonly until 1929 (see Seed, ed., *Anticipations: Essays on Early Science Fiction and Its Precursors,* 27–28). Accordingly, in America the terms "romance," "scientific fiction," and "invention stories" were used to describe Verne's writing (ibid., 28).

54. "On the Other Side," *New York World,* November 22, 1889.

55. Bell, *The Problem of American Realism,* 8.

56. Ibid.

57. Jones, "Jules Verne at Home," 670.

58. Also included in the president's survey of moon narratives is Sir John Herschel's "discovery" of "caverns frequented by hippopotamuses, green mountains bordered by golden lacework, sheep with horns of ivory, a white species of deer, and inhabitants with membranous wings, like bats"—or the Moon Hoax of 1835.

59. "Three Sundays in a Week" was not the only Poe story that Verne drew upon. He also wrote a "continuation" of *The Narrative of Arthur Gordon Pym* with his 1897 novel *Le Sphinx des Glaces,* or *The Ice Sphinx,* which began with the dedication, "A la memoire d'Edgar Poe. A mes amis d'Amèrique." Evans's "Literary Intertexts in Jules Verne's 'Voyages Extraordinaires'" provides a more extensive list of "concrete borrowings" from Poe.

60. Poe, "Three Sundays in a Week," 142.

61. The end of the century brought a huge increase in the number of scientific romances published in the United States and Britain. Over four hundred scientific fictions were published between 1880 and 1900 in America alone, and Verne's work was consistently the best selling of these (Seed, *Anticipations,* 34).

62. Costello, *Jules Verne,* 76. Verne even made the closing "date" within this serialized novel coincide with the date of the newspaper in which it appeared so that the question of veracity would doubtless be raised (Butcher, introduction to *Around the World in Eighty Days,* viii). The French novel inspired by an American work in turn led to another American novel—Taves argues *Five Weeks in a Balloon* in turn "clearly inspired" Mark Twain's *Tom Sawyer Abroad* (Taves and Michaluk, *Jules Verne Encyclopedia,* 6). Yet another Verne work, "A Drama in the Air," was also inspired by Poe's "Balloon Hoax."

63. Qtd. in Evans, "Literary Intertexts in Jules Verne's 'Voyages Extraordinaires,'" 178.

64. Review of *A Journey to the Center of the Earth,* by Jules Verne, 373.

65. Butcher, introduction to *Around the World in Eighty Days,* viii.

66. Ibid., 206.

67. Belloc, "Jules Verne at Home," 212.

68. Jones, *Jules Verne at Home,* 667. Other written sources for the novel included Poe's "Three Sundays in a Week" (1841), as noted above; Fogg's *Round the World* (1872), describing an 1869–71 circumnavigation; Cook's *Letters from the Sea and from Foreign Lands, Descriptive of a Tour Round the World* (originally serialized in 1872); and a scientific article in *Siècle* describing how a journey around the world

might be done in eighty days. In addition, contemporary technologies such as the redrawing of the world's map, the completion of rail lines across the United States and India, and the opening of the Suez Canal offered additional opportunities for success. Verne had already used the theme of circumnavigation himself in *Captain Grant's Children: A Voyage Round the World* (1865) and *Twenty-Thousand Leagues under the Sea: A Submarine Trip around the World* (1869). See William Butcher's notes in Verne, *Around the World,* appendix A, for further discussion of sources. As Butcher points out, no matter the sources that possibly influenced Verne, by 1870 the idea of circumnavigation was "common currency" and "even the minimum of 80 days seems to have been a commonplace" (206).

69. "Nellie Bly's Fame," *New York World,* January 9, 1890; Taves and Michaluk, *Jules Verne Encyclopedia,* 136–37.

70. "Nellie Bly's Fame," *New York World,* January 9, 1890.

71. Ibid.

72. "The Press and the Globe-Trotter," *New York World,* December 26, 1889.

73. "Verne's Bravo," *New York World,* January 26, 1890.

74. Belloc, "Jules Verne at Home," 208–9.

75. Jones, "Jules Verne at Home," 668–69.

76. Ibid., 669.

77. Lottman, *Jules Verne,* 282.

78. Wilson, *The Labor of Words,* 81.

79. Jules-Verne, *Jules Verne,* 178.

80. Taves and Michaluk, *Jules Verne Encyclopedia,* 15.

81. "Nellie Bly's Admirer," *New York World,* December 26, 1889.

82. Ibid.

83. Verne, *Claudius Bombarnac, or the Special Correspondent,* originally published in *Le Soleil* (Paris) from October 10 to December 7, 1892.

84. Ibid., 17, 183.

85. Ibid., 71, 103.

86. Wilson, *The Labor of Words,* 193.

87. Ibid., 82.

88. Sherard, *Twenty Years in Paris,* 316.

89. Ibid.

90. Kroeger, *Nellie Bly,* 185.

91. Ibid., 185–86.

92. Ibid., 186. It was fairly common for publishers to bring out a timely book version of articles previously published in the newspaper. What makes that practice particularly interesting is that it suggests readers could sit down with the collected newspaper stories and peruse them en masse, much as they might peruse a work of fiction. The newspaper stories, in other words, allowed a smooth transition from periodical form (a theoretically transitory form) to book form (a theoretically lasting form).

93. Ibid., 116.

94. Ibid., 186.

95. Bly's name was, however, kept in the public eye in any number of other ways. Manufacturers eagerly used her name to advertise, among countless other items, medications, crackers, caps, and travelers' checks (Kroeger, *Nellie Bly,* 179–80; Bly, *Nellie Bly's Book*). Textual references to Bly also abounded: Dora Keen published a book about European travel entitled *Three Little Maids from School versus Nellie Bly;* a character in Richard Harding Davis's "Van Bibber and the Swan-Boats" jokes he is "taking a trip around the world in 80 minutes" (208); an 1891 travel book invoked Bly implicitly with its title *Around the World in Seven Months;* and, more humorously, *Life* magazine ran a spoof describing its own girl reporter and her raucous trip around New York ("She's Home Again!"). Even today, Bly's name is invoked by enterprises as diverse as kaleidoscope manufacturing and amusement parks.

Journalist as Hero

1. Traxel, *1898,* 84.

2. Schudson, *Discovering the News,* 69.

3. Ibid., 67. As just one example, the *New York Herald* maintained a staff of at least forty war correspondents in southern states.

4. Philips, ed., *The Making of a Newspaper,* 263.

5. Schudson, *Discovering the News,* 69; Harrington and Frankenberg, *Essentials in Journalism,* 75.

6. Riis, *The Making of an American,* 204.

7. Getting the proverbial foot in the door at New York newspapers was a daunting task, given the competition of people who wanted to be the next Nellie Bly or Richard Harding Davis. James H. Collins's article "The American Grub Street," for instance, details the difficulties aspiring reporters faced (in *The Profession of Journalism,* ed. Bleyer, 243–63).

8. Smythe, "The Reporter, 1880–1900," 2. Many reporters in the 1890s were still paid "space and time rates," as they had been since the end of the Civil War. Under this arrangement, they were paid a fixed rate per printed column. If their writing was not published, they were paid a nominal hourly rate for the time spent preparing the story. Only when a reporter held great public sway with his popularity could he negotiate a fixed salary. Many journalism historians credit the space system with encouraging sensationalism because reporters turned to extensive description and storytelling in order to "pad" their dispatches.

9. Ibid., 2.

10. Wilson, *The Labor of Words,* 37.

11. Burgess, "Norris's Van Bubbles Story," 11.

12. Despite his literary talent, Davis scored consistently at the bottom of his class in all subjects, including English. This dismal record in literary studies is all the more amazing when, as Davis's biographer points out, one considers that Lehigh was a college specializing in the training of future engineers, not writers.

13. Bly would follow up with a stint on Blackwell Island in 1888, posing as an insane woman in order to expose the deplorable conditions there. Her harrowing experiences were published first in the *World* and then under separate cover as *Ten Days in a Mad-House.*

14. Dana had created the *Evening Sun* in 1887, partly in response to the pressures brought about by Pulitzer's success in New York.

15. Lubow, *The Reporter Who Would Be King,* 47.

16. Davis, "Our Green Reporter," *New York Evening Sun,* November 2, 1889.

17. Lubow, *The Reporter Who Would Be King,* 26; Burgess, "Norris's Van Bubbles Story," 11. Smythe notes that reporters "hired" false witnesses to sensational crimes so that they could scoop the competition; that newspapers manufactured news events and then "authenticated" them with "real participants" who had been hired to corroborate the non-event and make it appear true; and that reporters stole criminal evidence from the police so that they could solve crimes themselves and "break" the story ("The Reporter, 1880–1900," 7–8). In his own making of the news, Davis helped create a figure of the proper gentleman, crime-fighting reporter who appears, ultimately, as Clark Kent–Superman of the *Gotham Daily Planet.* For more about the reporter as a fictional character, see Good, *Acquainted with the Night.*

18. Lubow, *The Reporter Who Would Be King,* 64. Newsboys had, of course, appeared earlier in fiction, notably as stock figures for Horatio Alger. But Davis expanded and popularized newspaper fiction as a distinct genre.

19. The first edition of *Gallegher,* the collected stories brought together as a book in 1890, sold out within its first month of release. It had sold over fifteen thousand copies by the end of the first year. The first edition (four thousand copies) of *Van Bibber and Others* ran out by noon of its second day on the market. Davis followed up with two of the best sellers of the 1890s, the romantic novels *Soldiers of Fortune* (1897) and *The Princess Aline* (1899), both serialized in 1895.

20. Davis, *Gallegher and Other Stories,* 156.

21. Lubow, *The Reporter Who Would Be King,* 53.

22. Burgess, "Norris's Van Bubbles Story," 11.

23. Lubow, *The Reporter Who Would Be King,* 2.

24. Burgess, "Norris's Van Bubbles Story," 11.

25. Davis may have been irrepressibly popular with readers, but he was the target of sometimes ruthless mockery from fellow reporters and other writers. See, for example, Frank Norris's story "Van Bubble's Story," which satirizes Davis's obsession with himself as a half-fictionalized gentleman adventurer.

3. A Front Seat to Lizzie Borden

1. Green, *Leavenworth Case,* 193.

2. Some critics, including Michelle Slug in her introduction to the 1981 reprint of *The Leavenworth Case,* call this work the first detective novel written by

a woman in America. Others point out, as I explore later in this chapter, that a much older tradition of detection already existed, though it was often associated with sheer sensationalism and lower-class readers. Metta Fuller Victor, for instance, published *The Dead Letter* and other mysteries targeting lower-class readers as early as 1866.

3. Mott, *Golden Multitudes,* 263.

4. The similarities between the Borden case and *The Leavenworth Case* were striking. Both featured women accused of murdering a father or father figure, with a motive of protecting an inheritance. Both involved two female relatives, sisters in Borden's case and cousins in Green's novel. Both spun suspicions around the familiar scapegoat of an Irish maid. Both drew upon issues of class and the disbelief that women of high social standing and apparent moral uprightness could commit something as unseemly as murder. Also, both "murders" were played out in the press. In Green's novel, Mr. Raymond strives to solve the case against the cousins before the papers vilify them. He particularly notices a "pale-faced, seedy" reporter at the inquest, whose "ghoul-like avidity" in the crime makes his "flesh creep" (Green, *Leavenworth Case,* 10).

5. See Green's "A Fictionist Faces Facts," *Fall River Daily Herald,* August 22, 1892; and "I Believe Her Innocent," *New Bedford Evening Standard,* August 22, 1892.

6. David Papke theorizes that the Borden case drew such attention because it underscored "the struggle for and partial achievement of a new social coherence" (*Framing the Criminal,* 11). The Borden family was among Fall River's wealthiest inhabitants, and the brutal murder proved the vulnerability even of those people who were "models for social life and holders of power" (ibid., 12). Moreover, the possibility that a Borden daughter committed the crime raised uncomfortable questions about the sanctity of family in middle-class society—the "gender-based family, ballast in the hustling society, seemed, at least briefly, less reliable than before" (ibid., 12).

7. In the 1840s Edgar Allan Poe articulated a formula for mystery and detective stories, a formula that was used nearly without fail by subsequent writers well into the twentieth century. John Cawelti in *Adventure, Mystery, and Romance* describes these crucial formulaic elements as *situation* (beginning with an unsolved crime and moving toward "the elucidation of its mystery"), *pattern of action* (centering on "the detective's investigation and solution of the crime"), *characters and relationships* (including the victim, the criminal, the detective, and "those threatened by the crime but incapable of solving it"), and *setting* (taking place in isolated settings clearly marked off from the rest of the world; for instance, "the locked room in the midst of the city") (80–97). For the sake of simplification, I am conflating the categories of mystery and detection novels, which are sometimes studied as separate types of writing.

8. Curiously, despite its enormous implications in American folklore and criminality, the Lizzie Borden case has only recently become the subject of extended scholarly study. In addition to an intriguing number of twentieth-century novels and stories taking Borden as their subject, a number of popular "armchair

detective" books have been published, an example of which is David Kent's *Forty Whacks.* Kent's work, though lacking critical perspective, does provide a substantial bibliography of book-length works, short stories, plays, opera, ballet, and articles. Aside from Borden's passing treatment in scholarly studies of crime reportage, two recent dissertations investigate the Borden case: Plummer's "Witness for the Persecution" and Adler's "Our Beloved Lizzie." Two articles of note include Schofield's "Lizzie Borden Took an Axe," which surveys the gender politics involved in modern artistic revisions of the story; and Robertson's "Representing 'Miss Lizzie,'" which studies gendered representation in the trial transcripts.

9. My method for this chapter included reading every dispatch filed by Julian Ralph to the *Sun,* June 5–21, 1893, the duration of the trial; most of these articles were three to four full columns in length. In addition, I examined samples of trial dispatches in the *New York Times, New York Post, New York World,* and *Boston Globe.* While Ralph's dispatches were not formally published as a separate volume after their initial publication in the *Sun* (unlike Bly's and Cisneros's/Decker's), they were essentially given life as a separate text away from the context of the newspaper in that they were quoted at length in the nonfiction books about Lizzie Borden published after the trial, including Pearson's influential *The Trial of Lizzie Borden.*

10. This idea of first capturing readers' attention with sensationalism and then educating them was Pulitzer's—and to a less genuine extent Hearst's—editorial position as well. While the morning *Sun* tended to be somewhat more staid, the *Evening Sun* of the 1890s more closely resembled the *World* and the *Journal.* As one historian puts it, in the *Evening Sun* "the revenge or suicide of an outraged young woman would be lovingly detailed. Brawls among immigrants, fires in tenements, freaks of nature, fits of madness—the *Evening Sun* played up the weird, the piteous, the startling" (Lubow, *The Reporter Who Would Be King,* 45).

11. O'Brien, *The Story of the Sun,* 415.

12. Ibid., 245. Throughout his tenure at the *Sun,* Dana exhorted his reporters to "be interesting" (ibid., 238). One of Day's associate editors in the 1830s famously explained what constituted interesting news at the *Sun:* "When a dog bites a man, that is not news; but when a man bites a dog, *that* is news" (qtd. in Emery, Emery, and Roberts, *The Press and America,* 244). Dana schooled his men on the literary umbrella that hung over their work: "If I could have my way," he once lectured, "I had rather take a young fellow who knows the 'Ajax' of Sophocles, and has read Tacitus, and can scan every ode of Horace" (qtd. in O'Brien, *The Story of the Sun,* 242).

13. Qtd. in O'Brien, *The Story of the Sun,* 243.

14. Lancaster, *Gentleman of the Press,* 196.

15. Ralph was widely recognized among both fellow reporters and the reading public. The *Boston Globe,* for instance, included in its June 6, 1893, coverage a prominent illustration of the courtroom scene portraying "Julian Ralph, the Writer" as he sat adjacent to key players in the drama, implying that readers would understand his significance without further explanation.

16. Lancaster points out that Julian Ralph's favorite books included the Bible and *Robinson Crusoe*. "The story of the castaway soldier is an interesting choice," he posits. "Its author, Daniel Defoe, one of the outstanding journalists of the eighteenth century as well as a novelist, was a master of clear, forceful narrative, with an eye for the detail that makes a scene leap to life" (*Gentleman of the Press*, 32). Defoe practiced, that is, a style Ralph would strive to emulate throughout his career, a style evident also in his reportage for one of the other hugely sensational trials of the century—Henry Ward Beecher's trial for adultery in 1875, which Ralph covered to much acclaim for the *New York Daily Graphic*.

17. Ralph, *Making of a Journalist*, 3–4.

18. Ibid., 11; Connery, "Fusing Fictional Technique and Journalistic Fact," 111.

19. Pearson, *The Trial of Lizzie Borden*, 57.

20. See Moskowitz, *Science Fiction by Gaslight*, for more about the intertwining of science fiction and "respectable" mysteries.

21. Papke, *Framing the Criminal*, 12.

22. Ralph, "Lizzie Borden at the Bar," *New York Sun*, June 5, 1893.

23. Ibid.

24. Spiering, *Lizzie*, 58.

25. Ralph, "Lizzie Borden Was Cheery," *New York Sun*, June 8, 1893.

26. Ibid.

27. Ibid.

28. Ralph, "Lizzie Borden at the Bar."

29. Ibid.

30. Ralph, "The Borden Jury Chosen," *New York Sun*, June 6, 1893.

31. Ralph, "Lizzie Borden Swooned," *New York Sun*, June 7, 1893.

32. Ralph, "With Skulls and Hatchets," *New York Sun*, June 14, 1893.

33. Ibid.

34. Ralph, "Lizzie Borden Free," *New York Sun*, June 21, 1893. Ralph here perpetuated a falsehood common in the late nineteenth century regarding the manner in which witches were executed in America. References to burning witches in Salem had become a common misinterpretation of what happened to the convicted women and men in 1692—condemned witches were hanged, not burned, at Salem. Bernard Rosenthal points out that to this day, "no matter how often the mistake is corrected, the popular image of burning witches in Salem remains, because burning evokes the starkest image of ignorance and barbarity that we popularly associate with the superstitions of the past. The burning image of Salem pervades the way we imagine the Salem episode and utilize it metaphorically" (*Salem Story*, 209).

35. Ralph's casting of Borden in archetypal terms was but one way in which he constructed the case fictively. His characterizations of Borden's chief defense attorney, George Robinson, as well as his humorous and often scathing depiction of the Bristol County sheriff also echoed some formulas of 1890s detective stories. Ralph transformed Robinson into the character type of the forceful, heroic, puzzle-solving detective; ironically, he transformed the sheriff into the bumbling,

hateful, even nefarious villain. For their part, the defense and prosecution teams turned to models of fiction as well. In framing their cases for the jury, they used "literary allusion as well as . . . fiction of their own devising" (Robertson, "Representing 'Miss Lizzie,'" 393).

36. Papke, *Framing the Criminal,* 70.

37. Ralph, "The Borden Jury Chosen."

38. Ibid.

39. Ralph, "Lizzie Borden Swooned."

40. Ralph, "Turning Now to the Jury," *New York Sun,* June 19, 1893.

41. Ibid.

42. An even more compelling example of self-reference in the Lizzie Borden trial reports occurred in the dispatches of the popular reporter Joseph Howard. Discarding all pretense of objectivity, his writings for the *Boston Globe* (syndicated in Pulitzer's *World* as well as in other papers) were in first person and signed, literally, with a scrawled "Howard" at the end of the column. One Borden historian sneers that Howard "made himself look more important than judges, jury, and prisoner" with dispatches that "were eagerly read by those who prefer bubbling impressions to matter-of-fact reports" (Pearson, *The Trial of Lizzie Borden,* 58). Still, Howard's columns underscore the growing urge to commodify not only Lizzie Borden and crime in general, but to commodify the reporter of crime as well.

43. Frus, *The Politics and Poetics of Journalistic Narrative,* 99.

44. Ibid.

45. Ralph, "Lizzie Borden Free."

46. Ibid.

47. Halttunen, *Murder Most Foul,* 3.

48. The Jewett murder case, which tripled circulation for Bennett's *Herald,* "fueled a crime-reporting extravaganza unrivaled in the prior history of newspaper journalism in the United States" and introduced an "expansive new form of crime reporting" (Papke, *Framing the Criminal,* 41–42). See Tucher's *Froth and Scum* and Anthony's "The Helen Jewett Panic," 487–514, for further discussion of the Jewett murder in the penny press.

49. Schiller, *Objectivity and the News,* 102. See also Papke, *Framing the Criminal,* 26 and 61; and Lane, *Murder in America,* 95.

50. Qtd. in Schiller, *Objectivity and the News,* 105.

51. Ibid., 68.

52. For thorough readings of the actual Mary Rogers murder and Poe's version of it, see Srebnick, *The Mysterious Death of Marie Rogers;* and Walsh, *Poe the Detective.*

53. Reynolds, ed., *George Lippard,* 5.

54. Slug, introduction, iii.

55. Papke, *Framing the Criminal,* 68.

56. Williams, "The Collision of a Personality and an Era," 9. Other favorite books of Borden's included "sentimental romances of the '90s," especially medi-

evalist romances like Charles Major's *When Knighthood Was in Flower* and Maurice Thompson's *Alice of Old Vincennes*—novels that have their own kind of violence, as the chapter on Evangelina Cisneros suggests. See Marshall, "Librarians in the Life and Legend of Lizzie Borden," 303.

57. Mott, *Golden Multitudes*, 311.

58. Ibid., 265.

59. Papke, *Framing the Criminal*, 110.

60. Landrum, *American Mystery and Detective Novels*, 8.

61. Kalikoff, *Murder and Moral Decay in Victorian Popular Literature*, 1. Mark Twain's interest in the mystery novel provides further insight into its market potential at the end of the century. A number of his later novels, including *Pudd'nhead Wilson* (1894) and *Tom Sawyer, Detective* (1896), simultaneously spoof the genre's conventions and depend on those very conventions for their own marketability.

62. Kalikoff, *Murder and Moral Decay*, 131.

63. Ibid., 129.

64. Ibid.

65. Freeman, "The Long Arm," 32. This method of investigation is also preferred by the prefect of police in Poe's "The Purloined Letter" (1841). As he tells Poe's detective Dupin, in his search for a missing letter he divided the "entire surface" of the suspect's house "into compartments, which we numbered, so that none might be missed; then we scrutinized each individual square inch throughout the premises" ("The Purloined Letter," in *Selected Poetry and Prose of Edgar Allan Poe*, ed. Mabbott, 293–309).

66. Freeman, "The Long Arm," 27.

67. Ibid., 1.

68. For full discussion of "The Long Arm" in terms of the Borden crimes, see Shaw, "New England Gothic by Light of Common Day," 211–36.

69. See, for instance, Pearson, *The Trial of Lizzie Borden*, 58, and Radin, *Lizzie Borden*, 39–40.

70. The Borden murders occurred (as Clive Bloom writes about another infamous nineteenth-century murderer, Jack the Ripper) at "a correct psychological moment, for almost immediately" the deeds "became the stuff of legend" and became "a focus for numerous related fears among metropolitan dwellers across Europe and America" (Bloom et al., *Nineteenth-Century Suspense*, 120). A healthy dose of Borden-related fiction has nurtured that legend, including Edward Stratemeyer's "Dash Dare on His Mettle, or Clearing Up a Double Tragedy" (1892), Mary E. Wilkins Freeman's "The Long Arm" (1895), Elizabeth Jordan's "Ruth Herrick's Assignment" (in *Tales of the City Room*, 1898), Pauline Hopkins' "Talma Gordon" (1900), Lily Dougall's *Summit House Mystery, or the Earthly Purgatory* (1905), Edith Wharton's "The Confession" (1936), Gertrude Stein's *Blood on the Dining Room Floor* (1948) (as well as other Stein works), Marie Belloc Lowndes's *Lizzie Borden: A Study in Conjecture* (1930), Mary Roberts Rinehart's *The Album* (1933), Edward Hale Bierstadt's *Satan Was a Man* (1935), Robert Bloch's

"Lizzie Borden Took an Axe" (in *Skull of Marquis de Sade,* 1965), Robert Henson's "Lizzie Borden in the P.M." (1973), Evan Hunter's *Lizzie: A Novel* (1984), Angela Carter's "The Fall River Axe Murders" (in *Saints and Strangers,* 1986) and "Lizzie's Tiger" (in *American Ghosts and OldWorldWonders,* 1993), Walter Satterthwait's *Miss Lizzie* (1989), Gwendoline Butler's "The Sisterhood" (in *Murder in New England,* 1989), Elizabeth Engstrom's *Lizzie Borden* (1991), and Owen Haskell's *Sherlock Holmes and the Fall River Tragedy* (1997). Theatrical works include *Lizzie* (Donald Blackwell, 1930), *Nine Pine Street* (John Colton and Carlton Miles, 1933), *The Man Who Came to Dinner* (George Kaufman and Moss Hart, 1939), *Suspect* (Reginald Denham and Edward Percy, 1940), *The Trial of Lizzie Borden* (Donald Henderson, 1946), *Goodbye, Miss Lizzie Borden* (Lillian de la Torre, 1947), *Murder, Plain and Fanciful* (James Sandoe, 1948), *Murder Takes the Stage* (James Reach, 1957), *The Legend of Lizzie* (Reginald Lawrence, 1959), *Lizzie Borden of Fall River* (Tim Kelly, 1976), *The Lights Are Warm and Coloured* (William Norfolk, 1980), and *Blood Relations and Other Plays* (Sharon Pollock, 1981). Other creative works include the Agnes De Mille ballet *Fall River Legend* (1948); the Thomas Albert opera *Lizbeth: An Opera in One Act* (libretto by Linde Hayen Herman, 1976) and the Jack Beeson opera *Lizzie Borden: A Family Portrait in Three Acts* (libretto by Kenwood Elmslie, 1967); poems "To Lizzie" and "Bloody Versicles" (A. L. Bixby, *Driftwood,* 1971), "The Passion of Lizzie Borden" (Ruth Whitman, *The Passion of Lizzie Borden,* 1973), "Photographs Courtesy of the Fall River Historical Society" (Sharon Olds, *Satan Says,* 1980), *Our Lady of Fall River* (Stephen Ronan, 1983), and "Lizzie Borden: A Street Ballad" (Phyllis Parker, *How to Become Absurdly Well-Informed about the Famous and Infamous,* 1987); and numerous songs, essays, films, and made-for-TV movies. References collected from Nickerson, Ryckebusch, and independent database searching. In addition, a number of Borden research societies still labor over the facts and transcripts of the case, struggling to solve the mystery of whodunit. Today aficionados of the mystery can even take a virtual tour of the Borden house (www.halfmoon.org/borden/) or spend the night in Lizzie's own home, which has been turned into a "bed and breakfast" establishment.

71. In 1894 Edwin H. Porter, a reporter for the *Fall River Globe,* privately published a scathing exposé of Borden, *The Fall River Tragedy.* Tradition has it that Borden immediately purchased all the copies available, but this work was only a small portent of the flood of indicting narrative to come her way. New evidence, however, suggests that the legend of Lizzie's purchase is just that: a legend. See Smith, "Lizzie Borden on the Rare Book Market," 273–91.

72. Spiering, *Lizzie,* 201.

73. Lincoln, *A Private Disgrace,* 307. Borden also continued to suffer from a problem that had apparently plagued her during her entire adult life—kleptomania. While her stealing had been smoothed over and hushed up in the years before her father's death, after the murders the crime seemed little else than further evidence of Borden's generally guilty persona to suspicious Fall River citizens.

74. Williams, Smithburn, and Peterson, eds., *Lizzie Borden,* 259.

75. Ralph's other published works included the arguably fictional *The Sun's German Barber near the Cooper Institute* (1883), *The German Policeman; [or, A Leedle Blain English from Policeman Schneiderkase]* (1887), *"That Dutchman"; or, The German Barber's Humorous Sketches* (1889), *Dixie; or Southern Scenes and Sketches* (1896), *Alone in China, and Other Stories* (1897), *A Prince of Georgia and Other Tales* (1899), *An Angel in a Web* (1899), and *The Millionairess* (1902). Nonfiction works included *Long Island of To-Day* (1884), *Along the South Shore of Lake Superior* (1890), *The Chinese Leak* (1891), *On Canada's Frontier* (1892), *Our Great West* (1893), *Harper's Chicago and the World's Fair* (1893), *Towards Pretoria* (1900), *War's Brighter Side* (1901), *At Pretoria* (1901), *An American with Lord Roberts* (1901), *Famous Cures and Humbugs of Europe* (1903), and *The Making of a Journalist* (1903).

76. Lancaster, *Gentleman of the Press,* 267.

77. Ibid.

78. Bird and Dardenne, "News and Storytelling in American Culture," 34.

True Women and New Women

1. Bloom et al., eds., *Nineteenth-Century Suspense,* 129–30.

2. Welter, *Dimity Conviction,* 21.

3. Nelson, *British Woman Fiction Writers of the 1890s,* 1.

4. Dupree, "The New Woman, Progressivism, and the Woman Writer in Edith Wharton's *The Fruit of the Tree,*" 46.

5. Qtd. in Cunningham, *The New Woman and the Victorian Novel,* 1.

6. Jones, *Women Who Kill,* 232.

7. I am presuming here Borden's guilt, as most modern scholars do, and as the conclusion to which most of the criminal evidence points.

8. The Borden home, located in a crowded, unfashionable part of Fall River, lacked even some of the most standard conveniences of comfortable 1890s households, including indoor plumbing, except for a cold-water spout by the kitchen door and a thirty-year-old water closet in the cellar.

9. Psychological reconstructions of the Borden household reveal a collection of rather disturbed individuals—indeed, several of the family's friends and contemporaries considered them "odd" even before the murders. Jules Ryckebusch includes essays unlocking some of the possible psychodynamics of the Borden family, including the suggestion of incest (in *Proceedings: Lizzie Borden Conference, Bristol Community College, Fall River, Massachusetts*).

10. Jones, *Women Who Kill,* 111.

11. Ibid., 193.

12. Ibid., 111.

13. Knelman, *Twisting in the Wind,* 13.

14. Jones, *Women Who Kill,* 219. Careful contemplation does not seem to have been an issue at the conclusion of the Borden trial. The jury returned their verdict of not guilty in only an hour.

15. Robertson, "Representing 'Miss Lizzie,'" 416.

16. Ralph, "Lizzie Borden at the Bar."

17. Shaw, "New England Gothic by Light of Common Day," 211. Cawelti explains that formula stories, including tales of detection and mystery, do important cultural work because they "affirm existing interests and attitudes by presenting an imaginary world" that is in "alignment with those interests"—that is, they "resolve tensions and ambiguities resulting from the conflicting interests of different groups within the culture," they "enable the audience to explore in fantasy the boundary between the permitted and the forbidden" and control crossing over that boundary, and they "assist in the process of assimilating changes in values to traditional imaginative constructs" (*Adventure, Mystery, and Romance,* 35–36).

18. Eyebrows rose particularly when women chose to live with other women, especially if a hint of romantic involvement existed. By the end of the century, general acceptance of the "Boston marriage" had been cast aside. No longer could women live comfortably with one another in unmarried status, for such an act increasingly smacked of "deviant" sexuality (Shaw, "New England Gothic by Light of Common Day," 230). This attitude was apparent when Fall River citizens gossiped about Borden's relationship with actress Nance O'Neil.

19. Brett, "Murder at Jex Farm." Both Freeman's and Brett's stories were published in the same collection of prize-winning detective fiction in 1895.

20. Nickerson, *The Web of Iniquity,* 15.

21. Ibid., 22.

22. Ibid., 118.

23. Ibid., 155.

24. Robertson, "Representing 'Miss Lizzie,'" 356.

4. The Evangelina Cisneros Romance, Medievalist Fiction, and Journalism That Acts

1. "Saved from Death!" *San Francisco Examiner,* January 4, 1890.

2. Ibid.

3. Ibid.

4. "The Rescued Man," *San Francisco Examiner,* January 5, 1890.

5. "New journalism" and "yellow journalism" were not synonymous terms. "Yellow journalism" came to describe the newspaper style that Pulitzer pioneered and that Hearst and others eventually mimicked by taking the basic principles of new journalism to melodramatic and frequently unethical extremes. After about 1896 critics used the label "as shorthand for the blatant degeneration of a modern journalism gone wild in pursuit of profit" (Marzolf, *Civilizing Voices,* 22). The use of yellow as a symbol for this journalistic style arose when the *World* and the *Journal*—at the height of their circulation war—each published a comic strip featuring a boy dressed in yellow. The editor of the *New York Press,* deeply disapproving of all Hearst and Pulitzer represented, dubbed their style "yellow." Charles Dana picked up the term and made it popular. See Kanfer, "From the

Yellow Kid to Yellow Journalism," 32–37, for a full look at the emergence of the Yellow Kid comics.

6. Cisneros's correct name was Evangelina Cosio y Cisneros, but the American press almost inevitably (and incorrectly) shortened it.

7. Hearst was certainly not alone in thinking American journalism should act. Other editors, most obviously Pulitzer, also manufactured stories, and the *World* even had in the works its own plot to break Cisneros out of jail. See Milton, *The Yellow Kids*, 205. Additional reporters and editors asserted the place of newspapers in creating the news. Even the general manager of the normally staid Associated Press asserted: "I hold that a newspaper should make news, not merely report and chronicle passing events" (qtd. in "The Days of Knight Errantry Are Still with Us," *New York Journal,* October 13, 1897). Also, the famous reporter James Creelman argued that "the very nature of *Journalism* enables it to act in the very heart of events at critical moments and with knowledge not possessed by the general public. . . . There are times when public emergencies call for the sudden intervention of some power outside of governmental authority. Then journalism acts" (*On the Great Highway,* 188). Furthermore, "if it be right for a newspaper to urge others to act in any given direction, it is also right for the newspaper itself to act" (ibid., 193).

8. Hearst's politics were always ambiguous when it came to Cuba. By most accounts he was sincere in his opinion that the Spaniards were the scourge of the Western Hemisphere, and he felt real sympathy for the Cubans. One biographer suggests that "with his weakness for reducing complex phenomena to terms of sheerest simplicity, the struggle in Cuba was purely a case of hero vs. villain" (Swanberg, *Citizen Hearst,* 108). On the other hand, Hearst's sympathies were rather superficial and closely tied to how much sensational copy he could milk out of any given plight.

9. The medievalist historical romances of the late nineteenth century were frequently modeled on another literary vogue of an earlier day: the Indian captivity narrative. The next section highlights the captivity narrative as a path toward uncovering some of the imperialist concerns evident in this case study.

10. Procter, *William Randolph Hearst,* x.

11. Swanberg, *Citizen Hearst,* 19.

12. Qtd. ibid., 30.

13. Qtd. ibid.; qtd. in Nasaw, *The Chief,* 63.

14. Qtd. in Nasaw, *The Chief,* 63.

15. Swanberg, *Citizen Hearst,* 45.

16. Ibid., 56. Hearst, who had been galled that Pulitzer thought of the Nellie Bly stunt first, created his own travel adventure, selecting three schoolboys through "literary and athletic contests" and sending each on a worldwide race, starting from different American cities. See Commander, "The Significance of Yellow Journalism," 153. In another telling example of a "circulation-building sensation" that seems closer to the Moon Hoax of 1835 than to the Nellie Bly episode, Hearst directed his staff to invent a full-page feature about an orphan newsboy

and his brothers. Hearst's own mother, unaware the entire story was manufactured, was so moved by the pathetic tale that she sent a large sum of money to support the imaginary children. Thrilled by the possibilities, Hearst recruited three street children at random and depicted them in new clothing to demonstrate how the public awareness of the *Examiner* and "the generosity of Mrs. Hearst had saved them from squalor" (Swanberg, *Citizen Hearst,* 70). Mother Hearst was furious when she discovered her own son had duped her.

17. Swanberg, *Citizen Hearst,* 75; Procter, *William Randolph Hearst,* 52.

18. Swanberg, *Citizen Hearst,* 71.

19. Procter, *William Randolph Hearst,* 74.

20. Swanberg, *Citizen Hearst,* 60.

21. Nasaw, *The Chief,* 77.

22. Action and then self-congratulation was a favorite Hearst formula, which he continued in the *Journal.* To cite just two of countless instances, after a snowstorm wracked New York, headlines crowed, "*Journal*'s Relief Work Saves Many Poor Ones from Starvation" and "*Journal* Wagons Bring Life to Sufferers from Cold and Hunger" (*New York Journal,* January 29 and 30, 1897).

23. Hearst, editorial, *San Francisco Examiner,* October 30, 1897.

24. Hearst, editorial, *New York Journal,* April 21, 1897.

25. Hearst, editorial, *New York Journal,* March 19, 1897.

26. Hearst, editorial, *New York Journal,* April 21, 1897; Hearst, editorial, *New York Journal,* April 18, 1897.

27. Hearst, editorial, *New York Journal,* April 18, 1897.

28. Biographer Swanberg characterizes Hearst's journalistic "recipe" as "crime and underwear" and comments that if Pulitzer's *World* "was the organ of the underdog, the *Journal* fought for the *under* underdog" (*Citizen Hearst,* 102).

29. See earlier section for more information on the professionalization of authorship in terms of journalistic careers. Hearst recognized a thirst within the public for writer-heroes, and his brassy bylines both promoted and sated this thirst. Such editors as Pulitzer and Dana, who steadfastly refused to use bylines, lost readers to this cult of celebrity.

30. Qtd. in Swanberg, *Citizen Hearst,* 106.

31. Hearst, of course, was not the only editor who capitalized upon the conflict in Cuba. Pulitzer commissioned more than his share of Cuba-inspired stories. John Brisben Walker, editor of *Cosmopolitan* magazine, sent one of his reporters to the island in 1895 in an attempt to buy Cuban independence for $100,000,000 (Mott, *A History of American Magazines, 1885–1905,* 485).

32. Brown, *The Correspondents' War,* 93.

33. Swanberg, *Pulitzer,* 260.

34. Information about and by Cisneros came to the public in three stages, and I mix those three print sources in this section. First, various *Journal* reporters published articles about the imprisoned and newly freed Cisneros in August and October 1897. After her arrival in the United States, Cisneros wrote her own account of her tribulations for Sunday editions of the *Journal* (see figure p. 99). Finally, by

the end of 1897, the Continental Press published the stories of Cisneros and Decker, illustrated by Frederic Remington and with an introduction by Julian Hawthorne.

35. Swanberg, *Citizen Hearst,* 120.

36. Ibid.

37. Kendrick, "Better She Died than Reach Ceuta," *New York Journal,* August 18, 1897.

38. Creelman, "American Women Unite to Save Miss Cisneros," *New York Journal,* August 22, 1897.

39. Musgrave, "Miss Cisneros in Death's Shadow," *New York Journal,* August 23, 1897.

40. Swanberg, *Citizen Hearst,* 120.

41. Creelman, *On the Great Highway,* 180. An indication of the *Journal's* utter devotion to this story is evident by comparing how much space various New York papers devoted to Cisneros. While Hearst devoted 375 columnar inches of type to Cisneros, the *World* and *Times* provided only twelve and ten, respectively, much of that space given to attempts to debunk the validity of the *Journal* stories. The *Sun* devoted only a single column to Cisneros, and all other New York papers gave less than one inch to the story.

42. Cisneros and Decker, *The Story of Evangelina Cisneros,* 26.

43. Ibid., 65. In reality, Cisneros's prison conditions were far from squalid. She enjoyed her own room, which was, by most accounts, semi-luxurious, and she was catered meals separate from (and much superior to) those of the other inmates (Swanberg, *Citizen Hearst,* 124). Comparatively luxurious accommodations, however, simply would not suit a stereotypical romance. By embroidering the tale with sad details, Hearst's writers of course extended the motif of the innocent captive in its most logical direction.

44. Halstead, "Murat Halstead to the *Journal,*" *New York Journal,* October 10, 1897.

45. Musgrave, "Miss Cisneros in Death's Shadow," 1.

46. Despite the national fervor unleashed by the *Journal's* exposé of Cisneros's plight (their framing in romantic terms obviously struck a national nerve), most *Journal* employees "cursed the whole thing for a false bit of cheap sensationalism"—most, that is, except Hearst, who appropriately "felt himself in the role of Sir Galahad rescuing a helpless maiden" (Abbot, *Watching the World Go By,* 216).

47. Evangelina Cisneros and Karl Decker first published their own versions of captivity and escape in the October 17, 1897, *Journal*—the very day, coincidentally, that *New York Sun* editor Charles Dana died, as if symbolically conceding defeat to an ever brasher style of new journalism.

48. Cisneros and Decker, *The Story of Evangelina Cisneros,* 101. Cisneros was not the first woman rescued from jail by *Journal* reporters. In 1895 they freed a young woman wrongly accused, they claimed, of soliciting prostitution ("The Liberation of Lizzie Schauer," *New York Journal,* December 10, 1895).

49. Swanberg, *Citizen Hearst,* 125.

50. The *Journal* proudly reported that British novelist Anthony Hope—author of the wildly successful medievalist romance *The Prisoner of Zenda*—attended

and enjoyed the mass reception held for Cisneros at Madison Square Garden ("Greetings Pour in on the Heroine," *New York Journal,* October 18, 1897).

51. "Miss Cisneros to Be a U.S. Citizen," *New York Journal,* October 15, 1897. In medievalist stories of the 1890s, women were allowed some entry into the typically male preserve of warfare and military adventure. As T. J. Jackson Lears points out, "the heroines of chivalric fiction could sometimes ride, fight, and organize an army as well as any man"—a point illustrated by the frequency with which Joan of Arc appears as a character (*No Place of Grace,* 125). Another example is evident in Nellie Bly, who attempted two years before the Spanish-American War "to recruit a regiment of volunteers, officered by women, to fight for Cuban independence" ("Nellie Bly Proposes to Fight for Cuba," *New York World,* March 8, 1896). The *World* illustrated the announcement (featured in its weekly feature, "Daring Deeds by the Sunday *World*'s Intrepid Women Reporters") with a striking depiction of Bly as the "Fin de Siècle Joan of Arc." Cisneros first possessed the necessary pluck of this type of heroine; but when need for that "masculine" character passed, she slid seamlessly into her more naturally feminized role by blushing and shopping for dresses.

52. Milton, *The Yellow Kids,* 200.

53. Swanberg, *Citizen Hearst,* 125.

54. Milton, *The Yellow Kids,* 200.

55. "The Days of Knight Errantry Are Still with Us," *New York Journal,* October 13, 1897.

56. "America's Women and Statesmen Applaud the *Journal*'s Feat," *New York Journal,* October 11, 1897.

57. Halstead, "Murat Halstead to the *Journal,*" 2.

58. Editorial, *New York Journal,* October 11, 1897.

59. Editorial, *New York Journal,* October 15, 1897.

60. *New York Journal,* October 13, 1897.

61. Halstead, "Murat Halstead to the *Journal,*" 1.

62. Ibid.

63. Ibid.

64. Cisneros embarked on a tour of major U.S. cities to promote this book and the cause of Cuban liberation. The introduction to the book claimed that all profits from its sale would go to support Cisneros so that she would not need to rely on the continued generosity of her new American friends.

65. Hawthorne, introduction to *The Story of Evangelina Cisneros,* 17.

66. Ibid., 18.

67. Ibid.

68. Ibid., 19.

69. Ibid.

70. Ibid., 20.

71. Ibid.

72. It is important to note that the story was presented across America to an enormous audience, not simply to New Yorkers or even East Coast residents.

Newspapers across the nation carried the *Journal's* stories via the Associated Press wire service (Procter, *William Randolph Hearst*, 108).

73. Like the Lizzie Borden story, the Cisneros story appealed to readers so much because it relied on the elements of formula, or "familiar stories," in John Cawelti's words. Formula stories are sources of such pleasure because they "have highly predictable structures that guarantee the fulfillment of conventional expectations" (*Adventure, Mystery, and Romance* 1). These formulas work because they "establish a common ground between writers and audiences" (8). One of the most popular novels of the decade, *When Knighthood Was in Flower,* was published in the year following the Cisneros adventure and followed a specific formula of its own (Major, *When Knighthood Was in Flower*). This novel—which depicts a fictionalized love affair between a plucky Mary Tudor and a common knight—features Princess Mary's being held captive and attempting escape by disguising herself as a man. As I discuss in an earlier section, one other novelist who strove to break down barriers between what a novelist would do on paper and what he would do in real life was Richard Harding Davis. Critics lampooned Davis's genteelly chivalric demeanor as he strove to blend his life, art, and journalism into one seamless mass and provide further example of how to participate in romantic and martial ideals. To vast numbers of Americans, however, Davis was the modern hero "who would be accepted in the drawing rooms of the effete rich because his natural nobility gave him a place there," the hero "who could carry the principles of gentlemanliness into the most brutal situations and show that Americans, through birth and training, were adequate to them" (Ziff, *The American 1890s,* 174). Like the Cisneros story itself, Davis's life, work, and heroes (which were frequently indistinguishable) represented "a vision of life in which the old ideals" girding medievalism "could still work" (ibid., 182). Davis felt as though he "should have been born in the active days of knights-errant," just as he described one of his characters (qtd. as the epigram to this chapter; Davis, *The Princess Aline,* 5).

74. Lears, *No Place of Grace,* 103; Glazener, *Reading for Realism*; Link, "The War of 1893," 309–21; Ziff, *The American 1890s,* and Lears details the manner in which romance functioned at the turn of the century.

75. Mott, *Golden Multitudes,* 207, 311–12.

76. Ziff, *The American 1890s,* 78, 104. Some novels, like Major's and Crawford's, were set in medieval times. Others, like Hope's *The Prisoner of Zenda* (1894) and Richard Harding Davis's *The Princess Aline* (1895) and *Soldiers of Fortune* (1895) were contemporary but included an obvious "medieval" flair. For example, in Hope's novel, action occurs in the mythical kingdom of Ruritania, a land filled with crumbling old castles, in whose capital city "modern boulevards and residential quarters surround and embrace the narrow, tortuous, and picturesque streets of the original town" (Hope, *The Prisoner of Zenda,* 37). Furthermore, much of the inevitable swashbuckling adventure of the story involves detailed swordplay. Indeed, characters deliberately set aside their modern revolvers so that they can seek vengeance on one another using swords and daggers in a true show of

medievalist martial impulse. More directly, Davis's *Soldiers of Fortune,* set in a fictional, Cuba-like nation, is "an imperialistic rhapsody celebrating the triumph of the North American hero over his lethargic and corrupt Latin neighbors" (Lubow, *The ReporterWhoWould Be King,* 124). Davis's biographer speculates that the book was so popular and widely read that "in some unquantifiable way, it doubtless helped prime the national psyche for the collective adventure in Cuba" (124).

77. Mott, *Golden Multitudes,* 207. Edwin Arlington Robinson commented on medievalism more ironically in his poem "Miniver Cheevy" (1907):

> Miniver mourned the ripe renown
> That made so many a name so fragrant;
> He mourned Romance, now on the town,
> And Art, a vagrant.

78. Lears, *No Place of Grace,* 104.

79. Medievalism was displayed in such organizations as the Knights of Ak-Sar-Ben ("Nebraska" spelled backward), a fraternal organization of Omaha businessmen. Teddy Roosevelt enacted medievalism when he was training his men in Tampa before shipping out to Cuba by staging a mock battle complete with colorful banners and "with swords cutting gleaming curves in [the] bright sunshine" (Traxel, *1898,* 162). Medievalism even appeared in advertising at the 1893 Chicago World's Fair—the state of California, promoting its agricultural products, constructed a giant statue of a knight made entirely of prunes. The accompanying brochure asserted that California prunes "are being introduced victoriously into all lands, to the discomfiture of the products of other countries" (qtd. in Lears, *No Place of Grace,* 116).

80. Lears, *No Place of Grace,* 5.

81. Traxel, *1898,* 63.

82. Ibid., 63–64.

83. Ziff, *The American 1890s,* 87; Lears, *No Place of Grace,* viii.

84. Ziff, *The American 1890s,* 88.

85. Notably, even naturalism, as envisioned by its champion Frank Norris, grew from the artful synthesis of realism and romanticism. If realism dealt with "everyday" issues, romanticism picked up the "unplumbed depths of the human heart, and the mystery of sex, and the problems of life, and the black, unsearched penetralia of the soul of man" (qtd. in Pizer, introduction, 121). Naturalism transcended both realism and romance and drew from the best qualities of both forms of writing.

86. Lears, *No Place of Grace,* 98.

87. Ibid., 104.

88. Ibid., 102.

89. As journalism historian Milton points out, editors who highlighted the fabulous stories of new journalism "did not necessarily expect anyone to believe

them," especially if the stories originated in such "exotic" locales as Cuba. Rather, these news stories were considered "a form of good entertainment, a good source of fantasy and horror," much like medievalist novels (Milton, *The Yellow Kids,* 92).

90. Ziff, *The American 1890s,* 174.

91. "Greetings Pour in on the Heroine," *New York Journal,* October 18, 1897. Cisneros's husband, Carlos Carbonelle, was a U.S. citizen and Cuban junta agent in New York before the war. In 1898 he produced a letter for the *Journal* implicating Spain in the explosion of the battleship *Maine,* but the junta, from which most U.S. newspapers as well as the government took its official information, was a wellspring of completely manufactured news (Milton, *The Yellow Kids,* 231). After the war Cisneros and Carbonelle returned to Cuba for the remainder of their lives, and Carbonelle took up dentistry in Havana.

92. Milton, *The Yellow Kids,* 201–2.

Captive Cubans, International Impulses, and New Journalism

1. Bly, *Nellie Bly's Book,* 27.

2. The Borden case, for instance, unearthed the strong anxieties Anglo-Americans harbored about recent immigrants and violent crime in Fall River. Initial suspects in the case were a "disgruntled Portuguese laborer and a Swede who worked on Andrew Borden's farm" (Robertson, "Representing 'Miss Lizzie,'" 359). Class-based conflict arose after Borden's acquittal when the large Irish Catholic, French Canadian, and Portuguese populations in the city grew convinced that a native, wealthy woman had literally gotten away with murder.

3. VanDerBeets, *The Indian Captivity Narrative,* ix.

4. Ibid., ix–x; McCafferty, "Palimpsest of Desire," 43.

5. VanDerBeets, *The Indian Captivity Narrative,* 25.

6. "Straight" (i.e., clearly nonfiction) captivity narratives, such as Meginness's *Biography of Frances Slocum,* Fuller's *Left by the Indians,* and Baker's *True Stories of New England Captives,* also continued to find a popular audience.

7. American settlers in Hawaii overthrew the government of Queen Liliuokalani in 1893 and established the Republic of Hawaii in 1894. On August 12, 1898, as part of the pacts made at the close of the Spanish-American War, the United States negotiated a treaty of annexation with the republic, promising statehood in the future. Hawaii became a territory of the United States in 1900. Another territory ripe for American settlement efforts in the late nineteenth century was the immigrant portion of major cities. Writers and social reformers frequently "depicted the city as a new frontier or foreign territory to settle" (as in "settlement house") and to explore, and they "regarded its inhabitants—usually immigrants—as natives to civilize and control" (Kaplan and Pease, eds., *Cultures of United States Imperialism,* 45).

8. Lears, *No Place of Grace,* 102. This is not to say the *Journal* advocated outright territorial expansion. Americans—particularly East Coast Republicans—were wary

of traditional imperialism, but they did embrace the idea of economic expansion, which we see as one motivation for and outcome of the Spanish-American War. See Brands, *The Reckless Decade,* 295. Democrats and Populists had fewer scruples against expansionism, but even they were careful to distinguish themselves from outright imperialists.

9. Lears, *No Place of Grace,* 101.

10. Norris, "The Frontier Gone at Last," 1184.

11. Ibid.

12. Kendrick, "The Cuban Girl Martyr," 1.

13. Ibid.

14. Burnham, *Captivity and Sentiment,* 2.

15. Other forms of captivity narrative also inform this story. By the late nineteenth century, belief in the forced prostitution of white women by Eastern Europeans was a growing concern in America. Despite the slenderness of the evidence that such organized "white slavery" actually took place, an extensive set of captivity myths developed, growing out of this anxiety and leading to the 1910 Mann Act (the "White Slave Traffic Act"), which "prohibited interstate trafficking in women and girls for prostitution or 'any other immoral purpose'" (Grittner, "White Slavery," 2). The subtext of possible sexual violation running through the Cisneros narrative—with its accompanying emphasis on Cisneros's light complexion versus her captors' swarthiness—clearly operates within these same concerns. On a more theoretical level, Edward Griffin proposes interlocking layers of captivity in any captivity narrative, something we also see in the Cisneros story. Cisneros unwittingly held her Spanish captors captive in that they were under the intense scrutiny of the American public while the *Journal* focused attention on the imprisoned maiden. Furthermore, she "captivated" both Hearst and the American public, gaining an ironic power. However, her rescue from imprisonment was "not necessarily an escape from captivity" but "actually another version of captivity" since the captive becomes a commodity once a ransom has been paid for her (Griffin, "Women in Trouble," 46). Cisneros became a commodity in a most literal sense once the *Journal* reaped profit from her. So even after she was redeemed from her Havana prison cell, she was held captive by Hearst and by the American people. She was not an individual, but a persona with a set role to play: "The redeemed captive is henceforth purchased goods, owing his or her life to the people who put up the money. They all own a piece of her; she is their captive" (ibid.).

5. From There to Here

1. Cooke, "Jimmy's World," *Washington Post,* September 28, 1980.

2. All quotations in this paragraph are from Green, "The Players: It Wasn't a Game," *Washington Post,* April 19, 1981.

3. Simons, "Addict, 8, Is in Hiding, Mayor Says," *Washington Post,* October 1, 1980.

4. Ibid.

5. Ibid.

6. Simons and Knight, "Young 'Fagin' Is Nabbed," *Washington Post,* October 2, 1980.

7. Richburg, "Mayor Says City Ending Its Search for 'Jimmy,'" *Washington Post,* October 16, 1980.

8. Cooke, "Fear Stalks Oakwood Street," *Washington Post,* December 18, 1980.

9. Cooke, "Emotions High, Polished during Rally to Save Food Stamps," *Washington Post,* March 8, 1981.

10. Green, "The Players."

11. Ibid.

12. Ibid.

13. Ibid.

14. Editors recognized a variety of red flags only after Cooke's confession. In a prescient statement during a press conference on October 16, 1980, for instance, Marion Barry noted that "he and police department officials" were "convinced that the *Post* report . . . is at least part fabrication" (Richburg, "Mayor Says City Ending Its Search for 'Jimmy'"). It appears now that Cooke first heard reference to an eight-year-old child addict from social workers who operated a treatment program with Howard University psychiatrist Alyce Gullatte. Intrigued, Cooke tried to arrange a meeting with the boy, which Gullatte refused to set up. Later, investigators for the National News Council learned that Gullatte had called the *Post* after "Jimmy's World" was published to voice her suspicions that the story was fictitious. Though she later refused to speak further with police and investigating officials, Gullatte did denounce the *Post* on a mid-April television show "for having impugned her motives when she sought unsuccessfully to warn it about the story" (National News Council, *After "Jimmy's World,"* 40). Coincidentally, less than a month before her exposure, Cooke herself authored an article about the spread of a rumor that Vice President George H. W. Bush had been shot, remarking that "the story had everything going for it but the truth" (Cooke, "Anatomy of a Washington Rumor," *Washington Post,* March 22, 1981). Additionally, just before her resignation, Cooke had been working on yet another sensational story—this time the subject was a fourteen-year-old prostitute. When editors pressed Cooke to arrange a meeting between them and the fourteen-year-old, the reporter repeatedly set meeting times but then canceled them, providing only flimsy excuses for the cancellations. Apparently, Cooke was well on her way to creating another "fictionalized" story.

15. See, for instance, Grossberger and Howard, "The Pulitzer Prize Hoax," *Newsweek,* April 27, 1981; Griffith, "Washing Dirty Linen in Public," *Time,* April 16, 1984; Wright, "The Lie Machinery Stirs," *New Statesman,* May 1981; Nobile, "The Pulitzer Surprise: Janet Cooke's False Report," *New York,* April 27, 1981; McGrath, "A Fraud in the Pulitzers," *Time,* April 27, 1981; R. Emmett Tyreel Jr., "Bogus Operandi," *Washington Post,* May 8, 1981; Pianin, "Cooke's 'Today' Interview," *Washington Post,* January 30, 1982; Cattani and Malone, "Hoax Story Sparks

Soul-Searching among Nation's Media," *Christian Science Monitor,* April 20, 1981; Bates, "Why Embellishment Can Be So Tempting," *Los Angeles Times,* June 29, 1998; National News Council, *After Jimmy's World;* and "A Pulitzer Fake: The Echoes Linger," *U.S. News and World Report,* April 27, 1981. The shock and outrage were compounded by the facts that Cooke had won the highest award possible in the ranks of journalism; that the *Washington Post* was, along with the *New York Times,* a national paper of record (the very paper, no less, that had, having exposed the Watergate scandal, elevated itself as a symbol of truth); and that Cooke was a young black woman working precisely at a time when both women and African-Americans were struggling to defend their professional roles in an increasingly conservative society. Consequently, Cooke's name "has come to symbolize such diverse issues as plagiarism and fabrication, anonymity and unnamed sources, minority recruitment, newsroom ethics, résumé fraud, the precarious practice of New Journalism" (National News Council, *After Jimmy's World,* 203). At the same time, the fact that Cooke had committed professional fraud in composing false résumés appeared only as the insult added to a grievous injury, never as the primary cause of outrage.

16. Michener, "On Integrity in Journalism," *U.S. News and World Report,* May 4, 1981.

17. Sanoff, "Uneasy Press Sets Out to Refurbish Its Image," *U.S. News and World Report,* June 29, 1981. See also *After Jimmy's World*—in which National News Council chairman Norman Isaacs charged that the "permissiveness and arrogance" of new journalism was directly to blame for such embarrassments as "Jimmy's World"—and John Hersey's "The Legend on the License." Wolfe coined the term "new journalism" to characterize this group of writers; his label was, however, anti-historical and not reflective of any aspect of nineteenth-century new journalism (though they were in fact quite similar).

18. National News Council, *After Jimmy's World,* 49.

19. Mailer's publishers promoted *The Executioner's Song* as both "a novel" and "a model of precise and accurate reporting" (Fishkin, *From Fact to Fiction,* 208). Similarly, Capote insisted that he and the other new journalists of his generation invented a new literary form—the "nonfiction novel"—which offered a synthesis between fact and fiction that had never before been attempted.

20. Sims, ed., *The Literary Journalists,* 5.

21. National News Council, *After Jimmy's World,* 3.

22. See Cohen, "8-Year-Old Shoots Up: A Question of Caring," *Washington Post,* September 30, 1980; Milloy and Cooke, "Custody of Boy with Arm Marks Brings Dismay," *Washington Post,* November 30, 1980; Cooke and Simons, "Children and Drugs," *Washington Post,* October 5, 1980; Cooke and Richburg, "Drug Sales Probed at District Schools during Past Year," *Washington Post,* October 7, 1980; Simons, "D.C. Authorities Seek Identity of Heroin Addict, 8," *Washington Post,* September 30, 1980; and Simons and Knight, "Young 'Fagin' Is Nabbed."

23. See, for instance, Gold, "The Problem Is All Too Real," *Washington Post,* April 17, 1981; and Parnass, "News as Routinely Reconstituted Reality," *New York Times,* May 5, 1981.

24. Cooke's action has been, to my knowledge, universally read as a self-serving lie intended to further her own career. While this reading may be accurate to large degree, we should not discount other motives for her embroidery of the truth in "Jimmy's World." Cooke had already coauthored a number of very factually based stories about childhood drug abuse, and, given her work in the field, "Jimmy's World" may have grown out of her desire to bring this serious issue to life in readers' eyes. Her motives for fabricating may very well have been self-serving, or the latest example in a lifelong pattern of deception, but she may also have had more altruistic aims behind her article. She may, in other words, have been aiming for the "larger truths" that composite figures and human drama can illustrate in news articles. Perhaps Cooke intuitively understood, as Hearst did, that unless an issue needing public attention can be dramatized in narrative, it cannot compete successfully against the scores of other issues clamoring for attention. If this was in fact Cooke's understanding, her efforts in this case backfired. The public has to accept the news story, and, in the standards of contemporary journalism, if an audience doubts the veracity of the story, the issue will not achieve public acceptance, let alone action and policy.

25. Pulitzer provided for the prizes in his 1904 will, originally establishing awards in journalism, letters and drama, education, and traveling scholarship. The prizes for photojournalism and feature writing were added in 1942 and 1978, respectively.

26. Hoffman and Murphy, eds., *Critical Essays in American Modernism*, 8.

27. I do not intend in this chapter to write a complete history of press criticism at the turn of the century, nor do I intend to write a full study of modernism and its connection to newspaper aesthetics. Rather, I will examine some of the highlights of these histories in order to suggest their mutual dependence and development. For additional relevant studies, see works by Dicken-Garcia, Marzolf, Orvell, Strychacz, and Tichi.

28. Qtd. in Marzolf, *Civilizing Voices*, 11.

29. Thomas, "The Psychology of Yellow Journalism," *American Magazine* 65 (1908): 493.

30. Pallen, "Newspaperism," *Lippincott's Monthly Magazine* 32 (1886): 472.

31. Guerra, "Henry James's Paradoxical Bowl: The Reinstatement of Doubt in *Fin-de-Siècle* America," *Style* 32 (1998): 61.

32. Bleyer, ed., *Profession of Journalism*, xiv.

33. Ibid., xv, xix. See also Bleyer, *Newspaper Writing and Editing*, 242 and 406. Other fears led critics to argue for clear disciplinary boundaries, as Hersey was to articulate nearly a century later: "The moment the reader suspects" fictionalizing in any part of journalism, "the earth begins to skid underfoot, for the idea that there is no way of knowing what is real and what is not real is terrifying." Also, "even more terrifying is the notion that lies are truths" ("The Legend on the License," 2). Little lies lead to big lies, in Hersey's eyes, and catastrophes such as Watergate were the inevitable result.

34. Thomas, "The Psychology of Yellow Journalism," 492.

35. Ibid., 495.

36. Marzolf, *Civilizing Voices,* 4.

37. Warner, "Newspapers and the Public," *Forum* 9 (1890): 201.

38. Thomas, "The Psychology of Yellow Journalism," 491.

39. Warner, "Better Newspapers," *Journalist,* May 1, 1897, 14.

40. Of course, new journalism—which by this time was almost universally dubbed "yellow journalism"—continued to boast its supporters. In an echo of Hearst, famous editor Arthur Brisbane declared that "yellow journalism is the journalism of action, and responsibility. . . . Yellow journalism is simply Real journalism" (Brisbane, "Yellow Journalism," 400). Lydia Commander added that new journalism was a "living creature" that acts while "ordinary journalism talks" ("The Significance of Yellow Journalism," 151).

41. See Dicken-Garcia, *Journalistic Standards in Nineteenth-Century America,* 167. Lambert Wilmer (Edgar Allan Poe's partner in planning a doomed literary magazine) published *Our Press Gang,* an early scathing attack on American newspapers, in 1860. One of his principal arguments was that newspapers debased literature—an argument that gained force amongst well-heeled readers as the century progressed. The need to "defend" literature against the nefarious influence of the press became one of the most pronounced elements of fin-de-siècle press criticism.

42. Washington College offered a journalism course in 1869, Cornell awarded a "Certificate of Journalism" in 1875, and the University of Missouri developed a journalism curriculum in 1878. Missouri went on to establish the nation's first full school of journalism in 1908, and Columbia University opened its Department of Journalism in 1912 (although Pulitzer had provided the program's endowment nine years earlier). See Dicken-Garcia, Marzolf, and also Louis Dudek (*Literature and the Press*). By 1912 three professional schools were open (Missouri, Marquette, and Columbia), and by 1918 at least twenty American schools offered courses in journalism.

43. Editorial, *Dial* 15 (1893): 79.

44. "Equipment for Journalism," *Editor and Publisher,* August 20, 1910, 4.

45. Harrington and Frankenberg, *Essentials in Journalism,* ix.

46. Ibid., xv.

47. A 1900 content analysis of newspapers found that of 147 city newspapers from twenty-one urban areas surveyed, forty-seven were "yellow," forty-five "conservative," and the rest a combination of the two. "Crime, vice, illustrations, want ads, medical ads, and self-advertising belonged to the yellow press, while conservative papers"—to which I refer as information-model papers—"had more political news, business news, letters, exchanges, and miscellaneous advertisements" (Marzolf, *Civilizing Voices,* 28).

48. "Objective" was not a word that critics used in regard to journalism until after the 1920s. Before then, newspapers were praised or criticized depending on their treatment of facts, a word that simply signified information. This information, however, "was not objectivity; the attachment to information did not betray much anxiety about the subjectivity of personal perspective" until after developments in psychology called it into question (Schudson, *Discovering the News,* 120).

49. Ibid., 90.

50. Marzolf argues that press criticism "arises from certain most interested circles: culture critics and preservers; political and social advocates; journalists and scholars. Thus, it generally tends to reinforce both the elitist value of a press ideal and the popular value of a democratic, open society" (*Civilizing Voices,* 2).

51. Schudson, *Discovering the News,* 107. Again, we have no real way of determining absolutely what members of particular social sets actually read. Consider, for instance, that Joseph Pulitzer once answered Matthew Arnold's criticism of sensational papers by noting that "like everybody else, Matthew buys and reads the newspapers that are racy." Likewise, E. L. Godkin complained that new journalism drew readers from all levels of society; "This stuff is greedily read by all classes," he observed, adding that "the grumblers over the wicked journals are often their most diligent readers" (qtd. in Schudson, *Discovering the News,* 117). Commander concurs, asking, "Is not the difference between the readers and the critics of the yellow press one of cultivation, rather than of kind? The latter simply prefer scandal, crime and conflict that deal with imaginary or historical characters" ("The Significance of Yellow Journalism," 150). Critics retorted that while the favorite subjects of newspaper stories—"love, hate, fear, despair, intrigue, sentiment, adventure, and the marvelous"—also seemed to be common "subjects of art," newspaper fictions could never be called artful, for "art in the proper sense . . . handles its materials from a generalized or ideal standpoint" (Thomas, "The Psychology of Yellow Journalism," 493).

52. Ochs, "Business Announcement," *New York Times,* August 19, 1896.

53. Schudson, *Discovering the News,* 119.

54. Ibid., 114. In comparison, the *World's* circulation in 1896 was 600,000, the *Journal's* 430,000, and the *Sun's* 130,000. Ochs's efforts were supplemented by the increased power of press associations at the turn of the century. Of international importance, such associations as the Associated Press (which began in the midnineteenth century but reached its final form in 1900), the United Press (formed in 1907 by Edward Scripps), and International News Service (organized in 1909 by Hearst) helped standardize the way news was transmitted and delivered—the AP, for instance, instructed correspondents to "avoid fine writing, . . . wild rumours, unverified stories" and to write "as briefly as is consistent with an intelligent statement of facts" (Shudson, *Discovering the News,* 84). While the *Times's* rising circulation signaled its elevation to its current respected status, the other papers I have surveyed in this study did not survive. The *World* started its downward slide in 1923 and ceased publication in 1931, officially ending an era. The *Sun* went downhill quickly after Frank Munsey purchased it in 1916. Although Hearst built his powerful publishing empire of today by purchasing many large newspapers and magazines, his *Journal* died in 1967, having survived two major mergers prior to that time.

55. Qtd. in Berger, *The Story of the New York Times, 1851–1951,* 126. Susan E. Tifft and Alex S. Jones, in *The Trust,* argue that Ochs did not seek to lure readers away from new journalism, but that he lowered the price of the *Times* in order to

attract readers of other quality papers, namely the *Herald* and the *Tribune*. What this view ignores, however, is the subtext that underwrote the *Times's* success and the spread of "information" as the standard journalistic model. The paper "succeeded because it appeared on the scene at a time of widespread emulation and conspicuous consumption," leading less wealthy classes of people to read the paper because "the elite reads it" (Schudson, *Discovering the News*, 116). The information-model paper "attracted readers among the wealthy and among those aspiring to wealth and status, in part, because it was socially approved. It was itself a badge of respectability" awarded by cultural critics, who held the power to proclaim what was "the real thing" in society and what was just a bad replication. The *Times*, those critics maintained, was the best example of what "real" journalism should look like. New journalism, on the other hand, was just a cheap knock-off of fiction—and frequently "bad" fiction, at that.

56. Marzolf, *Civilizing Voices*, 31. While Pulitzer came around, to some degree, to Ochs's model of journalism, Hearst continued in the same track he had been following since moving to New York. Practicing the highest drama, he eventually built an enormous media conglomerate and gained incredible political power (he was elected to the U.S. House of Representatives twice, nearly won the Democratic nomination for president in 1904, and made an unsuccessful bid for New York governor in 1906).

57. Qtd. in Marzolf, *Civilizing Voices*, 31.

58. "The Pulitzer School," *Editor and Publisher*, August 22, 1903.

59. At the end of the nineteenth century, New York City alone was home to "over ten thousand illustrators and engravers, all employed by newspaper or publishing houses" (Lemagny and Rouillé, eds., *A History of Photography*, 76). By 1903 career advisor Edwin Shuman noted that "there is a brisk demand for good photographers with a nose for news and a genius for getting good pictures of the right kind" (*Steps into Journalism*, 145).

60. Carlebach, *The Origins of Photojournalism in America*, 1. By the end of the century some "sketch artists were carrying portable cameras with them on their assignments, for the purpose of 'taking notes'" (Lemagny and Rouillé, *A History of Photography*, 76). Other inventions that encouraged the portability of photography included dry plates, faster shutters, and artificial lighting (Carlebach, *The Origins of Photojournalism in America*, 159).

61. Carlebach, *The Origins of Photojournalism in America*, 159.

62. Ibid., 2. Less naïve Americans realized photographs could of course be altered and were in no way an absolute record of the real thing. The delightful story "Faking as a Fine Art" recounts the adventures of a reporter who "never wrote even one story that had the element of truth in it except as a possibility" ("Faking as a Fine Art," 89). The reporter's editor commonly illustrates these bogus stories with stock photographs he had purchased en masse during a European trip and altered to appear appropriate, for "readers will not believe a story if it is illustrated by drawings; but print a photograph, and they accept it" (96). The first half-tone photographic reproduction in a newspaper appeared in the weekly

New York Daily Graphic in 1880, but photographs did not debut in the dailies until the very end of the century. Lemagny and Rouillé attribute the first photographic image in a newspaper to an 1897 image published on the front page of the *New York Tribune* (*A History of Photography*, 78). During the Spanish-American War the *New York World* published several photographs taken by a reporter named, interestingly, William Randolph. These years saw artists attempting "to compete with photographs by executing their own 'instant' sketches," while "photographs, often very much retouched and in heavy halftones, really did come to look like engravings" (Lemagny and Rouillé, *A History of Photography*, 77). After 1900 "gelatin-based roll film created a national market for news pictures" (Carlebach, *The Origins of Photojournalism in America*, 2), and between 1900 and 1914 "many dailies converted to photographic illustrations" (Lemagny and Rouillé, *A History of Photography*, 78).

63. Thompson, "The Domain of Romance," 327; Carlebach, *The Origins of Photojournalism in America*, 1.

64. Borus, *Writing Realism*, 24.

65. Ibid., 691.

66. Howells, *Criticism and Fiction*, 160.

67. James, "The Art of Fiction," 170, 177.

68. Ibid., 173, 182.

69. James, "Question of Our Speech," 28–29.

70. Connection to that mass marketplace was most humorously illustrated by an 1896 *Journal* headline reviewing James's *The Other House:* "Henry James' New Novel of Immorality and Crime; The Surprising Plunge of the Great Novelist in the Field of Sensational Fiction" (qtd. in Emery, Emery, and Roberts, 200). Howells and James both created a fair share of journalist characters in their fiction, employing such figures as Basil March and Henrietta Stackpole to comment satirically on the state of the modern newspaper business.

71. James, "The Question of the Opportunities," 20–21.

72. Robertson, *Stephen Crane*, 17.

73. Ibid., 13.

74. Indeed, from at least the 1830s elite writers had complained that newspapers were stealing away literary audiences. Ralph Waldo Emerson, for instance, discounted the growing circulation of the *Boston Globe* in 1838, claiming the people who read it were "as yet in too crude a state of nonage to deserve any regard" (qtd. in Robertson, *Stephen Crane*, 11). Henry David Thoreau, likewise, remarked in 1854 that newspapers were the "only book[s] which America has printed, and which America reads." This, however, was not a point of pride in Thoreau's eyes, for those who read newspapers "are in the condition of the dog that returns to its vomit" (Thoreau, *Reform Papers*, 100).

75. Robertson, *Stephen Crane*, 17.

76. Park, "The Yellow Press," 3. High-toned and culturally powerful magazines like *Arena, Atlantic Monthly, Harper's Monthly, Scribner's, The Nation,* and *North American Review* likewise argued that new journalism further debased the literary

tastes of the masses. They envisioned themselves steadfastly upholding "a respectable literary tradition in America" precisely at a time when newspapers were considered literary material by many readers (Marzolf, *Civilizing Voices,* 10). America could be saved from its own mass reading tastes only by defining journalism around a strictly enforced information model and leaving literature to perform society's loftiest storytelling functions—all the while urging lower- and middle-class readers to reach for ever-higher planes of thought and taste. Meanwhile, truly genteel readers would continue to define themselves within the confines of a coterie system, indulging in and supporting the little magazines of the 1890s.

77. Singal, ed., *Modernist Culture in America,* 2, 4. It should go without saying that such large-scale classifications as "realism" and "modernism" did not constitute the whole story of literary practice before and after the turn of the century. These classifications, however, do provide insight into the most relevant influences on journalism and literary standards.

78. Ibid., 13; qtd. in Hoffman and Murphy, eds., *Critical Essays in American Modernism,* 25.

79. Orvell, *The Real Thing,* 240.

80. Ibid., 241–42, 249.

81. Williams, "A Beginning on the Short Story (Notes)," 303.

82. Qtd. in Kenner, *The Pound Era,* 174; Pound, *The Literary Essays,* 3. The modernists quite literally wrote manifestos in the true sense of the word: as an attempt to change the focus of current thought and practice. Beginning in the March 1913 issue of *Poetry,* Pound and F. S. Flint composed statements describing their new aesthetic and argued against romantic tradition.

83. Pound, *Literary Essays,* 4–5, 50.

84. Tichi, *Shifting Gears,* 257.

85. *Some Imagist Poets,* vi.

86. Fishkin, *From Fact to Fiction,* 138.

87. Garst and Bernstein, *Headlines and Deadlines,* 155.

88. Bleyer, *Newspaper Writing and Editing,* 406.

89. Harrington and Frankenberg, *Essentials in Journalism,* 3.

90. Lewis, "The Liberation of Words: Williams's Verbal Imagism," 19.

91. Pound, *Literary Essays,* 4.

92. Qtd. in Kenner, *The Pound Era,* 185.

93. Qtd. ibid.

94. Ezra Pound, "In a Station of the Metro," *Poetry* 2 (1913): 12.

95. *Some Imagist Poets,* vii.

96. Pound, *Literary Essays,* 43–44.

97. Ibid., 6.

98. Poe, "The Poetic Principle," 91.

99. Stein, *Selected Writings of Gertrude Stein,* 201.

100. Strychacz, *Modernism, Mass Culture, and Professionalism,* 6.

101. Several more notorious "scandals" of fiction have surfaced in subsequent

years, including the use of composites in nonfiction pieces in the *New Yorker* (see Sam Zagoria, "*New Yorker,* How Could You?" *Washington Post,* June 27, 1984); overly colorful writing in the *Miami Post*'s coverage of Columbian drug trafficking (see Zagoria, "When Facts Get Lost Amid Drama," *Washington Post,* April 3, 1985); Stephen Glass's fabrications for the *New Republic* (see William Powers, "The Use and Abuse of Fiction," *National Journal,* June 27, 1998); and Patricia Smith's invented quotations in the *Boston Globe* (see Powers). Even Teresa Carpenter of the *Village Voice,* who won the Pulitzer in place of Cooke, received criticism for "a writing style so colored and imaginative as to blur precise meanings" (see Ann L. Trebbe, "Personalities," *Washington Post,* November 21, 1981). See also Sanoff; Marvin Kalb, "News-for-Profit," *Minneapolis Star Tribune,* July 13, 1998; Daniel Schorr, "Journalism's Litany of Sins Against Unabsolving Public," *Minneapolis Star Tribune,* July 14, 1998; David Daley, "Journalists' Ethical Lapses Stain Media," *Arizona Republic,* September 14, 1999; David Parish, Michael Murphy, and Maureen Jenkins, "Untraceable Sources Are Columnist's Undoing," *Minneapolis Star Tribune,* August 26, 1999; "Their Fake Story," *Minneapolis Star Tribune,* December 9, 2000; and "*Globe* Suspends Columnist for Alleged Misconduct," *Minneapolis Star Tribune,* July 9, 2000. Janet Cooke's name, long the standard bearer for journalistic sin, may very well be eclipsed fully by that of another notorious fictionalizer—Jayson Blair, formerly of the *New York Times,* whom I discuss briefly below.

102. Hersey, "The Legend on the License," 3.

103. Liza Mundy, "The Second Chance Club," *Washington Post,* October 3, 1999; National News Council, *After Jimmy's World,* 58; Bruce Nolan, "Fallen Reporter's Quest Raises Ethical Questions," *New Orleans Times-Picayune,* May 18, 1996. Cooke's career never recovered, and the fact that her name continues to be associated with a cardinal professional sin ensures that she will never again work in journalism, despite her recent efforts to redeem herself and reenter the writing world. After fleeing the *Post,* Cooke married an American diplomat, floundered in Paris for several years, divorced bitterly, and struggled near destitution as a retail clerk in Toledo. By 1996 she was working for six dollars an hour in a department store in Kalamazoo, Michigan. In an interview that year with a former *Post* colleague and friend, Cooke attributed her "mistake" to her strict father, explaining that "lying, from a very early age, was the best survival mechanism available. . . . It was like, do you unleash the wrath of Dad's temper, or do you tell something that is not exactly true and be done with it?" (Sager, "Janet's World," 206). In this construction, then, "Jimmy's World" was not about hoaxing the public; rather, it was "a highly personal act in a highly personal drama, a choice of action best explained, perhaps, as a damaged person's attempt to right the wrongs of her past, to overcome the paralyzing condition of self-loathing and self-doubt" (ibid., 204).

104. Haynes Johnson, "A Wound That Will Be Long in Healing and Never Forgotten," *Washington Post,* April 19, 1981.

105. Parnass, "News as Routinely Reconstituted Reality," 22.

106. Eason, "On Journalistic Authority," 206.

107. Ibid., 207.

108. Ibid.

109. Commander, "The Significance of Yellow Journalism," 150.

110. Howard Kurtz, "More Reporting by *Times* Writer Called Suspect," *Washington Post,* May 8, 2003.

111. The parallels between Jayson Blair and Janet Cooke are indeed striking. Both are African American; both were accused of obtaining their positions because of "racial quotas" rather than skill; both rose in journalistic ranks at noteworthy speed; and both left trails of lies in their educational institutions.

112. Adler, "The Porch Overlooks No Such Thing," 16.

113. Woo, "Journalism's 'Normal Accidents,'" 51.

114. Baker and Bartosiewicz, "'Scoops' and Truth at the *Times,*" 20.

115. Some commentators suggest that this is, indeed, the path American journalism seems to be taking. Woo observes that despite editorial claims that accuracy always comes first, "what ties together Jayson Blair, Patricia Smith, Mike Barnicle, Janet Cooke, Stephen Glass," and other journalistic "fictionalizers" and plagiarizers is that "all were valued for their narrative skills, for their 'storytelling' ability. None was recognized for reporting skills" based on information gathering alone (Woo, "Journalism's 'Normal Accidents,'" 51). Alarmed by such emphasis on careless storytelling over fact, particularly in light of newspaper coverage leading to the Iraq war and increasingly partisan political reporting, media critics have called for more transparency in divulging how news is made and framed for American readers and viewers. Michael Tomasky points out that while politically conservative newspapers "have less of a problem of thinking of themselves as an organ of the party to which they're sympathetic," other national papers, including the *New York Times* and the *Washington Post,* "have a different attitude and a different model of journalism. It's an old-fashioned and antiquated . . . and maybe threatened model—trying to establish their independence and integrity and trying to show that by being critical more often." But what happens to these familiar standards if large portions of the American population define "news" not in terms of independence, integrity, and critical perspective, but in terms of reinforcement of the (often biased) opinions they already hold? Marvin Kalb comments that traditional newspapers now face a journalistic machine that functions to satisfy "Americans seeking not *news* when they turn on the news, but rather confirmation of what they already know, or think, or prefer" (Tomasky, "Who Slants More?").

BIBLIOGRAPHY

Abbot, Willis J. *Watching the World Go By.* Boston: Little, Brown, 1933.

Adler, Gabriela Schalow. "Our Beloved Lizzie: Constructing an American Legend." Ph.D. diss., University of Rhode Island, 1995.

Adler, Renata. "The Porch Overlooks No Such Thing." *American Spectator* 36 (2003): 14–22.

"America's Women and Statesmen Applaud the *Journal's* Feat." *New York Journal,* October 11, 1897.

Anthony, David. "The Helen Jewett Panic: Tabloids, Men, and the Sensational Public Sphere in Antebellum New York." *American Literature* 69 (1997): 487–514.

Arnold, Matthew. "Up to Easter." *Nineteenth Century* 21 (1887): 629–43.

"Around the World." *New York World,* November 14, 1889.

Baker, Charlotte Alice. *True Stories of New England Captives Carried to Canada during the Old French and Indian Wars.* Cambridge, Mass.: E. A. Hall, 1897.

Baker, Russ, and Petra Bartosiewicz. "'Scoops' and Truth at the *Times.*" *Nation* (June 23, 2003): 18–20.

Barnum, P. T. *The Humbugs of the World.* 1865. Detroit, Mich.: Singing Tree, 1970.

Bates, Karen Grigsby. "Why Embellishment Can Be So Tempting." *Los Angeles Times,* June 29, 1998.

Bell, Michael Davitt. *The Problem of American Realism: Studies in the Cultural History of a Literary Idea.* Chicago: Univ. of Chicago Press, 1993.

Belloc, Marie A. "Jules Verne at Home." *Strand* 9 (1895): 206–13.

Bennett, Maurice J. "Edgar Allan Poe and the Literary Tradition of Lunar Speculation." *Science-Fiction Studies* 10 (1983): 137–47.

Berger, Meyer. *The Story of the* New York Times, *1851–1951.* New York: Simon and Schuster, 1951.

Bird, S. Elizabeth, and Robert W. Dardenne. "News and Storytelling in American Culture: Reevaluating the Sensational Dimension." *Journal of American Culture* 13, no. 2 (1990): 33–37.

Bleeker, Ann Eliza. *The History of Maria Kittle.* Hartford, Conn.: Elisha Babcock, 1797.

Bleyer, Willard Grosvenor. *Newspaper Writing and Editing.* 1913. Boston: Houghton Mifflin, 1923.

————, ed. *The Profession of Journalism*. Boston: Atlantic Monthly, 1918.

Bloom, Clive, et al., eds. *Nineteenth-Century Suspense: From Poe to Conan Doyle*. New York: St. Martin's, 1988.

Bly, Nellie. *The Mystery of Central Park*. New York: G. W. Dillingham, 1889.

————. *Nellie Bly's Book: Around the World in Seventy-Two Days*. New York: Pictorial Weeklies, 1890.

————. *Ten Days in a Mad-House*. New York: Munro, 1887.

"Bly Versus Verne." *New York World,* November 16, 1889.

"A Boom for Geography." *New York World,* December 21, 1889.

Borus, Daniel H. *Writing Realism: Howells, James, and Norris in the Mass Market*. Chapel Hill: Univ. of North Carolina Press, 1989.

Boyesen, H. H. "Why We Have Got No Great Novelists." *Forum* 2 (1887): 615–22.

Brands, H. W. *The Reckless Decade: America in the 1890s*. New York: St. Martin's, 1995.

Brett, George Ira. "The Murder at Jex Farm." In *The Long Arm and Other Stories,* 67–138. London: Chapman and Hall, 1895.

Brigham, Clarence S. *Poe's Balloon Hoax*. Metuchen, N.J.: American Book Collector, 1932.

Brisbane, Arthur. "Yellow Journalism." *Bookman* 19 (1904): 400–404.

Brown, Charles H. *The Correspondents' War: Journalists in the Spanish-American War*. New York: Scribner's, 1967.

Budd, Louis J. "The American Background." In *The Cambridge Companion to American Realism and Naturalism,* ed. Donald Pizer, 21–46. New York: Cambridge Univ. Press, 1995.

Burgess, Douglas K. "Norris's Van Bubbles Story: Bursting the Bubble of the Davis Mystique." *Frank Norris Studies* 15 (1993): 10–13.

Burnham, Michelle. *Captivity and Sentiment: Cultural Exchange in American Literature, 1682–1861*. Hanover, N.H.: Univ. Press of New England, 1997.

Butcher, William. Introduction to *Around the World in Eighty Days,* by Jules Verne. Oxford, U.K.: Oxford Univ. Press, 1995.

Capote, Truman. *In Cold Blood: A True Account of a Multiple Murder and Its Consequences*. New York: Random, 1966.

Carlebach, Michael L. *The Origins of Photojournalism in America*. Washington, D.C.: Smithsonian Institution, 1992.

Carlson, Eric W., ed. *A Companion to Poe Studies*. Westport, Conn.: Greenwood, 1996.

"A Case of Conscience." *New York Sun,* August 11, 1835.

Cattani, Richard J., and Julia Malone. "Hoax Story Sparks Soul-Searching among Nation's Media." *Christian Science Monitor,* April 20, 1981.

Cawelti, John G. *Adventure, Mystery, and Romance: Formula Stories as Art and Popular Culture*. Chicago: Univ. of Chicago Press, 1976.

Cisneros, Evangelina, and Karl Decker. *The Story of Evangelina Cisneros*. New York: Continental, 1897.

Cohen, Richard. "8-Year-Old Shoots Up: A Question of Caring." *Washington Post,* September 30, 1980.

Collins, James H. "The American Grub Street." In *The Profession of Journalism,* ed. Willard Grosvenor Bleyer, 243–63. Boston: Atlantic Monthly, 1918.

Commander, Lydia Kingsmill. "The Significance of Yellow Journalism." *Arena* 34 (1905): 150–55.

Connery, Thomas B. "Fusing Fictional Technique and Journalistic Fact: Literary Journalism in the 1890s Newspaper." Ph.D. diss., Brown University, 1983.

Cook, Thomas. *Letters from the Sea and from Foreign Lands, Descriptive of a Tour Round the World.* New York: Thomas Cook, 1873.

Cooke, Janet. "Anatomy of a Washington Rumor." *Washington Post,* March 22, 1981.

———. "Emotions High, Polished during Rally to Save Food Stamps." *Washington Post,* March 8, 1981.

———. "Fear Stalks Oakwood Street." *Washington Post,* December 18, 1980.

———. "Jimmy's World." *Washington Post,* September 28, 1980.

Cooke, Janet, and Keith B. Richburg. "Drug Sales Probed at District Schools during Past Year." *Washington Post,* October 7, 1980.

Cooke, Janet, and Lewis M. Simons. "Children and Drugs." *Washington Post,* October 5, 1980.

Costello, Peter. *Jules Verne: Inventor of Science Fiction.* New York: Scribner's, 1978.

Crane, Stephen. "War Memories." In *Wounds in the Rain,* 229–308. New York: Frederick A. Stokes, 1900.

Crawford, Marion. *Via Crucis: A Romance of the Second Crusade.* New York: Grosset and Dunlap, 1899.

Creelman, James. "American Women Unite to Save Miss Cisneros." *New York Journal,* August 22, 1897.

———. *On the Great Highway: The Wanderings and Adventures of a Special Correspondent.* Boston: Lothrop, Lee, and Shepard, 1901.

Cunningham, Gail. *The New Woman and the Victorian Novel.* New York: Barnes and Noble, 1978.

Daley, David. "Journalists' Ethical Lapses Stain Media." *Arizona Republic,* September 14, 1999.

Darrow, Clarence. "Realism in Literature and Art." *Arena* 9 (1893): 98–113.

Davis, Richard Harding. *Gallegher and Other Stories.* New York: Scribner's, 1891.

———. "Our Green Reporter." *New York Evening Sun,* November 2, 1889.

———. *The Princess Aline.* New York: Harper, 1899.

———. *Soldiers of Fortune.* New York: Scribner's, 1897.

———. *Van Bibber and Others.* New York: Scribner's, 1892.

———. "Van Bibber and the Swan-Boats." *Gallegher and Other Stories.* 1891. New York: Garrett, 1968.

Day, Benjamin. "The Great Astronomical Discoveries." *New York Sun,* September 16, 1835.

"A Day More." *New York World,* January 24, 1890.

"The Days of Knight Errantry Are Still with Us." *New York Journal,* October 13, 1897.

De Forest, John W. "The Great American Novel." *Nation* 6 (1868): 27–29.

Dicken-Garcia, Hazel. *Journalistic Standards in Nineteenth-Century America.* Madison: Univ. of Wisconsin Press, 1989.

Doyle, Arthur Conan. *The Sign of the Four.* Philadelphia, Pa.: Lippincott, 1890.

———. *A Study in Scarlet.* Philadelphia, Pa.: Lippincott, 1890.

Dudek, Louis. *Literature and the Press: A History of Printing, Printed Media, and Their Relation to Literature.* Toronto: Ryerson, 1960.

Dupree, Ellen. "The New Woman, Progressivism, and the Woman Writer in Edith Wharton's *The Fruit of the Tree.*" *American Literary Realism* 31, no. 2 (1999): 44–62.

Eason, David L. "On Journalistic Authority: The Janet Cooke Scandal." In *Media, Myth, and Narrative: Television and the Press,* ed. James W. Carey, 205–27. Newbery Park, Calif.: Sage, 1988.

Editorial. *Dial* 15 (1893): 79.

Editorial. *New York Journal,* October 11, 1897.

Editorial. *New York Journal,* October 15, 1897.

Ellis, Edward Sylvester. *Seth Jones: or, The Captives of the Frontier.* New York: Beadle, 1860.

Emery, Michael, Edwin Emery, and Nancy L. Roberts, eds. *The Press and America: An Interpretive History of the Mass Media.* 8th ed. Boston, Mass.: Allyn and Bacon, 1996.

"Equipment for Journalism." *Editor and Publisher* (Aug. 20, 1910): 4.

Evans, Arthur B. "Literary Intertexts in Jules Verne's 'Voyages Extraordinaires.'" *Science-Fiction Studies* 23 (1996): 171–87.

———. "Science Fiction vs. Scientific Fiction in France: From Jules Verne to J. H. Rosny." *Science-Fiction Studies* 15 (1988): 1–11.

"Faking as a Fine Art." *American Magazine* 75 (1912): 89–98.

Falk, Doris V. "Thomas Low Nichols, Poe, and the 'Balloon Hoax.'" *Poe Studies* 5 (1972): 48–49.

"Father Time Outdone." *New York World,* January 26, 1890.

Fishkin, Shelley Fisher. *From Fact to Fiction: Journalism and Imaginative Writing in America.* New York: Oxford Univ. Press, 1985.

"Flying Home." *New York World,* January 23, 1890.

Fogg, William Perry. *Round the World: Letters from Japan, China, India, and Egypt.* Cleveland, Ohio: Cleveland Leader, 1872.

Freeman, Mary E. Wilkins. "The Long Arm." In *The Long Arm and Other Stories,* 1–66. London: Chapman and Hall, 1895.

Frus, Phyllis. *The Politics and Poetics of Journalistic Narrative: The Timely and the Timeless.* New York: Cambridge Univ. Press, 1994.

Fuller, Emeline. *Left by the Indians: Story of My Life.* In *Women's Captivity Narratives,* ed. Kathryn Zabelle Derounian-Stodola, 317–37. New York: Penguin, 1998.

Fusco, Richard. "Poe's Revisions of 'The Mystery of Marie Rôget': A Hoax?" In *Poe at Work: Seven Textual Studies,* ed. Benjamin Franklin Fisher IV, 91–99. Baltimore, Md.: Edgar Allan Poe Society, 1978.

Garland, Hamlin. "Productive Conditions of American Literature." *Forum* 17 (1894): 690–98.

Garst, Robert E., and Theodore Menline Bernstein. *Headlines and Deadlines: A Manual for Copyeditors.* New York: Columbia Univ. Press, 1933.

Gilder, Richard Watson. "Certain Tendencies in Current Literature." *New Princeton Review* 4 (1887): 1–20.

Glazener, Nancy. *Reading for Realism: The History of a United States Literary Institution, 1850–1910.* Durham, N.C.: Duke Univ. Press, 1997.

"*Globe* Suspends Columnist for Alleged Misconduct." *Minneapolis Star Tribune,* July 9, 2000.

Gold, Bill. "The Problem Is All Too Real." *Washington Post,* April 17, 1981.

Good, Howard. *Acquainted with the Night: The Image of Journalists in American Fiction, 1890–1930.* Metuchen, N.J.: Scarecrow, 1986.

Green, Anna Katharine. "A Fictionist Faces Facts." *Fall River Daily Herald,* August 22, 1892.

———. "I Believe Her Innocent." *New Bedford Evening Standard,* August 22, 1892.

———. *The Leavenworth Case: A Lawyer's Story.* 1878. Intro. Michelle Slug. New York: Dover, 1981.

Green, Bill. "The Players: It Wasn't a Game." *Washington Post,* April 19, 1981.

"Greetings Pour in on the Heroine." *New York Journal,* October 18, 1897.

Griffin, Edward M. "Women in Trouble: The Predicament of Captivity and the Narratives of Mary Rowlandson, Mary Jemison, and Hannah Dustan." In *Für Eine Offene Literaturwissenschaft: Erkundungen und Erprobungen am Beispiel US-Amerikanischer Texte,* ed. Leo Truchlar, 41–51. Salzburg, Austria: Verlag Wolfgang Neugebauer, 1986.

Griffith, Thomas. "Washing Dirty Linen in Public." *Time* (Apr. 16, 1984): 83.

Grittner, Frederick Karl. "White Slavery: Myth, Ideology, and American Law." Ph.D. diss., University of Minnesota, 1986.

Grossberger, Lewis, and Lucy Howard. "The Pulitzer Prize Hoax." *Newsweek* (Apr. 27, 1981): 62.

Guerra, Gustavo. "Henry James's Paradoxical Bowl: The Reinstatement of Doubt in *Fin-de-Siècle* America." *Style* 32 (1998): 60–79.

Halstead, Murat. "Murat Halstead to the *Journal.*" *New York Journal,* October 10, 1897.

Halttunen, Karen. *Murder Most Foul: The Killer and the American Gothic Imagination.* Cambridge, Mass.: Harvard Univ. Press, 1998.

Harrington, H. F., and T. T. Frankenberg. *Essentials in Journalism: A Manual in Newspaper Making for College Classes.* Boston, Mass.: Ginn, 1912.

Harris, Neil. *Humbug: The Art of P. T. Barnum.* Boston: Little, Brown, 1973.

Hawthorne, Julian. Introduction to *The Story of Evangelina Cisneros,* by Evangelina Cisneros and Karl Decker. New York: Continental, 1897.

Hearst, William Randolph. Editorial. *New York Journal,* March 19, 1897.

———. Editorial. *New York Journal,* April 18, 1897.

———. Editorial. *New York Journal,* April 21, 1897.

———. Editorial. *San Francisco Examiner,* October 30, 1897.

Herschel, John. *A Treatise on Astronomy.* Philadelphia, Pa.: Carey, Lea, and Blanchard, 1834.

Hersey, John. "The Legend on the License." *Yale Review* 70 (1980): 1–25.

"Highway Robbery." *New York Sun,* August 14, 1835.

Hoffman, Michael J., and Patrick D. Murphy, eds. *Critical Essays in American Modernism.* New York: G. K. Hall, 1992.

Hope, Anthony. *The Prisoner of Zenda: Being the History of Three Months in the Life of an English Gentleman.* 1894. New York: Heritage, 1966.

Howells, William Dean. *Criticism and Fiction.* New York: Harper, 1891.

———. *The Rise of Silas Lapham.* 1885. New York: Penguin, 1984.

———. *Years of My Youth.* Ed. David J. Nordlon. Bloomington: Indiana Univ. Press, 1975.

James, Henry. "The Art of Fiction." In *The Art of Criticism: Henry James on the Theory and the Practice of Fiction,* ed. William Veeder and Susan Griffin, 32–58. Chicago: Univ. of Chicago Press, 1986.

———. "Question of Our Speech." In *French Writers and American Women,* ed. Peter Buitenhuis, 18–31. Branford, Conn.: Compass, 1960.

———. "The Question of the Opportunities." *Literature* 26 (1898): 20–21.

Johanningsmeier, Charles. *Fiction and the American Literary Marketplace: The Role of the Newspaper Syndicates, 1860–1900.* New York: Cambridge Univ. Press, 1997.

Johnson, Haynes. "A Wound That Will Be Long in Healing and Never Forgotten." *Washington Post,* April 19, 1981.

Jones, Ann. *Women Who Kill.* New York: Fawcett Columbine, 1980.

Jones, Gordon. "Jules Verne at Home." *Temple Bar* 129 (1904): 664–71.

"*Journal* Wagons Bring Life to Sufferers from Cold and Hunger." *New York Journal,* January 30, 1897.

"*Journal's* Relief Work Saves Many Poor Ones from Cold and Hunger." *New York Journal,* January 29, 1897.

Juergens, George. *Joseph Pulitzer and the "New York World."* Princeton, N.J.: Princeton Univ. Press, 1966.

Jules-Verne, Jean. *Jules Verne: A Biography.* Trans. Roger Greaves. New York: Taplinger, 1976.

Kalb, Marvin. "News-for-Profit." *Minneapolis Star Tribune,* July 13, 1998.

———. "The Right-Left Struggle of Media News." *Morning Edition.* National Public Radio, October 11, 2004.

Kalikoff, Beth. *Murder and Moral Decay in Victorian Popular Literature.* Ann Arbor, Mich.: UMI, 1986.

Kanfer, Stefan. "From the Yellow Kid to Yellow Journalism." *Civilization* 2 (1995): 32–37.

Kaplan, Amy, and Donald E. Pease, eds. *Cultures of United States Imperialism.* Durham, N.C.: Duke Univ. Press, 1993.

Keen, Dora. *Three Little Maids from School versus Nellie Bly.* N.p., 1890.

Kendrick, Marion. "Better She Died than Reach Ceuta." *New York Journal,* August 18, 1897.

———. "The Cuban Girl Martyr." *New York Journal,* August 17, 1897.

Kenner, Hugh. *The Pound Era.* Berkeley: Univ. of California Press, 1971.

Kent, David. *Forty Whacks: New Evidence in the Life and Legend of Lizzie Borden.* Emmaus, Pa.: Yankee, 1992.

Ketterer, David. *New Worlds for Old: The Apocalyptic Imagination, Science Fiction, and American Literature.* Bloomington: Indiana Univ. Press, 1974.

———. "Poe's Usage of the Hoax." *Criticism* 13 (1971): 377–85.

———. *The Rationale of Deception in Poe.* Baton Rouge: Louisiana State Univ. Press, 1979.

Kirkland, Joseph. "Tolstoi and the Russian Invasion of the Realm of Fiction." *Dial* 7 (1886): 79–81.

Knelman, Judith. *Twisting in the Wind: The Murderess and the English Press.* Toronto: Univ. of Toronto Press, 1998.

Kroeger, Brooke. *Nellie Bly: Daredevil, Reporter, Feminist.* New York: Random House, 1994.

Kurtz, Howard. "More Reporting by *Times* Writer Called Suspect." *Washington Post,* May 8, 2003.

Lancaster, Paul. *Gentleman of the Press: The Life and Times of an Early Reporter, Julian Ralph of the "Sun."* Syracuse, N.Y.: Syracuse Univ. Press, 1992.

Landrum, Larry. *American Mystery and Detective Novels: A Reference Guide.* Westport, Conn.: Greenwood, 1999.

Lane, Roger. *Murder in America: A History.* Columbus: Ohio State Univ. Press, 1997.

Lang, Andrew. *The Culture and Commerce of the American Short Story.* Cambridge, U.K.: Cambridge Univ. Press, 1993.

Lears, T. J. Jackson. *No Place of Grace: Antimodernism and the Transformation of American Culture, 1880–1920.* New York: Pantheon, 1981.

Lemagny, Jean-Claude, and André Rouillé, eds. *A History of Photography: Social and Cultural Perspectives.* Trans. Janet Lloyd. Cambridge, U.K.: Cambridge Univ. Press, 1986.

Levine, Stuart, and Susan Levine, eds. *The Short Fiction of Edgar Allan Poe.* Indianapolis: Bobbs-Merrill, 1976.

Lewis, Ethan. "The Liberation of Words: Williams's Verbal Imagism." *South Dakota Review* 31, no. 3 (1993): 18–42.

"The Liberation of Lizzie Schauer." *New York Journal,* December 10, 1895.

Lincoln, Victoria. *A Private Disgrace: Lizzie Borden by Daylight.* New York: Putnam's, 1967.

Link, Eric Carl. "The War of 1893; or, Realism and Idealism in the Late Nineteenth Century." *American Transcendental Quarterly* 11 (1997): 309–21.

Lippard, George. *The Quaker City: A Romance of Philadelphia Life, Mystery, and Crime.* 1843. Philadelphia, Pa.: Leary, Stuart, 1876.

Locke, Richard Adams. *The Moon Hoax; or, a Discovery That the Moon Has a Vast Population of Human Beings.* 1835. New York: William Gowans, 1859.

Lottman, Herbert R. *Jules Verne: An Exploratory Biography.* New York: St. Martin's, 1996.

Lubow, Arthur. *The Reporter Who Would Be King.* New York: Scribner's, 1992.

Lynch, Lawrence. *Jules Verne.* New York: Twayne, 1992.

Mailer, Norman. *The Executioner's Song.* Boston, Mass.: Little, Brown, 1979.

Major, Charles. *When Knighthood Was in Flower.* New York: Grosset and Dunlap, 1898.

Marshall, John David. "Librarians in the Life and Legend of Lizzie Borden." In *Proceedings: Lizzie Borden Conference, Bristol Community College, Fall River, Massachusetts,* ed. Jules R. Ryckebusch, 303–10. Portland, Maine: King Philip, 1993.

Marzolf, Marion Tuttle. *Civilizing Voices: American Press Criticism, 1880–1950.* New York: Longman, 1991.

Mason, Monck. *Account of the Late Aeronautical Expedition from London to Weilburg.* New York: Theodore Foster, 1837.

Matthew, Marie-Louise Nickerson. "Forms of Hoax in the Tales of Edgar Allan Poe." Ph.D. diss., Columbia University, 1974.

McCafferty, Kate. "Palimpsest of Desire: The Re-emergence of the American Captivity Narrative as Pulp Romance." *Journal of Popular Culture* 27, no. 4 (1994): 43–56.

McGrath, Ellie. "A Fraud in the Pulitzers." *Time* (Apr. 27, 1981): 52–53.

Meginness, John Franklin. *Biography of Frances Slocum, the Lost Sister of Wyoming.* Williamsport, Pa.: Heller, 1891.

Meyers, Jeffrey. *Edgar Allan Poe: His Life and Legacy.* New York: Scribner's, 1992.

Michener, James A. "On Integrity in Journalism." *U.S. News and World Report* (May 4, 1981): 80.

Miller, Linda Patterson. "Poe on the Beat: *Doings of Gotham* as Urban, Penny Press Journalism." *Journal of the Early Republic* 7 (1987): 147–65.

Milloy, Courtland, and Janet Cooke. "Custody of Boy with Arm Marks Brings Dismay." *Washington Post,* November 30, 1980.

Milton, Joyce. *The Yellow Kids: Foreign Correspondents in the Heyday of Yellow Journalism.* New York: Harper and Row, 1989.

"Miss Bly's Home-Coming." *New York World,* January 8, 1890.

"Miss Cisneros to Be a U.S. Citizen." *New York Journal,* October 15, 1897.

Monk, Maria. *Awful Disclosures of Maria Monk, of the Hotel Dieu Nunnery of Montreal.* New York: M. Monk, 1836.

Moskowitz, Sam, ed. *Science Fiction by Gaslight: A History and Anthology of Science Fiction in the Popular Magazines, 1891–1911.* Westport, Conn.: Hyperion, 1968.

Moss, Sidney P. *Poe's Literary Battles: The Critic in the Context of His Literary Milieu.* Durham, N.C.: Duke Univ. Press, 1963.

Mott, Frank Luther. *Golden Multitudes: The Story of Best Sellers in the United States.* New York: Macmillan, 1947.

———. *A History of American Magazines, 1885–1905.* Cambridge, Mass.: Harvard Univ. Press, 1957.

Mundy, Liza. "The Second Chance Club." *Washington Post,* October 3, 1999.

Musgrave, George Clark. "Miss Cisneros in Death's Shadow." *New York Journal,* August 23, 1897.

Nasaw, David. *The Chief: The Life of William Randolph Hearst.* Boston, Mass.: Houghton Mifflin, 2000.

National News Council. *After "Jimmy's World": Tightening Up Editing.* New York: National News Council, 1981.

"Nellie Bly Is Off." *New York World,* November 15, 1889.

"Nellie Bly on Time." *New York World,* December 19, 1889.

"Nellie Bly Proposes to Fight for Cuba." *New York World,* March 8, 1896.

"Nellie Bly's Admirer." *New York World,* December 26, 1890.

"Nellie Bly's Fame." *New York World,* January 9, 1890.

"Nellie Meets Verne." *New York World,* November 23, 1889.

Nelson, Carolyn Christensen. *British Woman Fiction Writers of the 1890s.* New York: Twayne, 1996.

"New Society." *New York Sun,* August 7, 1835.

Nickerson, Catherine Ross. *The Web of Iniquity: Early Detective Fiction by American Women.* Durham, N.C.: Duke Univ. Press, 1998.

Nobile, Philip. "The Pulitzer Surprise: Janet Cooke's False Report." *New York* (Apr. 27, 1981): 22.

Nolan, Bruce. "Fallen Reporter's Quest Raises Ethical Questions." *New Orleans Times-Picayune,* May 18, 1996.

Norris, Frank. "The Frontier Gone at Last." In *Novels and Essays.* 1902. New York: Library of America, 1986.

———. "Van Bubble's Story." In "Perverted Tales," *Wave* (Dec. 18, 1897): 5–7.

O'Brien, Frank M. *The Story of the Sun.* New York: George H. Doran, 1918.

Ochs, Adolph. "Business Announcement." *New York Times,* August 19, 1896.

"On the Other Side." *New York World,* November 22, 1889.

"On Time!" *New York World,* January 22, 1890.

Orvell, Miles. *The Real Thing: Imitation and Authenticity in American Culture, 1880–1940.* Chapel Hill: Univ. of North Carolina Press, 1989.

Pahl, Dennis. "De-composing Poe's 'Philosophy.'" *Texas Studies in Language and Literature* 38 (1996): 1–25.

Pallen, Condé Benoist. "Newspaperism." *Lippincott's Monthly Magazine* 32 (1886): 470–77.

Papke, David Ray. *Framing the Criminal: Crime, Cultural Work and the Loss of Critical Perspective, 1830–1900.* Hamden, Conn.: Archon, 1987.

Parish, David, Michael Murphy, and Maureen Jenkins. "Untraceable Sources Are Columnist's Undoing." *Minneapolis Star Tribune,* August 26, 1999.

Park, Robert E. "The Yellow Press." *Sociology and Social Research* 12 (1927): 3–11.

Parnass, John. "News as Routinely Reconstituted Reality." Letter to the editor. *New York Times,* May 5, 1981.

Pearson, Edmund, ed. *The Trial of Lizzie Borden.* London: William Heinemann, 1937.

Philips, Melville, ed. *The Making of a Newspaper.* New York: Putnam's, 1893.

Pianin, Eric. "Cooke's 'Today' Interview." *Washington Post,* January 30, 1982.

Pierstorff, Don K. "Poe as Satirist: An Apology." *Studies in Contemporary Satire* 10 (1983): 32–34.

Pizer, Donald, ed. *Documents of American Realism and Naturalism.* Carbondale: Southern Illinois Univ. Press, 1998.

———. Introduction to *The Cambridge Companion to American Realism and Naturalism.* New York: Cambridge Univ. Press, 1995.

Plummer, Laura A. "Witness for the Persecution: Reading the Wilde and Borden Trials." Ph.D. diss., Indiana University, 1995.

Poe, Edgar Allan. "The Balloon Hoax." In *Tales,* 462–76. New York: Dodd, Mead, 1952.

———. *Doings of Gotham.* Ed. Jacob E. Spannuth. Pottsville, Pa.: Jacob E. Spannuth, 1929.

———. *The Letters of Edgar Allan Poe.* Ed. John Ward Ostrom. 2 vols. 1948. New York: Gordian, 1966.

———. *The Literati: Some Honest Opinions about Autorial Merits and Demerits.* New York: J. S. Redfield, 1850.

———. "The Murders in the Rue Morgue." In *Selected Tales,* 92–122. New York: Oxford Univ. Press, 1998.

———. "The Mystery of Marie Rogêt." *Ladies Companion* (Nov. 1842): 15–20; (Dec. 1842): 93–99; (Feb. 1843): 162–67.

———. *The Narrative of Arthur Gordon Pym.* New York: Harper and Brothers, 1838.

———. "The Poetic Principle." In *Poems and Essays on Poetry,* ed. C. H. Sisson, 88–95. Manchester, U.K.: Fyfield, 1995.

———. "The Purloined Letter." In *Selected Poetry and Prose of Edgar Allan Poe,* ed. T. O. Mabbott, 293–309. New York: Modern Library, 1951.

———. "Three Sundays in a Week." In *Extravaganza and Caprice,* ed. Edmund Clarence Stedman and George Edward Woodberry, 139–49. New York: Scribner's, 1914.

———. "The Unparalleled Adventure of One Hans Pfaall." In *Tales of Edgar Allan Poe,* 179–243. New York: Scribner's, 1927.

———. *The Works of the Late Edgar Allan Poe: With Notices of His Life and Genius.* Ed. N. P. Willis Jr., R. Lowell, and R. W. Griswold. New York: J. S. Redfield, 1850.

Pollin, Burton P. Introduction to *The Imaginary Voyages,* by Edgar Allan Poe. New York: Gordian, 1994.

Pound, Ezra. "In a Station of the Metro." *Poetry* 2 (1913): 12.

———. *The Literary Essays.* 1918. Norfolk, Conn.: New Directions, 1954.

Powers, William. "The Use and Abuse of Fiction." *National Journal* (June 27, 1998): 1520.

"The Press and the Globe-Trotter." *New York World.* December 26, 1889.

Procter, Ben. *William Randolph Hearst: The Early Years, 1863–1910.* New York: Oxford Univ. Press, 1998.

"A Pulitzer Fake: The Echoes Linger." *U.S. News and World Report,* April 27, 1981.

Pulitzer, Joseph. Editorial. *New York World,* May 11, 1883.

"The Pulitzer School." *Editor and Publisher* (Aug. 22, 1903): 1–2.

Radin, Edward D. *Lizzie Borden: The Untold Story.* New York: Simon and Schuster, 1961.

Ralph, Julian. "The Borden Jury Chosen." *New York Sun,* June 6, 1893.

———. "Lizzie Borden at the Bar." *New York Sun,* June 5, 1893.

———. "Lizzie Borden Free." *New York Sun,* June 21, 1893.

———. "Lizzie Borden Swooned." *New York Sun,* June 7, 1893.

———. "Lizzie Borden Was Cheery." *New York Sun,* June 8, 1893.

———. *The Making of a Journalist.* New York: Harper, 1903.

———. *People We Pass: Stories of Life among the Masses of New York City.* New York: Harper and Brothers, 1896.

———. "Turning Now to the Jury." *New York Sun,* June 19, 1893.

———. "With Skulls and Hatchets." *New York Sun,* June 14, 1893.

"The Rescued Man." *San Francisco Examiner,* January 5, 1890.

Review of *A Journey to the Centre of the Earth,* by Jules Verne. *Illustrated Review* (Dec. 16, 1872): 373–74.

Reynolds, David, ed. *George Lippard: Prophet of Protest: Writings of an American Radical, 1822–1854.* New York: P. Lang, 1986.

Reynolds, David S. *Beneath the American Renaissance: The Subversive Imagination in the Age of Emerson and Melville.* New York: Knopf, 1988.

Richardson, Charles F. *American Literature, 1607–1885.* Vol. 2. New York: Putnam's, 1889.

Richburg, Keith B. "Mayor Says City Ending Its Search for 'Jimmy.'" *Washington Post,* October 16, 1980.

Riis, Jacob. *The Making of an American.* New York: Grosset and Dunlap, 1901.

Robertson, Cara. "Representing 'Miss Lizzie': Cultural Convictions in the Trial of Lizzie Borden." *Yale Journal of Law and the Humanities* 8 (1996): 351–416.

Robertson, Michael. *Stephen Crane, Journalism, and the Making of Modern American Literature.* New York: Columbia Univ. Press, 1997.

Robinson, Edwin Arlington. "Miniver Cheevy." In *Tilbury Town: Selected Poems of Edwin Arlington Robinson,* ed. Lawrance Thompson, 6–7. New York: Macmillan, 1953.

Rosenthal, Bernard. *Salem Story: Reading the Witch Trials of 1692.* Cambridge, U.K.: Cambridge Univ. Press, 1993.

Ryckebusch, Jules R., ed. *Proceedings: Lizzie Borden Conference, Bristol Community College, Fall River, Massachusetts.* Portland, Maine: King Philip, 1993.

Sager, Mike. "Janet's World." *GQ* 6, no. 6 (1996): 200–211.

Sanoff, Alvin P. "Uneasy Press Sets Out to Refurbish Its Image." *U.S. News and World Report,* June 29, 1981.

"Saved from Death!" *San Francisco Examiner,* January 4, 1890.

Schiller, Dan. *Objectivity and the News: The Public and the Rise of Commercial Journalism.* Philadelphia: Univ. of Pennsylvania Press, 1981.

Schlipp, Madelon Golden, and Sharon M. Murphy. *Great Women of the Press.* Carbondale: Southern Illinois Univ. Press, 1983.

Schofield, Ann. "Lizzie Borden Took an Axe: History, Feminism, and American Culture." *American Studies* 34 (1993): 91–103.

Schorr, Daniel. "Journalism's Litany of Sins Against Unabsolving Public." *Minneapolis Star Tribune,* July 14, 1998.

Schriber, Mary Suzanne. *Writing Home: American Women Abroad, 1830–1920.* Charlottesville: Univ. Press of Virginia, 1997.

Schudson, Michael. *Discovering the News: A Social History of American Newspapers.* New York: Basic, 1978.

———. "Why News Is the Way It Is." *Raritan* 2, no. 3 (1983): 109–25.

Scudder, Harold H. "Poe's 'Balloon-Hoax.'" *American Literature* 21 (1949): 179–80.

Seavey, Ormond, ed. Introduction to *The Moon Hoax; Or, a Discovery That the Moon Has a Vast Population of Human Beings,* by Richard Adams Locke. 1859. Boston: Gregg, 1975.

Seed, David, ed. *Anticipations: Essays on Early Science Fiction and Its Precursors.* Syracuse, N.Y.: Syracuse Univ. Press, 1995.

Seitz, Don C. *Joseph Pulitzer: His Life and Letters.* New York: Simon and Schuster, 1924.

Shaw, S. Bradley. "New England Gothic by Light of Common Day: Lizzie Borden and Mary E. Wilkins Freeman's 'The Long Arm.'" *New England Quarterly* 70 (1997): 211–36.

Sherard, Robert Harborough. *Twenty Years in Paris: Being Some Recollections of a Literary Life.* Philadelphia, Pa.: George W. Jacobs, n.d.

"She's Home Again!" *Life* (Jan. 23, 1890): 47.

Shi, David E. *Facing Facts: Realism in American Thought and Culture, 1850–1920.* New York: Oxford Univ. Press, 1995.

Shuman, Edwin L. *Practical Journalism: A Complete Manual of the Best Newspaper Methods.* New York: D. Appleton, 1903.

———. *Steps into Journalism.* Evanston, Ill.: Evanston, 1894.

Simons, Lewis. "Addict, 8, Is in Hiding, Mayor Says." *Washington Post,* October 1, 1980.

———. "D.C. Authorities Seek Identity of Heroin Addict, 8." *Washington Post,* September 30, 1980.

Simons, Lewis, and Athelia Knight. "Young 'Fagin' Is Nabbed." *Washington Post,* October 2, 1980.

Sims, Norman, ed. *The Literary Journalists.* New York: Ballantine, 1984.

Singal, Daniel Joseph, ed. *Modernist Culture in America.* Belmont, Calif.: Wadsworth, 1991.

Slug, Michelle. Introduction to *The Leavenworth Case: A Lawyer's Story,* by Anna Katharine Green. New York: Dover, 1981.

Smith, Patterson. "Lizzie Borden on the Rare Book Market." In *Proceedings: Lizzie Borden Conference, Bristol Community College, Fall River, Massachusetts,* ed. Jules R. Ryckebusch, 273–91. Portland, Maine: King Philip, 1993.

Smythe, Ted Curtis. "The Reporter, 1880–1900: Working Conditions and Their Influence on the News." *Journalism History* 7 (1980): 1–10.

Some Imagist Poets: An Anthology. Boston, Mass.: Houghton Mifflin, 1915.

Spiering, Frank. *Lizzie.* New York: Random House, 1984.

Srebnick, Amy Gilman. *The Mysterious Death of Marie Rogers: Sex and Culture in Nineteenth-Century New York.* New York: Oxford Univ. Press, 1995.

Stein, Gertrude. *Selected Writings of Gertrude Stein.* Ed. Carl Van Vechten. New York: Modern Library, 1962.

Stovall, James Glen. "Richard Adams Locke." In *American Newspaper Journalists, 1690–1872,* ed. Perry J. Ashley, 309–12. Detroit, Mich.: Gale Research, 1985.

Stratemeyer, Edward. "Dash Dare on His Mettle, or Clearing Up a Double Tragedy." *Old Cap Collier Library,* October 15, 1892.

Strunk, William, Jr. *The Elements of Style.* Ithaca, N.Y.: Thrift, 1918.

Strychacz, Thomas. *Modernism, Mass Culture, and Professionalism.* New York: Cambridge Univ. Press, 1993.

"Success to Nellie Bly." *New York World,* November 17, 1889.

Swanberg, W. A. *Citizen Hearst: A Biography of William Randolph Hearst.* New York: Scribner's, 1961.

———. *Pulitzer.* New York: Scribner's, 1967.

Taves, Brian, and Stephen Michaluk Jr. *The Jules Verne Encyclopedia.* Lanham, Md.: Scarecrow, 1996.

"Their Fake Story." *Minneapolis Star Tribune,* December 9, 2000.

Thomas, Dwight, and David K. Jackson. *The Poe Log: A Documentary Life of Edgar Allan Poe, 1809–1849.* Boston, Mass.: G. K. Hall, 1987.

Thomas, W. I. "The Psychology of Yellow Journalism." *American Magazine* 65 (1908): 491–97.

Thompson, Maurice. "The Domain of Romance." *Forum* 8 (1889): 326–36.

Thoreau, Henry David. *Reform Papers.* Princeton, N.J.: Princeton Univ. Press, 1973.

Tichi, Cecelia. *Shifting Gears: Technology, Literature, Culture in Modernist America.* Chapel Hill: Univ. of North Carolina Press, 1987.

Tifft, Susan E., and Alex S. Jones. *The Trust: The Private and Powerful Family behind the* New York Times. Boston, Mass.: Little, Brown, 1999.

Tomasky, Michael. "Who Slants More?" Interview with Bob Garfield. *On the Media.* National Public Radio, August 8, 2003.

Traxel, David. *1898: The Birth of an American Century.* New York: Knopf, 1998.

Trebbe, Ann L. "Personalities." *Washington Post,* November 21, 1981.

Tucher, Andie. *Froth and Scum: Truth, Beauty, Goodness, and the Ax Murder in America's First Mass Medium.* Chapel Hill: Univ. of North Carolina Press, 1994.

Tucker, George. *A Voyage to the Moon: With Some Account of the Manners and Customs, Science and Philosophy, of the People of Morosofia, and Other Lunarians.* New York: E. Bliss, 1827.

Turner, Hy B. *When Giants Ruled: The Story of Park Row, New York's Great Newspaper Street.* New York: Fordham Univ. Press, 1999.

Twain, Mark. *Personal Recollections of Joan of Arc.* New York: Harper and Brothers, 1896.

———. *Tom Sawyer Abroad: Tom Sawyer, Detective and Other Stories.* New York: Harper and Brothers, 1896.

————. *The Tragedy of Pudd'nhead Wilson: and the Comedy of Those Extraordinary Twins.* Hartford, Conn.: American, 1894.

Tyreell, R. Emmett, Jr. "Bogus Operandi." *Washington Post,* May 8, 1981.

Vance, Robert H. *Catalogue of Daguerreotype Panoramic Views in California.* New York: Baker, Godwin, 1851.

VanDerBeets, Richard. *The Indian Captivity Narrative: An American Genre.* Lanham, Md.: Univ. Press of America, 1984.

Verne, Jules. *Around the World in Eighty Days.* Trans. William Butcher. 1873. Oxford, U.K.: Oxford Univ. Press, 1995.

————. *Captain Grant's Children: A Voyage Round the World.* 1865. London: Arco, 1964.

————. *Claudius Bombarnac, or the Special Correspondent.* New York: Hurst, 1892.

————. "Edgar Poe et Ses Oeuvres." *Musée des Familles* 31 (1864): 193–208.

————. *Five Weeks in a Balloon: A Voyage of Exploration and Discovery in Central Africa.* 1863. New York: Appleton, 1869.

————. *From the Earth to the Moon.* 1865. N.p.: Didier, 1947.

————. *Round the Moon.* 1870. New York: George Munro, 1877.

————. *Le Sphinx des Glaces.* Paris: J. Hetzel, 1897.

————. *Twenty-Thousand Leagues Under the Sea: A Submarine Trip Around the World.* 1869. London: Arco, 1960.

"Verne and His Works." *New York World,* November 23, 1889.

"Verne's Bravo." *New York World,* January 26, 1890.

Victor, Metta Fuller. *The Dead Letter, An American Romance.* New York: Beadle, 1866.

Wadsworth, Sarah. "Excel-ing the Seaside Library: Database Design and Queries." Paper presented at the annual meeting of the Midwest Modern Language Association, Minneapolis, Minnesota, November 6, 1999.

Walsh, John. *Poe the Detective: The Curious Circumstances Behind the Mystery of Marie Rogêt.* New Brunswick, N.J.: Rutgers Univ. Press, 1968.

Warner, Charles Dudley. "Better Newspapers." *Journalist* (May 1, 1897): 14.

————. "Newspapers and the Public." *Forum* 9 (1890): 198–207.

Weber, Ronald. *Hired Pens: Professional Writers in America's Golden Age of Print.* Athens: Ohio Univ. Press, 1997.

Weiner, Bruce I. *The Most Noble of Professions: Poe and the Poverty of Authorship.* Baltimore, Md.: Enoch Pratt Free Library, 1987.

Weissbuch, Ted N. "Edgar Allan Poe: Hoaxer in the American Tradition." *New York Historical Society Quarterly* 45 (1961): 291–309.

Welter, Barbara. *Dimity Conviction: The American Woman in the Nineteenth Century.* Athens: Ohio Univ. Press, 1976.

Whalen, Terence. *Edgar Allan Poe and the Masses: The Political Economy of Literature in Antebellum America.* Princeton, N.J.: Princeton Univ. Press, 1999.

White, Hayden. "The Historical Text as Literary Artifact." In *The Writing of History: Literary Form and Historical Understanding,* ed. Robert H. Canary and Henry Kozicki, 41–62. Madison: Univ. of Wisconsin Press, 1978.

Whitman, Walt. *Uncollected Poetry and Prose.* Vol. 1. Ed. Emory Holloway. Garden City, N.Y.: Doubleday, Page, 1921.

Wilkinson, Ronald Sterne. "Poe's 'Balloon-Hoax' Once More." *American Literature* 32 (1960): 313–17.

Williams, Joyce G. "The Collision of a Personality and an Era." In *Proceedings: Lizzie Borden Conference, Bristol Community College, Fall River, Massachusetts,* ed. Jules R. Ryckebusch, 3–10. Portland, Maine: King Philip, 1993.

Williams, Joyce G., J. Eric Smithburn, and M. Jeanne Peterson, eds. *Lizzie Borden: A Case Book of Family and Crime in the 1890s.* Bloomington, Ind.: TIS, 1980.

Williams, William Carlos. "A Beginning on the Short Story (Notes)." In *Selected Essays,* 295–310. New York: New Directions, 1969.

Wilson, Christopher P. *The Labor of Words: Literary Professionalism in the Progressive Era.* Athens: Univ. of Georgia Press, 1985.

Wolfe, Tom. *The Right Stuff.* New York: Farrar, Straus, and Giroux, 1979.

Woo, William F. "Journalism's 'Normal Accidents.'" *Nieman Reports* 57, no. 3 (2003): 47–53.

Wright, Claudia. "The Lie Machinery Stirs." *New Statesman* (May 1981): 6–7.

Zagoria, Sam. "*New Yorker,* How Could You?" *Washington Post,* June 27, 1984.

———. "When Facts Get Lost amid Drama." *Washington Post,* April 3, 1985.

Zboray, Ronald J. *A Fictive People: Antebellum Economic Development and the American Reading Public.* New York: Oxford Univ. Press, 1993.

Ziff, Larzer. *The American 1890s: Life and Times of a Lost Generation.* New York: Viking, 1966.

INDEX